Privacy Journal's

COMPILATION OF STATE AND FEDERAL PRIVACY LAWS, 2013 Edition

By

ROBERT ELLIS SMITH

This edition replaces the 2002 edition and all subsequent supplements

Published by PRIVACY JOURNAL

An Independent Monthly on Privacy in a Computer Age

Library of Congress Classification Data:

KF1262.A3   342'.73'085

ISBN: 978-0-930072-56-8

Published by

PRIVACY JOURNAL

P.O. BOX 28577

Providence RI 02908

401/274-7861

orders@privacyjournal.net

www.privacyjournal.net

A supplement to this book is published annually.
Call or write for information.

CONTENTS

About This Book
About Privacy Journal

State and Federal Laws Described

ABOUT THIS BOOK

This edition of *Compilation of State and Federal Privacy Laws* includes citations and descriptions of *all* of the laws affecting privacy, surveillance, and data collection that the researchers of **PRIVACY JOURNAL** can find. This book replaces all previous editions and supplements. It includes material from all previous supplements.

We continually publish supplements to describe laws enacted since the publication of our latest edition of the *Compilation*. These are available from **PRIVACY JOURNAL**. In addition, by subscribing to our monthly newsletter, **PRIVACY JOURNAL**, you will learn immediately about new laws enacted in this field. A yearly subscription is available by calling or writing **PRIVACY JOURNAL**.

PRIVACY JOURNAL's survey of state and federal laws affecting the confidentiality of personal information is a continuing project, just as the development of fair information standards is an on-going process in each of the state capitals and in Washington.

Our hope is to provide a readable book that will give attorneys, citizens interested in privacy, legislators, public interest groups, lobbyists, business persons, journalists, and researchers an idea of the diverse sorts of privacy protections that exist in the 50 states.

Each statute has been cited by title, article (art.), chapter (ch.), paragraph (para.) and/or section (sec.) so that you may look it up in a statute book or online, in a revised (rev.) or annotated (ann.) version. You may visit a law library or write to the state capitol for a copy of a law or search on the Internet. Many times you can enter the statute number in a search engine and find the full text. Or you can use a search engine to find the laws of a particular state; then you can search or browse the text of the state's code. Any county or state law library can help you find the texts of the laws if you have the citation. Many public libraries have state laws on file or can find them on-line.

We have not included the "boiler plate" language requiring confidentiality in many state laws on specific topics, like drug treatment or adoption. And because of the universal nature of the husband-wife and attorney-client privilege, only a few were included in the category on privileges. Likewise we have not listed the varying laws in most stated punishing "cyberstalking" or "cyberharassment."

All states have constitutional provisions similar to the First Amendment and Fourth Amendment of the United States Constitution; some have written into their state constitutions specific language protecting the right to privacy. These are included in this compilation.

PRIVACY JOURNAL's *Compilation of State and Federal Privacy Laws* is written and edited by Robert Ellis Smith, publisher of **PRIVACY JOURNAL,** a lawyer, and author of *Ben Franklin's Web Site: Privacy and Curiosity From Plymouth Rock to the Internet*.

Robert Ellis Smith

ABOUT PRIVACY JOURNAL

PRIVACY JOURNAL, an independent newsletter, has been published monthly since it was founded in Washington in November 1974. *The Washington Post* called it "the most talked about Washington newsletter since *I. F. Stone's Weekly*."

Since 1986, **PRIVACY JOURNAL** has been based in Providence, R.I.

PRIVACY JOURNAL maintains an extensive research collection of materials about privacy, in each of the areas cited in this book. Newsletter subscribers may take advantage of this research service and receive materials as they need them.

You should also call or write us to reserve a copy of a future edition of our supplement to this edition of the *Compilation of State and Federal Privacy Laws*. If you wish to know when new editions of the supplement or the book are published, simply send us a note now or call, and we'll notify you when a new edition is published.

For a list of **PRIVACY JOURNAL**'s other publications, look at the end of this book or call or write us. **PRIVACY JOURNAL**, PO Box 28577, Providence RI 02908, 401/274-7861, fax 401/274-4747, orders@privacyjournal.net, www.privacyjournal.net.

ARREST AND CONVICTION RECORDS

Alabama–An individual may have access to his or her criminal record. Ala. Code 41-9-643.

Alaska–In a case of mistaken identity or false accusation, a person may seek sealing of past conviction or current offender information. Alaska Stat. 12.62.180.

Arizona–Any person wrongfully arrested, indicted, or otherwise charged may petition superior court for an entry of notation upon any and all records that the person has been cleared. Ariz. Rev. Code sec. 13-1761.

California–Whenever a person is acquitted of a charge and it appears to a judge that the person was factually innocent of the charge, the judge may order the case sealed and later destroyed. The person may then state that he was not arrested. Cal. Penal Code sec. 851.8. Records of minor drug offenses prior to 1976 may be destroyed upon petition to a court. Cal. Health & Safety Code sec. 11361.5.

Law enforcement agencies may not disclose criminal history information with the intent of affecting a person's employment prospects. Cal. Labor Code sec. 432.7. Public and private employers may not inquire into arrests of applicants (nor certain marijuana convictions), nor may public agencies inquire into arrests on applications for a license, certificate, or registration. Cal. Labor Code sec. 432.7 and Cal. Bus. & Prof. Code sec. 461. Nor may auto insurers inquire. Cal. Ins. Code sec. 11580.08. Securities broker-dealers may inquire. Cal. Corp. Code sec. 25221. Mere detentions, not regarded as arrests, must be accompanied by a record of release and the individual is entitled to a certificate labeling the incident a detention. Cal. Penal Code sec. 851.6(b).

There is a right to inspect and challenge one's record. Cal. Penal Code 11126.

It is a misdemeanor to disclose, for financial gain, information that a peace officer or prosecutor obtains in the course of a criminal investigation, the disclosure of which is prohibited by law. It is also a misdemeanor to solicit the exchange of information. Penal Code sec. 146g.

Colorado–Any person may petition the appropriate court to seal his or her record, except for the basic identifying information, if the person is not guilty of an additional crime within a certain number of years. Employers and educational institutions may not inquire about sealed records. Colo. Rev. Stat. sec. 24-72-308.

Connecticut–State law mandates erasure of all court and police records of arrests, including photos and fingerprints, of persons acquitted, pardoned, dismissed or not prosecuted. Conn. Gen. Stat. Ann. sec. 54-142a. See also **Employment Records**.

A 1994 law prohibits police from disclosing any details about a suspect's "personal possessions or effects" at the time of arrest if not relevant to the charge. Sec. 1-206.

Delaware–For $5, a person may receive a copy of his or her Delaware criminal history record. Del. Code title 11, sec. 8511(4). There is a procedure for expunging records. Title 11, sec. 4371.

A court may order destruction of a record if there is no conviction nor prior record. Title 11, sec. 3904.

District of Columbia–Police records of complaints are open to public inspection and the police commissioner may order obsolete records destroyed. D.C. Code Ann. sec. 4-131. There is a right to expunge by court order.

Florida–Fla. Stat. Ann. sec. 901.33 provides a right for the expunction of arrest records of acquitted or released persons. [See 1978-79 book.] Illegal to discriminate in public employment on the basis of a prior conviction unless it is directly related to the position sought. Sec. 112.011.

Employees and applicants may answer questions about arrests and expunged convictions in the negative. Sec. 943.058.

Georgia–Arrest information may be disclosed to certain employers and others, but an individual rejected on that basis has a right to be told of the information disclosed. Ga. Code Ann. Sec. 35-3-34.

Hawaii–"The attorney general, upon application from a person arrested for, but not convicted of, a crime, shall issue an expunction order annulling, canceling, and rescinding the record of arrest." The record must then be placed in a confidential file in the attorney general's office or erased from magnetic tape or computer memory, to be seen again only under court order. The individual is provided a certificate of annulment and may answer inquiries about an arrest record in the negative. Haw. Rev. Stat. 831-3.2. An individual may not be denied a state job nor license to do business solely because of a criminal conviction. Government employers and license issuers may not use arrest records for which no jail term may be imposed. Other convictions may be considered if job-related. Haw. Rev. Stat. 831-3.1.

Illinois–A person charged but not convicted may petition a court for expunction of the arrest record. Criminal records are generally not public. ILCS 2630/5 and 7. It is a civil rights violation to inquire whether a job applicant has ever been arrested. A distinction is drawn between arrests and convictions. 775 ILCS 5/4-103.

Indiana–Upon written request of an individual with no prior arrests and no criminal charges pending, a law enforcement agency must destroy or return fingerprints and photographs connected with an arrest in which no charges were pressed. The agency must also request any other agencies to which it has sent the arrest materials to do the same. And no record of the arrest may be kept in an alphabetical file. Ind. Code Ann. sec. 35-4.8.

Kansas–State law permits expunction of arrest records. Kans. Stat. Ann. 12-4516a. See also **Criminal Justice Information Systems**.

Kentucky–Individuals have access to their own arrest records. Ky. Rev. Stat. Ann. sec. 61.884.

Louisiana–La. Rev. Stat. Ann. sec. 44:9 provides for the destruction of misdemeanor records for persons later acquitted or released.

Maryland–An individual may answer arrest record inquiries in the negative if acquitted, or the case is not prosecuted or dismissed and if he had petitioned a court to seal his record–either three years after the arrest, or earlier, when he waives his right to civil claims arising from the incident. An employer may not fire a person if he discovers such arrest information. Md. Crim. Proced. 10-101 to 10-109.

Massachusetts–Employers must notify applicants that they may respond "no record" if they have been arrested but never convicted; if they have not been convicted within five previous years and have only misdemeanors more than five years old on their records; or if they have only one conviction for simple assault, traffic offenses or drunkenness (misdemeanors). The law applies also to university admissions applicants. Offenders may have criminal records sealed 15 years after release for a felony, ten years after release for a misdemeanor. Mass. Gen. Laws ch. 276, sec. 100 A-C. First convictions for marijuana and other drug offenses may be sealed under certain circumstances. Ch. 94C, sec. 34.

Michigan–See **Employment Records**.

Minnesota–Records of arrests without conviction, convictions that have been expunged, and misdemeanors without jail sentences shall not be used by the state in connection with any application for public employment or license. Minn. Stat. Ann. sec. 364.04.

Missouri–Arrest records are to be sealed if no charge is filed within 30 days. They are then unavailable to the public. Mo. Ann. Stat. sec. 610.100.

Nevada–Fifteen years after release from custody for felony, ten years after release for gross misdemeanor, five years after release for misdemeanor an individual may petition court to seal all records. Nev. Rev. Stat. sec. 179.245. Thirty days after acquittal or dismissal of charges a person may petition for sealing. Sec. 179.255.

New Jersey–Persons convicted (except for serious offenses) may petition the court, ten years later, to expunge the record, if there is no law enforcement objection. N.J. Rev. Stat. sec. 2A:164-28.

New Mexico–Criminal records of arrests not followed by valid conviction and misdemeanor convictions not involving moral turpitude shall not be used, distributed, or disseminated in connection with an application for any public employment, license, or authority. Convictions may be considered, but are not a bar to employment. N.M. Stat. Ann. sec. 28-2-3.

New York–Upon the termination of a criminal proceeding in favor of a person, all records are sealed unless the district attorney shows the court cause not to, or the person applies for a gun license. It is an unlawful discriminatory practice to inquire about the proceeding. N.Y. Crim. Proc. Law sec. 160.50 McKinney). Marijuana misdemeanors shall be sealed by a court, even if there is a dismissal. Sec. 170.56.

It is unlawful for an employer, insurance company, or credit bureau to inquire into an arrest that resulted in a favorable outcome for the individual. N.Y. Exec. Law 296.16.

Ohio–First offenders may petition a court for expunction of convictions after release. Ohio Rev. Code Ann. sec. 2953.32. Applicants are not to be asked about expunged criminal records. An applicant may respond in the negative if an employer or licensing body asks about expunged or sealed criminal records. Sec. 2953.43. Similar requirements apply to juvenile records. Sec. 2151.358 (I) and (J).

Oregon–First offenders may petition the court after release for the conviction to be set aside so that it is "deemed not to have occurred." Or. Rev. Stat. sec. 137.225. An employer must notify a person before getting access to criminal records. Sec. 181.555(2). Arrest records are not subject to disclosure if there is a good reason to delay. Sec. 192.500(1)(c).

Pennsylvania–Arrest information may not be used for licensing. Only criminal information relevant to the employment may be used in hiring decisions, and the applicant shall be notified when this is done. Pa. Stat. Ann. title 18, sec. 9124.

Rhode Island–The law requires destruction, within 45 days of acquittal, of any fingerprints, photographs and other records of the accused taken by law enforcement. R.I. Gen. Laws sec. 12-1-12. An employment application form may inquire into convictions, but not arrests. 28-5-7(7).

South Carolina–Arrest records and accompanying fingerprints and mug shots shall be destroyed if no conviction. S.C. Code sec. 17-4.

Tennessee–Upon petition to a court, arrest records may be destroyed if there is no finding of guilt, but "non-public" law enforcement records remain on file. Tenn. Code Ann. sec. 40-32-101. See also 40-15-106.

Utah–Arrest records may be sealed one year after a charge has been dropped. An individual not convicted may petition a court to expunge an arrest record and certain convictions. Utah Code Ann. sec. 77-18-9 through 14, 77-26-16.

Virginia–Similar to Maryland's law. Va. Code 19.2-392.4(a) and (c).

Washington–An individual may ask a court for destruction of records after release or acquittal. Wash. Rev. Code Ann. sec. 43.43.730.

West Virginia–An individual is entitled to have returned to him arrest records, fingerprints, and photographs in state files, if acquitted. W. Va. Code sec. 15-2-24(h).

Wisconsin–Employment law prohibits inquiring into arrest records, except for bonding. Wis. Stat. Ann. sec. 111.335.

BANK AND FINANCIAL RECORDS

Alabama–A bank shall disclose financial records of its customers pursuant to a lawful subpoena, summons, warrant, or court order issued by or at the request of a government agency. No bank shall be held civilly liable or criminally responsible for disclosure of financial records pursuant to such legal process when it appears on its face to be valid. A note to the law says that customer records should be disclosed only upon legal process. Ala. Code sec. 5-5A-43.

Alaska–All books and records of savings and loan associations pertaining to accounts and loans of members shall be kept **confidential**. Alaska Stat. sec. 06.30.120. Bank records are confidential and shall not be made public except by court order, as required by state or federal law, when authorized, or to holder of negotiable instrument. When disclosure is required, the depositor must be notified unless disclosure is made under a search warrant. Sec. 06.05.175.

California–A bank customer is entitled to a ten-day notice before a state investigator can obtain records about the customer's financial affairs from the bank. Notice not required if a judge determines that law or state regulation has been or is about to be violated. Cal. Govt. Code sec. 7460.
The Financial Information Privacy Act prohibits financial institutions from sharing or selling personally identifiable non-public information without obtaining a consumer's consent ("opt-in"). It provides for a plain-language notice of the privacy rights it confers. Consumers must be given the opportunity to "opt out" of sharing with a financial institution's affiliates. Fin. Code sec. 4050.

Connecticut–A customer's records may not be disclosed by a financial institution without legal process or other specifically listed circumstances. Conn. Gen. Stat. Ann. 36a-41 through 45. The disclosure provisions of the federal Financial Services Modernization Act of 1999 are incorporated into state law applicable to banks, credit unions, and out-of-state trust companies.

Florida–The state may require banks operating electronic funds transfer systems to inform customers of their protection policies including "protection against wrongful or accidental disclosures of confidential information." In its annual report a bank must "disclose procedures for the protection of a customer's privacy and confidentiality of account information and discuss who has access to a customer's account information and under what circumstances." In addition, a customer's Social Security number may not be used as a personal identifying number in electronic systems. Fla. Stat. Ann. sec. 659.062.

Illinois–Bank disclosure of customer information is prohibited without customer authorization, a subpoena or regulatory agency request, or credit exchange. $1000 fine. 205 ILCS 5/48.1.

Iowa–Satellite terminals or data processing centers are not to permit any person to obtain information concerning the account of any person with a financial institution, unless such information is essential to complete or prevent the completion of a transaction then being engaged in through the use of that facility. Iowa Code Ann. sec. 527.10.

Louisiana–A financial institution or credit card company may not release personal credit or financial information except under subpoena with advance notice to the customer, except for exchanges among credit grantors and other businesses and for non-tax law enforcement investigations. La. Rev. Stat. Ann. sec. 9:3571.

Maine–Bank records are confidential, except for matching of government records, for supervisory audit, with consent of the individual, or by legal process. Me. Rev. Stat. Ann. title 9-B, sec. 161.

Maryland–A fiduciary institution may not disclose any financial records unless customer has authorized disclosure or unless records are subpoenaed; subpoena must be directed to institution and customer at least 21 days prior to disclosure. Md. Fin. Inst. Code Ann. sec. 1-302. See also **Credit Reporting**.

Massachusetts–No person may (1) condition the extension of credit on participation in an electronic funds transfer system, (2) require a consumer to accept an electronic fund transfer service or establish an account as a condition of employment or receipt of government benefits, or (3) condition the sale of goods or services on a customer's paying by electronic means. Mass. Gen. Laws Ann. ch. 167B, sec. 7.
A provider of electronic banking services may not disclose customer information except to the customer or with his authorization, to a party to the transaction, to government regulators, to auditors, to a consumer reporting agency, to the representative of a collection agency, or pursuant to legal process. There must be "reasonable procedures" to prevent unauthorized disclosure. Ch. 167B, sec. 16.
Banks are required to disclose, when requested by the state, the amount of deposits held by a recipient of, or an applicant for, public assistance. Ch. 18, sec. 15.

Minnesota–All banks must report quarterly the Social Security number, address, and "all account information" on any non-custodial parent owing child support. A bank may comply by providing the state a list of all its account holders and identifying numbers. Minn. Stat. Ann. Sec. 13B.06.

New Hampshire–No state or local investigator may get "financial or credit" information about an individual from a financial institution or credit reporting agency unless "described with particularity and consistent with the scope and requirements of the investigation." N.H. Rev. Stat. Ann. sec. 359-C.

New Mexico–All financial services and insurance companies must receive permission ("opt-in") from customers before disclosing account information to unaffiliated entities. Customer data may be disclosed to process a transaction or to comply with a legal process, according to a rule issued by the Public Regulation Commission. N. M. Stat. Ann. sec. 59A-4-3.

North Carolina–"It is the policy of this state that financial records should be treated as confidential and that no financial institution may provide to any government authority and no government authority may have access to any financial records... unless the financial record is described with reasonable specificity and access is sought pursuant to... customer authorization" or 12 U.S. C. 3401 or court order. There are other exceptions. N.C. Gen. Stat. 53B-1.

North Dakota–Banks may not disclose personal information to anyone (even the government) if a customer "opts out," unless there is valid legal process or other specific conditions are met. N. D. Cent. Code sec. 6-08.1-03.

Bank customer information may not be disclosed for marketing and other purposes unless a customer provides consent ("opt-in"). Cent. Code secs. 6-08.1-01 to 6-08.1-08.

Oklahoma–"A financial institution is prohibited from giving, releasing or disclosing any financial record to any [state] government authority unless it has written consent from the customer for the specific record requested; or it has been served with a subpoena" and a copy of the subpoena is served on the customer before it is served on the financial institution. The customer has 14 days to challenge the demand for his or her financial records. Okla. Stat. title 6, sec. 2201-2206. [See 1981 book.]

Oregon–A financial institution is prohibited from disclosing customer information to a state or local agency, unless there is a suspected violation of law, unless the customer consents, or unless the government follows procedures similar to those in the federal Right to Financial Privacy Act. Or. Rev. Stat. sec. 192.550.

Utah–Any bank may report to any other bank or credit reporting agency in the state that an "unsatisfactory demand deposit account has been closed out." There is no liability for any error or omission in such reports. Utah Code Ann. sec. 7-14-1.

Vermont–There is a limitation on disclosure of personal information by financial institutions, except to certain governmental agencies, credit bureaus, or check-authorization services. 8 Vt. Stat. Ann. 10203.

Federal law–Financial institutions and their service organizations must provide customers a "clear and conspicuous" description of their disclosure policies and provide a means for customers to "opt out" of such disclosures. But institutions may disclose customer information to an outside marketing firm if it promises not to re-disclose it. And the 1999 law permits free exchanges of customer data within a corporate family ("affiliate sharing"). Under the law, states may enact stiffer restrictions. 15 U.S.C. 6801-6809. [See 2002 book.]

Nearly all federal investigators must present proper legal process or "formal written requests" to inspect the financial records of an individual kept by a financial institution, including a credit card company. The federal agent must give simultaneous notice to the individual, who then has an opportunity to challenge the access, under the federal Right to Financial Privacy Act of 1978. 12 U.S.C. 3401. [See 1981 book.]

Within 120 hours, banks and credit-card companies must give the government access to any account information demanded in any investigation into money laundering. 31 U.S.C. 5318.

Banks must conduct due diligence to report transactions that look suspiciously like money laundering. Financial institutions must "know your customer" and report unusual or suspicious patterns by customers. Sec. 314(b) of PL 207-56.

"Any person engaged in a trade or business" must file a government report if a customer spends $10,000 or more in cash. 31 U.S.C. 5331.

Financial institutions must meet minimum standards set by the Department of Treasury for identifying any person opening a new bank account. 31 U.S.C. 5318.

The Internal Revenue Service must provide a customer 14 days' notice when it issues an administrative summons to see records at a bank or other financial institution. After receiving this notice, the customer then has a right to intervene in any proceeding with respect to enforcing the summons and may suspend compliance with the summons if he notifies the IRS and the bank within the 14-day period. In that case, a federal district judge will decide on whether to enforce the summons. The court may allow IRS to waive the notice requirement in exceptional circumstances. The law also requires IRS to notify a court when it seeks the financial records of a class of persons under a "John Doe" summons without specific names. Credit unions, consumer reporting agencies, credit card companies, brokers, attorneys and accountants are subject to these same provisions when they are holders of a third party's business records. 26 U.S.C. 7609. [See 1978-79 book.]

Intentionally accessing a computer without authority and thereby obtaining information from a financial institution, card issuer, or consumer reporting agency is a crime. 18 U.S.C. 1030. See **Computer Crime**.

The Electronic Funds Transfer Act requires institutions operating electronic banking services to inform customers of the circumstances under which automated-banking account information will be disclosed to third parties in the ordinary course of business. 15 U.S.C. 1693c(a)(9). See also 12 Code of Federal Regulations 205.10.

Amendments to the Fair Credit Reporting Act in 2003 allow financial institutions to disclose account information for marketing purposes to affiliated companies only if they offer an "opt-out" opportunity. 15 U.S.C. 6801-6809.

A regulation states that the Financial Services Modernization Act, 15 U.S.C. 6801-6809, requires financial institutions to make security-breach notifications to customers.

CABLE TELEVISION

California–State law prohibits a cable-television or satellite-TV company from using any electronic device to record, transmit, or observe events inside a subscriber's premises and from disclosing any information regarding a subscriber, without consent. Companies may sell lists of subscribers and addresses if they permit a subscriber to be deleted from such lists. Customers have a right to inspect and correct information about themselves. Cal. Penal Code 637.5. [See 1984-85 book.]

Connecticut–It is illegal to install a device to observe or listen inside a residence without the knowledge or permission of the cable television subscriber; to release subscriber lists unless subscribers have a chance to delete their names; to disclose subscribers' viewing habits without consent; and to install security scanning devices without express written consent. Conn. Gen. Stat. Ann. 53-421.

District of Columbia–A provider of cable television services shall not install any equipment that permits transmission of an aural, visual, or digital signal from the subscriber's premises without written permission of the subscriber. "The franchisee shall exercise the highest possible standard of care in protecting the privacy of data in its possession with respect to an individual subscriber's financial transactions, viewing selections, and utilization of other computer-based interactive services. This individual subscriber data shall not be subject to subpoena or other compulsory process." D.C. Code Ann. sec. 43-1845. [See 1984-85 book.]

Illinois–It is unlawful for a cable company to use equipment that would permit observation or listening inside the household; to provide any private or public organization with a list containing the name of a subscriber, unless prior notice is given to subscribers; to "disclose the television viewing habits of any individual subscriber" without consent; or to install any scanning device within a home without written consent. 720 ILCS 110/2. [See 1984-85 book.]

New Jersey–Individual information held by cable television providers must be confidential. N.J. Rev. Stat. sec. 48:5A-1.

Wisconsin–Every cable TV connection must have a device allowing the subscriber to shut off completely any reception or transmission. "No person may intrude on the privacy of another" by, without consent, monitoring use of a subscriber's equipment, disclosing names or addresses that describe behavior or viewing habits, conducting covert research over the system. List may be disclosed if the subscriber has a "negative check-off" option to be deleted. Wisc. Stat. Ann. 134.43. The wiretap law covers cable communications. 968.27(1). [See 1984-85 book.]

Federal law–Cable operators must abide by a code of fair information practices and provide a subscriber with the opportunity to limit disclosure of name and address for mail solicitation and similar purposes. In no case may a cable television company release viewing choices, retail transactions, or other personally identifiable information, without written or electronic consent. A subscriber may check information on file about him or herself for accuracy. Aggrieved individuals have a right to sue for damages. A governmental entity may obtain personally identifiable information only pursuant to a court order based on clear and convincing evidence that the subject of the information sought will be material evidence *and* if the subscriber has had an opportunity to be heard to contest the government's claim. 47 U.S.C. 551.

COMPUTER CRIME
Including 'Security-Breach Notifications'

Alabama–The Computer Crime Act punishes offenses against intellectual property – accessing, communicating, examining, modifying, or destroying computer data without authorization. Unauthorized disclosure of data is a crime. Ala. Code 13A-8-101.

Alaska–"Property" in the state's criminal code includes "intangible personal property including data or information stored in a computer program, system, or network." Alaska Stat. sec. 11.81.900(b)(48). Sec. 11.46.200(a)(3) defines the unauthorized use of computer *time* as "theft of services."

An entity must report to an individual affected any losses of personal data unless it determines that no harm will result. Stat. sec. 45.48.010.

Arizona–State law defines types of crimes using computers and makes them punishable as felonies. Ariz. Rev. Stat. sec. 13-2301E. Also, sec. 13-2316.

"When a person that conducts business in this state and that owns or licenses unencrypted computerized data that includes personal information becomes aware of an incident of unauthorized acquisition and access to unencrypted or unredacted computerized data that includes an individual's personal information, the person shall conduct a reasonable investigation to promptly determine if there has been a breach of the security system. If the investigation results in a determination that there has been a breach in the security system, the person shall notify the individuals affected." Financial and medical establishments subject to federal laws are not covered. Rev. Stat. Ann. sec. 44-7501.

Arkansas–Accessing a system to defraud or obtain money or services is a felony. Ark. Code Ann. sec. 5-41-103. Trespassing without authorization is a misdemeanor. Sec. 5-41-104.

Medical information in combination with a name is regarded as personal information, along with Social Security numbers, driver's license numbers or state

ID numbers, account numbers, and passwords, under the law that requires entities to notify persons when personal information is breached. The wrongful disclosure of this information will trigger the requirement to notify persons following a leak. Law enforcement must be advised before the security-breach notice, which need not be made if a business determines that no harm is likely. Code 4-110-102 through 106.

"A person or business shall take all reasonable steps to destroy or arrange for the destruction of a customer's records within its custody or control containing personal information that is no longer to be retained by the person or business by shredding, erasing, or otherwise modifying the personal information in the records to make it unreadable or undecipherable through any means."

"A person or business that acquires, owns, or licenses personal information about an Arkansas resident shall implement and maintain reasonable security procedures and practices appropriate to the nature of the information to protect the personal information from unauthorized access, destruction, use, modification, or disclosure." Sec. 4-110-104.

California–It is a crime to "intentionally access... any computer system or computer network for the purpose of devising or executing any scheme or artifice; to defraud or extort or obtain money, property or services with false or fraudulent intent, representations, or promises; or to maliciously access, alter, delete, damage, or destroy, any computer system, computer network, computer program, or data." Cal. Penal Code sec. 502.

Publishing a Personal Identification Number (PIN), password, access code, debit card number, or bank account number is a crime. Penal Code sec. 484j. Persons convicted of computer-related offenses are denied computer access. Penal Code 2702.

Stalking by use of a computer modem is a tort. Civil Code sec. 1708.7. See also **Mailing Lists**.

Government and private organizations must notify consumers if a security breach has occurred in their systems. Medical facilities and financial institutions are covered; the definition of protected "personal information" includes medical histories and health-insurance data. A 2011 law spells out which key details must be included in the notification letter and assures that the state Attorney General hears about the breach. If more than 500 persons must be notified, so must the state attorney general electronically, according to the 2011 amendment. Civ. Code sec. 1798.29 and 1798.82.

A company must dispose of personal information properly. Civ. Code sec. 1798.81.

It is illegal, without consent, to install "spyware" (1) taking control of the computer, (2) modifying certain settings on the computer, (3) collecting personally identifiable information, (4) preventing a user's reasonable efforts to block its installation or disable it, (5) misrepresenting that it will be uninstalled or disabled by a user's action, or (6) removing or rendering inoperative security, anti-spyware or anti-virus software on the computer. Bus. and Prof. Code sec. 22947.

Colorado–This law, similar to Florida's, creates a Class 3 misdemeanor for computer crimes. Colo. Rev. Stat. sec 18-5.5-101.

Using a computer network to disturb a person or to direct obscene language to another is the crime of harassment. Rev. Stat. sec. 18-9-111.

Entities must notify individuals when a breach of security occurs, leaking personal information (limited to a name with Social Security number, driver's license number, or account number). Sec. 6-1716.

Connecticut–Computer crime is a misdemeanor or a felony, depending on the dollar amount involved. Conn. Gen. Stat. Ann. sec. 53a-250. The victim of such a crime may sue. 52-5-570b.

A business must send notices to individuals named in a database where there has been a breach of security or access. It may be delayed for a criminal investigation. Failure is an unfair trade practice. Stat. Ann. sec. 36a-701b. The same law covers "credit freezes."

The law penalizes any individual or business that intentionally fails to protect personal information, Social Security numbers, driver's license numbers, and bank-account, credit-card, and insurance account numbers. The intentional failure to "destroy, erase or make unreadable" personal information during disposal of records is punishable, but not negligent or unintentional violations. Companies that collect SSNs must have privacy policies in place. Government entities are not subject to the requirement. Sec. 42-471. See **Credit Reporting**.

Delaware–Accessing a computer system for defrauding or obtaining money or services is computer fraud, and intentionally accessing, altering, destroying or attempting to do so for an improper purpose is computer misuse, both felonies. Del. Code title 11, sec. 931 to 939.

The law on notifications of security breaches is "borrowed from California." Code title 6, sec. 12B-101.

District of Columbia–Individuals must be notified when there is an unauthorized disclosure of personal information, narrowly defined. D.C. Code Ann. sec. 28-3851.

Florida–It is a felony to commit offenses against intellectual property; against computer equipment or supplies; or against computer users. The law prohibits willful modification, destruction, and disclosure. Fla. Stat. Ann. sec. 815.01. [See 1984-85 book.]

Businesses maintaining computerized data that include personal information must provide notice after breaches of system security under certain circumstances. Stat. Ann. sec. 817.568.

Georgia–Accessing or attempting to access a computer system owned by the state or under state contract or owned by any business is punishable by a fine and up to 15 years. Ga. Code Ann. sec. 16-9-90.

Stalking by computer is a crime. Code Ann. sec. 16-5-90.

State law requires information brokers like ChoicePoint, not all companies, to notify persons of breaches of any password or other identifier that permits access to an account without the name. Sec. 10-1-910.

Hawaii–Computer fraud is a felony or misdemeanor depending upon the amount of money or damages involved. Computer fraud includes accessing a system with intent to defraud or to obtain money, get credit information, or introduce false information. Also, to wrongfully damage or enhance the credit rating of any person is a crime. Unauthorized computer use is a separate crime. Haw. Rev. Stat. 708-890.

Businesses must notify individual of inadvertent breaches of personal information (undefined). Rev. Stat. sec. 487N-2.

Idaho–The law distinguishes between accessing or altering information with fraudulent purposes (a felony) and access only (a misdemeanor). Idaho Code sec. 18-2202.

Businesses must notify individuals of inadvertent breaches of personal information (undefined). Code sec. 28-51-105.

Illinois–Without the consent of the owner, it is illegal to alter a computer program, access a system, or to obtain uses or benefits from it. There is a civil right of action for victims of computer crime. The law now also includes two offenses: insertion of a computer virus that will damage or destroy a computer or data or cause harm to the users and "aggravated computer virus insertion," which would disrupt the functioning of state or local government or a public utility or cause bodily harm. There are penalties for unleashing a virus into a computer system. 720 ILCS 5/16D-1.

"Any data collector that owns or licenses personal information [SSNs, driver's license number, or account numbers] concerning an Illinois resident shall notify the resident that there has been a breach of the security of the system data following discovery or notification of the breach. The disclosure notification shall be made in the most expedient time possible and without unreasonable delay, consistent with any measures necessary to determine the scope of the breach and restore the reasonable integrity, security, and confidentiality of the data system." 815 ILCS 505/1.

The security-breach notification law was amended in 2011. 815 ILCS 530/5.

Indiana–A person who knowingly alters a computer program or data that is part of a system commits the felony of computer tampering. A person who accesses a system without consent commits a misdemeanor. Ind. Code Ann. sec. 35-43-1-2.

The law restricting use of SSNs by state agencies also requires "a state agency to notify: (1) an individual of a security breach of the agency's computer system if the individual's unencrypted personal information was or is reasonably believed to have been acquired by an unauthorized person; and (2) all consumer reporting agencies if notice is provided to more than 1,000 people." IC 4-1-11-2.

Iowa–Accessing a system without authority to obtain information and altering information with intent to defraud are crimes. Iowa Code Ann. sec. 716A.

A business must make a consumer notification in the event of a breach of security. Code Ann. sec. 715C.1.

Kansas–"Willfully exceeding the limits of authorization and damaging, modifying, altering, destroying, copying, disclosing, or taking possession" are crimes, as well as using a computer to defraud or to obtain money fraudulently. Kans. Stat. Ann. sec. 21-3755.

Businesses and government agencies must report to affected individuals unauthorized access to systems with personal information, if misuse has or will occur. Stat. sec. 50-7a01.

Kentucky–Fraudulently accessing a system to defraud, to obtain money or services, or to alter, damage, or attempt to alter information is a felony. Access for the sole purpose of gaining information is a misdemeanor. A person is guilty of "misuse of computer information" when he or she receives, conceals, or uses any proceeds from an act in violation of the law (or aids another in doing so). Ky. Rev. Stat. sec. 434.840.

Louisiana–Computer-related offenses are defined in La. Rev. Stat. 14:73.1 through 5.

Companies must notify individuals when unintended disclosures have occurred of their Social Security numbers, driver's license data, account numbers, passwords, or PINs, unless there is no likelihood of harm. Companies with a notification policy in place are not subject to the law. Rev. Stat. Ann. sec. 51:3071.

Maine–The unauthorized invasion of a computer system, including copying, damaging, or introducing a virus is a crime. Me. Rev. Stat. Ann. title 17A, sec. 432. Sec. 357 concerns theft of services.

Businesses must notify Maine residents and (if more than 1000 records are involved) notify credit bureaus of security breaches involving consumers' data. Rev. Stat. title 10, sec. 137.

Maryland–"No person shall intentionally, willfully, and without authorization access, attempt to access, or cause access to a computer, computer network, computer software..." Personal home computers and dedicated computers are excluded. Md. Crim. Law sec. 7-302. It is illegal to harass a person or to transmit obscene material by way of electronic mail. Crim. Law sec. 3-805.

A business shall notify individuals of a security breach of data (limited to a name with Social Security number, driver's license number, or account number) if it believes that misuse will result. It must notify the nationwide credit bureaus as well. Contractors shall notify the principal company of a breach of personal data. Comm. Law 14-3504.

Massachusetts–"Property" in the larceny statute includes "electronically processed or stored data, either tangible or intangible, [and] data while in transit." Mass. Gen. Laws Ann. ch. 266, sec. 30(2). Obtaining computer services fraudulently is a crime. Sec. 33-A.

A business must notify the attorney general and an individual of a "breach of security," narrowly defined as involving a name with Social Security number, driver's license number, or account number. Gen. Laws Ann. Ch. 93H.

Michigan–Trespassing into a computer system without authority and fraudulent use of a computer are crimes. It is illegal to circulate stone phone and credit-card numbers by computer. Law enforcement may seize equipment used wrongfully. Mich. Comp. Laws Ann. sec. 752.791. Harassment by mail, telephone or electronic communications is a crime (stalking). Sec. 750.411h.

Notification of a breach of personal information, widely defined, if injury or ID theft is likely requires notification. Falsely claiming a breach is punishable. Comp. Laws Ann. sec. 445.72.

Minnesota–Whoever intentionally and without authority damages or alters computer media is subject to a fine, depending on the loss involved, and a prison term. Minn. Stat. Ann. sec. 609.87. Inserting a computer virus into a system is a crime, as is theft by computer and unauthorized access. Sec. 609.89. Providers of computer services may not divulge the content of messages. Sec. 626A.27.

There must be notification of security breaches by businesses. Stat. Ann. sec. 325E. 61. And by government agencies. Sec. 13.055.

Personal information involved in an automated payments transaction must be deleted within 48 hours. Institutions that issue credit or debit cards may sue merchants for expenses incurred from a breach of security involving their payment cards. Sec. 325E.64.

Mississippi–Computer fraud is a crime, as well as intentionally denying an authorized user effective use of a computer system or disclosure or misuse of codes or passwords. Miss. Code Ann. sec. 97-45-1.

"A person who conducts business in this state shall disclose any breach of security to all affected individuals. The disclosure shall be made without unreasonable delay." Sec. 75-24-29.

Missouri–It is a crime to tamper with intellectual property. Mo. Ann. Stat. sec. 569.093.

Montana–The criminal code prohibits unlawful use of a computer, and "property" as defined in the criminal code on theft includes "any tangible or intangible thing of value... electronic impulses, electronically processed or produced data." Mont. Code Ann. 45-6-310.

The security-breach notification law is at Code Ann. 33-19-321 and 30-14-1704. See also **Social Security Numbers**.

Nebraska–Unauthorized access or disruption of a computer system is a felony. Neb. Rev. Stat. sec. 28-1343.

The breach notification law covers disclosures of a name with Social Security number, driver's license number, or account number, as well as "unique biometric data, such as a fingerprint, voice print, or retina or iris image, or other unique physical representation." Rev. Stat. sec. 87-802.

Nevada–A person who without authority denies the use of a computer to a person who has the duty and the right to use it is guilty of a misdemeanor. Also, using a computer without authority, to get personal information on another or to enter false information about another person in order to alter a credit rating is a crime. Nev. Rev. Stat. sec. 205.473.

Notification of security breaches is required. If a leak affects 1000 or more persons, credit bureaus must be notified. Rev. Stat. sec. 603A.

All "data collectors' including government agencies, universities, and businesses must use encryption when transferring personal data electronically, except for fax transmission. Businesses accepting credit cards must abide by the industry security standard. Sec. 597.970.

New Hampshire–Accessing, intercepting, or adding to computer data is a crime, unless the person believed that he had authority. N.H. Rev. Stat. Ann. sec. 638:16.

A business or government agency shall notify individuals of a security breach of data (limited to a name with Social Security number, driver's license number, or account number) if it believes that misuse will result. Rev. Stat. Ann. sec. 359-C:19.

New Jersey–There is a civil liability for computer-related fraud (N.J. Rev. Stat. sec. 2A:38A-1) and criminal liability (2C:20-1).

"Any business or public entity that compiles or maintains computerized records" shall notify New Jersey customers of breaches in security or any unauthorized access. Rev. Stat. sec. C.56: 8-164.

New Mexico–Misuse of a computer is a felony. N.M. Stat. Ann. sec. 30-45-1.

New York–Intruding into a computer system that contains confidential medical or personal information is a crime. Also, tampering with computer data while trying to commit a felony is itself an offense, as well as making unauthorized duplications of data. The law permits the state to prosecute a person in another state who taps into a computer in New York without authorization. N.Y. Penal Law 156.

Entities must notify affected persons of security breaches. Gen. Bus. Law art. 39-F.

The Department of Consumer Affairs in New York City may revoke or suspend licenses of businesses in the city found to have engaged in acts of identity theft. Int. 139-A, 2004. City agencies must immediately notify the police and then individuals involved after any unauthorized disclosure. Int. 140-A, 2004. All businesses licensed by the department have identical obligations. Int. 141-A, 2004.

North Carolina–The law punishes computer-related offenses, including physical damage to a unit, wrongfully accessing a computer or network, and altering or damaging computer software, and seeking to extort by use of a computer. N.C. Gen. Stat. 14-453.

There must be notifications of security breaches including, in cases involving 1000 or more persons, to the Attorney General consumer office. Gen. Stat. sec. 75-65.

North Dakota–Computer fraud by accessing, altering, damaging, destroying without authority with intent to defraud or deceive or control property or services is a Class B felony. Doing so with false pretense is a Class C felony. N.D. Cent. Code sec. 12.1-06.1-08.

Companies must notify individuals of breaches involving electronic data showing date of birth, mother's maiden name, employee ID number, or an individual's electronic or digital signature. The new law also includes ID-theft protections. Cent. Code sec. 12.1-23-11.

Ohio–In the criminal code, computer media is included in the definition of stolen property. Ohio Rev. Code Ann. sec. 2901.01 and 2913.01.

Rev. Code sec 1347.12 defines security breaches and sec. 1349.19 requires notice when it is reasonably believed that a breach will cause a material risk of identity theft or other fraud to the resident of the state. Notice must be within 45 days unless law enforcement delays it.

Oklahoma–Like Pennsylvania's, this law distinguishes computer hacking (a misdemeanor) from fraudulent alteration of, or damage to, computer data (a felony). Okla. Stat. Ann. 21, sec. 1951-1956.

The requirement on notification of security breaches covers computerized personal data, narrowly defined. Stat. 74-3113.1.

Oregon–Two classes of computer fraud are defined, prohibiting unauthorized access to systems. Or. Rev. Stat. sec. 164.377.

The requirement on notification of security breaches covers computerized personal data, narrowly defined. Rev. Stat. 646A.602 through 628.

Pennsylvania–Accessing, altering, damaging, or destroying any computer, system, or data base with criminal intent is a third-degree felony. Tampering, where no greater crime occurs, is a misdemeanor. Pa. Stat. Ann. title 18, sec. 3933.

The Breach of Personal Information Notification Act regards failure to make notification, to individuals and to statewide news media, an unfair trade practice. Stat. Ann. Title 73, sec. 2303.

Rhode Island–The computer crime law is similar to California's law. R.I. Gen. Laws sec. 11-52-1.

The security-breach notice law is at Gen. Laws 11-49.2-3.

South Carolina–The law defines "computer hacking." S.C. Code sec. 16-16-10.

Businesses must make notification of security breaches. Code Ann. sec. 1-11-490, 37-20-180.

South Dakota–The law punishes "computer hacking," including the use or disclosure of passwords without the consent of the owner. It also punishes wrongful access to computerized information, as well as altering or disclosing. S.D. Codified Laws Ann. 43-43B-1.

Tennessee–The law prohibits damaging or altering computers or computer data. Tenn. Code Ann. 39-14-602. [See 1984-85 book.]

State law requires businesses to notify customers of security breaches and provides a right to sue. Code Ann. sec. 47-18-21.

Texas–It is a misdemeanor to use a computer or gain access to it without consent when there is a computer security system in place; or to alter or damage a program or cause a system to malfunction. It is a felony if the loss exceeds $2500. Tex. Penal Code Ann. sec. 33.01.

It is a misdemeanor to disclose a secure password to another person. Legislative records are protected by Tex. Civ. Stat. Ann. art. 5429b.

A business must send written or electronic notices to victims of unauthorized disclosure of personal information. This protects residents of Texas as well those in states without security-breach notification laws. Bus. and Com. Law. sec. 521.053.

Utah–The altering, damaging or wrongful access of computer records is a misdemeanor or felony. Utah Code Ann. sec. 76-6-701.

"Spyware" companies must specify to users what is being installed on their computers as well as what information or behavior about them it is recording, under the Spyware Control Act. Companies face fines up to $10,000 each time they install spyware on a user's computer without consent. Code Ann. sec. 13-39-102.

Individuals must be notified of "an unauthorized acquisition of computerized data maintained by a person that compromises the security, confidentiality, or integrity of personal information," narrowly defined. Sec. 13-44-102.

Vermont–It is a crime to access a computer without authority or for a fraudulent purpose or to damage, interfere, or alter. Vt. Stat. Ann. tit 13, sec. 4101.

The Security Breach Notice Act is similar to Connecticut's law. It exempts law enforcement. Stat. Ann. 2435. "A business shall take all reasonable steps to destroy or arrange for the destruction of a customer's records within its custody or control containing personal information which is no longer to be retained by the business." 9 Vt. Stat. Ann. 2445.

Virginia–Fraudulent use of a system as well as trespassing in a system so as to cause a malfunction, alter data, or affect a financial transaction, is prohibited. It is a crime to invade one's privacy by perusing medical, employment, salary, credit or other financial or personal data relating to another person and stored in a computer. Va. Code sec. 18.2-152.2. [See 1984-85 book.] See also **Mailing Lists**.

Breaches of personal data must be reported to the individual and the attorney general. Code sec. 18.2-186.6.

Washington–Gaining access to a system for a criminal purpose or accessing any government computer is the crime of computer trespass Wash. Rev. Code Ann. Sec. 9A.52.110 and 9A.52.120.

Also, the criminal code defines "physical damage" as including "the total or partial alteration, damage, obliteration, or erasure of records, information, data, computer programs, or their computer representations, which are recorded for use in computers or the impairment, interruption, or interference with the use of such records, information, data, or computer programs, or the impairment, interruption, or interference with the use of any computer or services provided by computers," or "any diminution in the value of any property as the consequence of an act." Sec. 9A.48.100.

The law on breach notification is very similar to California's, but covers only government agencies. It allows an individual to sue when a breach occurs. Rev. Code sec. 19.255.010.

West Virginia–Fraud, tampering and unauthorized access are covered by W. Va. Code sec. 61-3c-4 through 12.

Security-breach notifications are required. Code sec. 46A-2A-101.

Wisconsin–It is a crime to modify, destroy, access, take, or copy data, programs or supporting documentation in a computer. Wisc. Stat. Ann. sec. 943.70.

There is a requirement to notify individuals of breaches of personal data. Stat. Ann. sec. 895.507.

Wyoming–The law defines crimes against intellectual property and makes it crime to wrongfully access a system or to deny computer services to an authorized user. Another section prohibits crimes against equipment, including impairing government or public services. A third section defines crimes against computer users. Wyo. Stat. sec. 6-3-501 through 504.

The security-breach law is triggered when there is a likelihood of misuse of the leaked data. Stat. Ann. sec. 40-12-501.

Federal law–It is a felony to trespass into a computer system across state lines or to receive classified information by computer with intent to injure the U.S. or to further a fraud by computer or to hack into a bank or credit-bureau computer; and a misdemeanor to trespass and obtain information from a computer system, across state lines. Trafficking in stolen computer passwords is a crime. 18 U.S.C. 1030.

It is a crime to transmit a virus to another computer system. 18 U.S.C. 1030(a)(5)(A).

Each federal agency is required to provide mandatory training in computer security awareness. The National Institute of Standards and Technology develops guidance and sets standards for encryption of data. 40 U.S.C. 759.

The Department of Veterans Affairs shall make timely notifications in the event of most breaches of personal data. P.L. 109-461, sec. 5726.

A regulation states that the Financial Modernization Act, 15 U.S.C. 6801-6809, requires security-breach notifications to customers by financial institutions.

See also **Medical Records.**

NOTE: All 50 states have laws that explicitly address electronic forms of stalking, harassment or cyberbullying. Cyberstalking is generally defined as use of electronic media with a pattern of threatening or malicious behavior. Cyberharassment generally refers to less threatening behavior online that annoys or torments another person. Cyberbullying generally refers to electronic harassment or bullying among minors within a school context.

CREDIT REPORTING AND INVESTIGATION
(Including 'Credit Repair,' 'Credit Clinics,' Check-Cashing, and Credit-Card Use)

Alaska–State law has procedures for any consumer to get a "security freeze" placed on his or her account. Alaska Stat. sec. 45.48.100.

Arizona–The sources of **investigative consumer reports** must be furnished to the consumer upon request, along with the contents of any reports. Within 15 days of written notice of an inaccuracy, the investigative company must respond to the consumer. If the facts in the dispute cannot be verified, the company must alter its file in accord with the consumer's version and notify any companies to whom the prior version was sent. Ariz. Rev. Stat. sec. 44-1693(A)(4).

Arkansas–A contract between a credit clinic and customer must include a list of rights, and a clinic may not charge for merely referring a customer to a credit grantor. Ark. Code Ann. sec. 4-91-101.

"A consumer may request that a security freeze be placed on his or her consumer report by sending a request in writing by certified mail to a consumer reporting agency at an address designated by the consumer reporting agency to receive such requests." The consumer reporting agency must place such a freeze within five days. Code 4-112-103.

California–Cal. Civil Code sec. 1785.1 regulates consumer credit reporting agencies, which gather credit-oriented information for consumer reports to third parties, usually grantors of credit. These companies must allow visual inspection of all files about an individual, including the sources of information. [See 1978-79 book.]

Sec. 1786 regulates investigative consumer reporting agencies, which gather personal information for reports to employers or insurers. Such companies must give the individual the opportunity to inspect visually the files on him or her, except for medical information, which need be disclosed only upon authorization by the individual's doctor. Sources of information need not be disclosed either. Special precautions are necessary when processing information in background checks overseas.

Users of an investigative consumer report must certify that they have notified the individual that a report will be made. An individual who is the subject of an investigative consumer report (used by insurers and employers) has many of the same protections available to the subject of a credit report. An employer must provide an investigative report to the applicant or employee who is the subject of the report. Sec. 1786. A credit bureau (for a reasonable fee) or a mortgage lender must disclose a person's credit score or credit rating. A consumer may opt-out of pre-screening. Sec. 1785.10. A consumer may opt out permanently from having information in a credit record provided to companies selling credit cards or credit services. Credit bureaus must have toll-free numbers to permit an individual to exercise this option. "Information brokers" must disclose "the ultimate end user" when they procure a credit report and they must certify the purpose for which a report will be used and that it will not be used for any other purposes. A credit bureau must reinvestigate within 30 days, and then the consumer may have a free corrected copy. Only verified information may be inserted into credit records. A credit *grantor*, like a bank or retail store, must reinvestigate disputed information and must notify a consumer before submitting negative information to a credit bureau. Sec. 1785.1 through 1785.11.

A credit bureau may not report bankruptcies after ten years. Sec. 1785.13.

A person may get a free copy of his or her credit report when it is requested by an employer. Sec. 1785.20.5.

As in federal law, a consumer may not sue for privacy invasions based on information seen under the *consumer credit reporting act* (Sec. 1785.1), but there is no similar waiver of a right to action in California's law with respect to *investigative consumer reporting agencies* (Sec. 1786).

Credit-card issuers must give card-holders "clear and conspicuous notice" if they are selling customer information. There must be an easy opportunity for a customer to get off rented lists. Sec. 1748.12.

"Credit repair" services must refrain from deceptive claims and from charging a fee for doing no more than referring customers to credit grantors when customers seek help in straightening out problems with credit-bureau reports. Repair services may not charge fees prior to performing services unless they are bonded. Customers have a five-day period in which to back out of a written agreement. A clear statement of consumer rights must be provided to potential customers. They must post a bond with the state Department of Justice. Sec. 1789.10.

A **merchant** may not require a credit card as a condition of paying by check or cashing a check. A merchant may ask to see a credit card, but the customer may refuse and still pay by check. The merchant may not copy the credit-card account number on the check. Sec. 1725.

Merchants may not require a customer's personal information, like address and phone number, as a condition of making a credit-card transaction. Sec. 1747.8. Users of an investigative consumer report must certify that they have notified the individual that a report will be made. An individual who is the subject of an investigative consumer report (used by insurers and employers) has many of the same protections available to the subject of a credit report. Sec. 1786.2-.50. See also **Mailing Lists**.

A credit issuer that discovers that key identifying information (first and last name, address, SSN) on an application for credit does not match the information in the credit report must take reasonable steps to stop and verify the accuracy of the information on the application. Consumer credit reporting agencies must place a freeze on a credit report within three days of receiving the request. Civ. Code sec. 1785.20.3.

Credit bureaus must honor fraud alerts placed by consumers who suspect they are victims of identity theft. Civ. Code sec. 12785.10 through 19.5. But they may continue to report data they collected from government sources.

A prospective employer may not use a consumer credit report in the hiring process unless directly related to the job, except for management positions, law enforcement, and jobs involving handling significant amounts of money. Civ. Code sec. 1785.20.

Colorado–A consumer is entitled to a free credit report for himself or herself once a year. Credit bureaus must provide a live operator for complaints. They must notify a consumer if three or more inquiries are made about him or her in a 12-month period or if adverse information is added to a credit report. A consumer may submit a dispute over the accuracy of a report to arbitration. Col. Rev. Stat. 12-14.3-101.

When payment is made by check, a person shall not require the maker of the check to record a SSN for ID or proof of creditworthiness, except for payment of a student loan. Rev. Stat. Ann. sec. 4-3-506.

A consumer may elect to place a "security freeze" on a credit report corrupted by fraudulent activity. Sec. 12-14.3-102.

Connecticut–The state consumer credit reports law requires a **credit bureau** to investigate a dispute within 30 days and correct any misinformation in its files upon satisfactory presentation of proof of error. A notice identifying the credit bureau must be given to the individual before adverse action is taken. The fee for access to one's own file is limited to $5. There is a right to sue for willful misuse of a credit report. Conn. Gen. Stat. Ann. sec. 36a-699a.

As in California, Connecticut requires an advisory to customers of credit clinics that federal and state law require similar benefits without charge or with a small charge. Sec. 36-435l.

The sale of credit-card names is prohibited. Sec. 42-133gg.

'Security freeze' means a notice placed in a consumer's credit report, at the request of the consumer, that prohibits the credit rating agency from releasing the consumer's credit report or any information from it without the express authorization of the consumer.

"Any consumer may submit a written request... to a credit rating agency to place a security freeze on such consumer's credit report. Such credit rating agency shall place a security freeze on a consumer's credit report not later than five business days after receipt of such request. Not later than ten business days after placing a security freeze on a consumer's credit report, such credit rating agency shall send a written confirmation of such security freeze to such consumer that provides the consumer with a unique personal identification number or password to be used by the consumer when providing authorization for the release of such consumer's report to a third party or for a period of time.

"In the event such consumer wishes to authorize the disclosure of such consumer's credit report to a third party, or for a period of time, while such security freeze is in effect, such consumer shall contact such credit rating agency and provide: (1) Proper identification, (2) the unique personal identification number or password described in subsection (a) of this section, and (3) proper information regarding the third party who is to receive the credit report or the time period for which the credit report shall be available. Any credit rating agency that receives a request from a consumer pursuant to this section shall lift such security freeze not later than three business days after receipt of such request.

"Except for the temporary lifting of a security freeze as provided in subsection (b) of this section, any security freeze authorized pursuant to the provisions of this section shall remain in effect until such time as such consumer requests such security freeze to be removed. A credit rating agency shall remove such security freeze not later than three business days after receipt of such request provided such consumer." Stat. Ann. sec. 36a-701a.

Utilities and telecommunications carriers may not report to credit bureaus payment delinquencies of less than 60 days or without a 30-day written notice to the customer. It may not report delinquencies once a person has filed a complaint about service. 16-262d(g).

The law prohibits certain employers from using credit reports in making hiring and employment decisions, unless "substantially related to the employee's current or potential job." 31-51tt.

Delaware–As a condition of accepting a credit card, a **merchant** may not record the address or phone number of a customer except to facilitate delivery, for special orders, when authorization is *not* required by the card issuer, or when the merchant processes transaction by mailing forms to a bankcard center. Del. Code title 11, sec. 914. As a condition for accepting a check, a merchant may not request or record a customer's credit-card number unless the card issuer is guaranteeing the check. The merchant may ask for it to show identification or credit worthiness and may record the type and issuer of the card and the expiration date. Sec. 915.

A request for a credit freeze or "security freeze" may be made electronically. Code title 6, sec. 2201.

District of Columbia–Merchants may not copy personal information on a credit-card slip. D.C. Code Ann. sec. 47-3153.

"A credit reporting agency shall place a security freeze on a consumer's credit report [within three days] if a consumer, providing proper identification, makes a request to the credit reporting agency by certified mail. In addition, a credit reporting agency shall make available an Internet-based method of requesting a security freeze and shall accept requests by one of the following methods: telephone or regular mail." Code Ann. sec. 28-3862.

Florida–Merchants may not record or request a credit-card number when a customer pays by check unless the card issuer is guaranteeing the check. Fla. Stat. Ann. sec. 832.075.

The law on credit repair is identical to Arkansas'. Sec. 817.7001-704.

A person must be informed if genetic information was used to deny a mortgage, credit, loan or educational opportunity. Sec. 760.40.

State law prohibits a collection agency from revealing that a debt exists if the debt is in dispute, without also revealing the fact of the dispute. Sec. 559.72(3) and (6).

Chap. 8A, Art. XII, Secs. 8A-271–275, Code of Miami-Dade County requires an investigative firm to provide a consumer with all the names of persons contacted in an investigation. Uninvited credit investigators are declared a nuisance.

The law describes procedures for placing a freeze on a credit report. Stat. Ann. sec. 501.005.

Georgia–"Each **consumer reporting agency** which compiles and maintains files on consumers on a nationwide basis shall furnish to any consumer who had provided appropriate verification of his or her identity two complete consumer reports per calendar year, upon request and without charge." It is a crime to receive a credit report under false pretenses or to provide credit information to someone not authorized to receive it. Ga. Code Ann. sec. 10-1-392 (29). [See 1997 book.].

It is a crime to operate a "credit repair service." Ga. Code Ann. 16-9-59.

The law on **merchants** recording credit-card numbers on checks is similar to Delaware's. Merchants may record addresses and phone numbers of credit-card slips only to facilitate delivery or to take special orders. A merchant may not require a phone number to accept a credit card, nor imprint a credit card number on a customer's check. 10-1-393.3.

State law requires information brokers like ChoicePoint to notify persons of breaches of any password or other identifier that permits access to an account without the name. Code Ann. 10-1-910.

Hawaii–A credit report in employment may be used only after a person has received a conditional offer of employment, which may be withdrawn then if information in the credit history reflects on job qualifications (and presumably is negative). Exceptions: management positions, regulated financial institutions, and companies permitted by federal or state law to inquire into credit histories. Haw. Rev. Stat. sec. 378-2.7. See also **Computer Crime**.

Idaho–Credit-reporting agencies must block information in the file of a person who presents a police report showing victimization of theft of identity. Idaho Code sec. 28-51-102.

Illinois–The victim of ID theft may place a security freeze on a credit report. 815 ILCS 505/MM.

An employer may not hire, recruit, discharge or discriminate against an employee due to an individual's credit history or even inquire into credit histories. 820 ILCS 70/10.

Iowa–No credit-card number may be required to use **a check**, nor may it be recorded on the check. Iowa Code Ann. sec. 537.8101.

Kansas–State **credit-reporting** law is identical to federal law. Unfair credit reporting is a criminal act. Kans. Stat. sec. 50-720.

Merchants may not copy a customer's credit-card account number on personal checks presented for purchase. Kans. Stat. Ann. sec. 50-669.

Only victims of ID theft may ask for a credit freeze on their credit records, with a police investigative report or complaint filed with a law enforcement agency. Stat. Ann. 21-4018. See also sec. 50-723.

Kentucky–Ky. Rev. Stat. Ann. sec. 431.350 provides that no **consumer reporting agency** shall maintain in its files any information concerning criminal charges unless those charges resulted in a conviction.

The law allows for credit freezes on credit reports in a way similar to Kansas law. Rev. Stat. 367.363 through .367.

Louisiana–The law on credit repair is similar to Arkansas'. La. Rev. Stat. Ann. sec. 9:3573.1.

Sec. 9:3571.1 regulates credit freezes.

Maine–State **credit-reporting** law is stronger than federal law. Two provisions that go beyond federal law were invalidated by the State Supreme Court in 1980. One would require a customer to give his or her consent before an investigation could be conducted, and the other would prohibit consumer reporting firms from collecting certain information, including "personal life style," "philosophy," "political beliefs," "and "hearsay." Me. Rev. Stat. title 10, sec. 1312. [See 1978-79 book.] The Bureau of Consumer Protection is responsible for compliance.

Consumers may place a freeze on their credit records if there has been fraud involved. Rev. Stat. title 10, sec. 1313-C through E.

Maryland–The state law is similar to the federal **fair-credit-reporting law**. It provides that an exact copy of any file (except for medical information and sources) is to be given to the consumer without charge. Md. Comm. Law Code Ann. sec. 14-1209.

The law on credit-service businesses is similar to California's law on credit repair. Comm. Law 14-1901.

It is illegal to disclose another person's credit-card or automatic-teller number to another. Md. Crim. Law sec. 8-213. A **merchant** may not record a telephone number on a credit-card transaction form unless the merchant is not required to get telephone authorization for the charge or unless the merchant mails its transaction forms to a bank to process. 13-317.

The law on **merchants** recording credit-card numbers on checks is similar to Delaware's. Md. Com. Law Code Ann. 10-318.

Employers are prohibited from using an applicant's or present employee's credit report or credit history in determining whether to deny employment, to discharge, or to determine compensation or conditions of work. A major exception: information related to a "bona fide purpose that is substantially job-related," generally thought to mean involving money or confidentiality. Where an employer chooses to request or use credit information for a bona fide purpose, it must disclose its intent to do so in writing to the employee. Md. Labor & Empl. Code sec 3-711.

Massachusetts–Mass. Gen. Laws Ann. ch. 93, sec. 51 limits **credit-report access** to third parties; sec. 52 limits content in consumer credit reports–no arrest record over seven years old, bankruptcies over 14 years; sec. 53 demands that the consumer be informed when an investigative report is being filed; sec. 54 and 55 limit access or provide protection for the consumer in the dissemination of the investigative report; sec. 56 and 57 force disclosure to the consumer, upon request, of the nature and sources (except "sources of information acquired solely for use in preparing an investigative consumer report") of information maintained; sec. 58 creates a right to challenge contents of a report. A national credit bureau must provide one free copy of a credit report to a consumer who asks and must investigate and correct errors within 30 days of a request and establish a toll-free line for inquiries. Consumers may opt out of targeted marketing lists based on credit-bureau files and may sue credit grantors that provide erroneous information.

Merchants may not copy personal identification information on credit-card forms nor copy credit-card information on a customer's check. Sec. 104.

The law on credit repair is similar to Arkansas'. Sec. 68A-E.

Consumers have a right to have a "security freeze" placed in their credit files and to have it lifted later. Gen. Laws Ann. Ch 66, sec. 8A.

Michigan–The Identity Theft Protection Act of 2005 prohibits denial of credit simply because a person is victimized by identity theft. Mich. Comp. Laws Ann. sec. 445.71.

Minnesota–A person may have a copy of his or her own **credit report** for no more than $8. As in California, an employer must give notice to a person when a credit report is used to evaluate an applicant and the applicant may get a copy of the report directly from the employer. Minn. Stat. Ann. Sec. 13C.01.

The law on **merchants** recording information on credit-card slips is the same as Georgia's, and the law on check cashing is similar to Delaware's. Minn. Stat. Ann. 325F.981 and 982.

The law provides the procedure for a credit freeze (called a "security freeze" in the law). Stat. sec. 13C.016 through 13C.019.

Mississippi–A victim of identity theft with an investigative report may place a security freeze in his or her credit file, meaning that the file will not be provided to credit grantors without notifying the consumer and the will be notified of name or address changes in the file. Miss. Code Ann. sec 75-24-201.

Montana–The purpose of the state law is to "require that **consumer reporting agencies** adopt reasonable procedures for meeting the needs of commerce for consumer credit... with regard to confidentiality, accuracy, relevancy, and proper utilization of such information." Further, the law's purpose is to "guard an individual's right to privacy guaranteed in... the Montana constitution." Mont. Code Ann. sec. 31-3-101 through 153. "A credit rating is a property right with full constitutional protection."

Identity-theft victims get a credit freeze without charge. Code Ann. sec. 30-14-1726 through 1736. See also **Identity Theft**.

Nebraska–The attorney general enforces the statute providing for security freezes in credit reports. Neb. Rev. Stat. sec. 8-2603 through 2615.

Nevada–As a condition of accepting a check, a **merchant** may not record a person's credit-card number, with exceptions similar to Delaware's. The law on check cashing is similar to Delaware's. Nev. Rev. Stat. sec. 598.088.

The law on credit repair is similar to Arkansas'. Sec. 598.281.

The request for a credit freeze must be in writing by certified mail. Rev. Stat. Ann. sec. 598C. Businesses accepting credit cards must abide by the industry security standard. Sec. 597.970.

New Hampshire–The law regulating **consumer credit reporting** is similar to federal law. In addition, investigative companies must give the individual a copy of any report requested on him or her, including the names of sources used and names of persons who were sent copies of the report. Credit bureaus and users of credit-bureau sales lists must publish a toll-free number permitting a consumer to prevent his or her name from being disclosed for that purpose. N.H. Rev. Stat. Ann. sec. 359-B. See also **Bank Records**.

Credit bureaus must notify residents of the opportunity for a security freeze in their credit files and how to remove it. All consumers are eligible; no fees for identity theft victims who submit a copy of a police report. Rev. Stat. Ann. sec 359-B:22.

New Jersey–A consumer is entitled to a free credit report himself or herself. N.J. Stat. Ann. 56:11-29.

A **merchant** may not record any personal information on a credit-card slip unless authorization is *not* required by the card issuer. Sec. 56:11-17. A **merchant** may not request a credit card in order to cash a check. Sec. 358-M:1.

State law allows a consumer to place a freeze on his or her credit record if a victim of identity theft. A credit bureau must send a notice of rights under this state law when making a consumer disclosure under the federal Fair Credit Reporting Act. Rev. Stat. sec. 56:11-45.

New Mexico–"Credit bureau** shall disclose the content of all information about that particular consumer which is included in this credit report or rating, if the consumer making the request presents adequate identification." The credit investigating firm must reinvestigate, update, and correct information at no cost ($5 if you were not denied credit).

After receiving written notice of inaccuracies, a credit bureau is liable for any subsequent report that fails to correct the inaccuracies. A credit bureau may give only name, address, former addresses and names of employers to government agencies; to others it may provide credit, employment or other data for a bona fide business use. A bureau must segregate credit and personnel-type investigative data. After seven years, data must be purged, including criminal data seven years after release (14 years for bankruptcy information). Punitive damages are possible for abuses. N.M. Stat. Ann. sec. 56-3-1.

The law on security freezes resembles New Hampshire's. Stat. Ann. sec 56-3A-1.

New York–The **credit-reporting law** is identical to Maine's, except for the restriction on types of information gathered. There is no bar to the consumer suing for invasion of privacy based on information in his or her file. Gen. Bus. Laws sec. 380.

The law also includes an elaborate set of restrictions on the reporting of accusations of shoplifting. These accusations may be reported to others only if the person admitted wrongdoing without coercion and the information is used only for employment purposes. The retail store that provides such information to a consumer-reporting agency must notify the individual in writing, with the name of the company.

Introducing false information into a consumer reporting agency file to damage or enhance the credit standing of an individual is punishable by fine or one-year imprisonment. Gen. Bus. Laws sec. 387.

New York's law on "credit service businesses" is similar to California's. Such services may not charge a fee in advance. Gen. Bus. Laws sec. 458a.

Merchants are restricted when they collect addresses on credit-card transaction slips and when they collect personal information on checks. N.Y. Gen. Bus. Law sec. 520-a.

The law on security freezes resembles New Hampshire's. There is no fee for the first request. Gen. Bus. Laws sec 380-a.

North Carolina–Credit repair is regulated. N.C. Gen. Stat. 66-220.

Consumers may have a freeze put on their credit records, and credit bureaus may charge $10. Gen. Stat. sec. 75-63.

North Dakota–The law on **checks and credit-card slips** is identical to New York's sec. 520-a. N.D. Cent. Code 51-14.1-03.

There are no fees for removing a credit freeze on a credit record. Cent. Code 51-33.

Ohio–A **merchant** may not record the address, phone number, or Social Security number of a credit-card holder in credit-card sales "except for legitimate business purposes," including when a card is given as a deposit, when the customer consents, when a debt is being collected, and when data will not be released to third parties except for collections and not used for marketing. Ohio Rev. Code Ann. 1349.17.

Oklahoma–Prior to sending a credit standing of any person to a retail concern, a **credit reporting agency** must first mail a copy of its opinion to the person about whom the opinion is given. A consumer may collect damages for false ratings. Okla. Stat. title 24, sec. 82.

No pre-payment is required and a person may have a statement of rights when dealing with a "credit clinic." title 24, sec. 131.

The fee for a credit freeze is waived for seniors and victims of identity theft. A consumer may request a temporary lift of the freeze. Stat. Ann. title 24, sec. 149.

Oregon–A person may elect to place a freeze on his or her credit report, free to victims of identity theft, no more than $10 for others. Or. Rev. Stat. 646A.602 through 628.

A credit history may not be the basis of an employment decision, except in financial or public-safety jobs, of if credit is job related and the applicant is informed. Sec. 659A.885.

Pennsylvania–**Merchants** may not copy personal information on a credit-card slip. Pa. Stat. Ann. title 69, sec. 2602.

The law on credit freezes, enforced by the attorney general, is similar to Oklahoma's. A freeze expires after seven years. Stat. Ann. 73-2503.

Rhode Island–Anybody requesting a **credit report** must first notify a consumer that a credit report may be requested. All credit bureaus must register with the Secretary of State. A credit bureau must give a consumer access to his or her credit report within four days. R.I. Gen. Laws Sec. 6-13.1-21.

Merchants may not copy personal information on credit-card slips. 6-13-16. Merchants may not record Social Security numbers on checks. R.I. Gen. Laws 6-13-17.

Seniors and ID-theft victims are exempt from a fee for placing a credit freeze in their credit reports. Gen. Laws 6-48-5.

"No credit bureau doing business in this state shall use all or part of a consumer's Social Security number as the sole factor when determining whether a credit report in its files matches the identity of a person who is the subject of a credit inquiry from a user of credit reports. When a Social Security number is used as a factor, a credit bureau may disclose a credit report in its files to an inquiring user of credit reports only if the name and, at a minimum, at least one other identifier such as address, prior address, date of birth, mother's maiden name, place of employment, or prior place of employment, also match the identity of the person who is the subject of the inquiry." Gen. Laws 6-13.1-29.

South Carolina–Credit freezes are authorized. S.C. Code sec. 37-20-180.

South Dakota–The law allowing credit freezes applies to identity-theft victims with a police report. There are no fees; the freeze expires after seven years or upon a consumer's request, if earlier. S.D. Codified Laws Ann. sec. 54-15 through 54-15-6.

Tennessee–Same law as New Hampshire's on **merchants** cashing checks. Sec. 47-22-104.

Texas–Furnishing false credit information is illegal. Tex. Finance Code sec. 391.002.

Credit-repair businesses may not charge in advance nor charge for merely referring a customer to a retail credit grantor. Fin. Code Ann. 393.105.

Credit bureaus are regulated by Bus. and Comm. Code 20.02, which also allows a "security alert" notifying credit grantors that a consumer may be the victim of ID theft and a "security freeze" prohibiting a credit bureau from releasing a consumer report for victims of theft of identity.

Utah–The law on "credit repair" is similar to California's (1789.10). Utah Code Ann. 13-21-1.

Credit grantors must notify consumers that negative information may be reported to **credit bureaus**. Sec. 70C-7-107.

The law on credit freezes permits consumers temporarily to lift freezes electronically. Code Ann. sec. 13-42-102, 13-42-201 through 205, 13-41-401.

Vermont–A company must get the consent of a consumer before obtaining a credit report. **Credit bureaus** "shall adopt reasonable procedures to assure maximum possible compliance" with this requirement. A consumer is entitled to a free credit report. 9 Vt. Stat. Ann. 2480b and e.

Consumers are entitled to be notified of their rights to place a security freeze in their credit reports, to stop the use of their credit report to open new accounts unless the consumer gives the business specific authority to review the credit report. An executor or next of kin may notify credit reporting agencies when a consumer is deceased, so that the credit report is not used inappropriately. 9 Vt. Stat. Ann. 2480h.

Except for financial institutions, employers may not use or inquire into an applicant's or employee's credit report, credit history, or credit score, unless the person has access to confidential financial information. Sec. 495i.

Virginia–State law sets forth rights when a consumer suspects there has been a billing error. The creditor must reply within 30 days or face loss of its right to collect. During this time, the creditor may not communicate to others unfavorable information about the consumer's ability to pay. Va. Code sec. 6.1-366(c).

An insurance company must notify an applicant in writing that he or she may have reasons for an adverse decision stated in writing and may have access to information used in making that decision. The company must disclose the nature and substance of all information, including medical information. Va. Code 38.1-52(11). [See 1981 book.]

The law on credit repair is similar to California's. 6.1-369.1.

Retailers (as distinguished from credit-card companies or direct marketers) may not disclose customer transaction information without notice to the customer or an opportunity "to opt out." Sec. 59.1-442.

No **credit-card numbers** may be recorded on checks used by customers. Sec. 11-33.1, 11-34.

The law on credit reporting allows for a credit freeze. Code sec. 18.2-186.3:1.

Washington–A **credit bureau** must convey notice of a consumer's dispute to the company that provided the disputed information. Wash. Rev. Code Ann. sec. 19.182.090.

No **credit-card numbers** may be recorded on checks, unless the card is provided as a security deposit. Sec. 62.A-512.

Credit repair clinics are regulated. Sec. 19.134.010.

A person may not procure a consumer report for employment purposes where any information bears on the consumer's creditworthiness, credit standing, or credit capacity, unless the information is either (1) substantially job related and the employer's reasons for the use of such information are disclosed to the consumer in writing; or (2) required by law. Rev. Code sec. 19.182.020(2)(c).

A victim of theft of identity may have a credit freeze placed on a credit-bureau report. Sec. 19.182.

Wisconsin–**Merchants** may ask for a credit card for ID but may not note the number on a check that is presented. Wis. Stat. Ann. sec. 423.402. Nor may they require address, phone or other ID as a condition of accepting a credit card. 423.401.

All consumers qualify for credit freezes, but there is no fee for an individual who submits "evidence satisfactory to the credit reporting agency" that the individual made a report to a law enforcement agency. Stat. Ann. sec. 138.25.

Wyoming–A consumer may place "a security freeze" on his or her credit file. A credit bureau must be able to apply a block on a credit report within 15 minutes of a request. Wyo. Stat. Ann. sec. 40-12-503.

Federal law–Consumers have the right to have a copy of a **credit report**. Medical information need not be disclosed to the consumer, according to the Fair Credit Reporting Act, 15 U.S.C. 1681. [See 1997 book.] See also 15 U.S.C. 6801-6809.

An $8 fee may be charged, but there is no charge if the consumer has been refused credit, insurance or employment, and the individual may take an adviser with him or her. Victims of identity fraud, poor persons, and unemployed persons may obtain a free credit report once a year.

Companies must purge obsolete information and must reinvestigate disputed information. If a dispute remains, the consumer may have his or her version of the facts included in subsequent consumer reports.

Credit reports may go only to companies that will use them for credit, insurance, employment, or "a legitimate business need." A credit report may not be used for an employment decision without the consent of the individual. Before any adverse action is taken (like denial of a job) the consumer must receive a copy of the report. All users are immune from libel or privacy lawsuits.

The nationwide credit bureaus must establish a system for notifying each other of reinvestigations of information disputed by a consumer so that the consumer need not contact all three.

When credit bureaus reinvestigate inaccuracies they must give weight to information provided by consumers. The national credit bureaus' toll-free lines must be staffed with real people. The bureaus must complete reinvestigations requested by consumers within 30 days. The bureaus and credit grantors must clearly label accounts in good standing that are closed by the consumer himself or herself. Banks and stores that furnish information to credit bureaus have obligations to report accurately. Credit-card companies, catalogers, and insurance companies may conduct "pre-screening," in which they send their mailing lists to a credit bureau to eliminate bad credit risks before an offer is sent. The major credit bureaus must establish a joint toll-free number so that consumers may choose not to be a part of pre-screening.

It is a felony to procure a credit report under false pretenses. Information brokers must take precautions not to disclose credit information to users without a legal, permissible purpose for a credit report. State attorneys general have authority to enforce the FCRA. So-called "credit repair" firms may not collect a fee before performing their services.

Consumers are entitled to a free copy of their credit score or credit ranking if adversely affected by it. P.L. 111-203, amending Sec. 615 of the Fair Credit Reporting Act.

Guidelines for complying with the Fair Credit Reporting Act are published by the Federal Trade Commission. 16 Code of Federal Regulations 600.

The federal Equal Credit Opportunity Act prohibits credit discrimination on the basis of race, color, religion, national origin, sex, marital status, welfare payments or age (unless you're not old enough to enter into a binding contract). Married persons may have credit information listed in husband's and wife's names separately, and creditors may see only the file of the spouse who applied for credit. 15 U.S.C. 1691.

The Fair Credit Billing Act provides a procedure for settling disputes of bills. If you send a written notification of the problem to the company that billed you, it may not report the unpaid amount to a credit bureau or other firms as delinquent. Installment credit or commercial credit are not covered by this law. 15 U.S.C. 1666.

The U.S. Department of Education is authorized to "enter into cooperative agreements with credit bureau organizations providing for the exchange of information concerning student borrowers." No information may be disclosed by the Department of Education unless it has been verified and a reasonable attempt has been made to collect the debt in question. Information is not to be used for collection efforts that "are not fair or reasonable or that involve harassment, intimidation, false or misleading representations, or unnecessary communication." 20 U.S.C. 1080.

The Department of Veterans Affairs may exchange information with credit bureaus and consumer reporting agencies on defaulted payment obligations. 38 U.S.C. 3301(a).

The Debt Collection Act of 1982 permits all federal agencies to exchange information on recipients of government loans and grants, and to disclose identities of delinquent debtors to private collection firms. It permits access to Internal Revenue Service files for the whereabouts of debtors, and requires Social Security numbers of all loan applicants. 28 U.S.C. 1 (note).

Bill collectors may not use false pretenses to collect consumer debts, nor may they call continually, nor at inconvenient hours. Collection agencies may not disclose the fact of a consumer debt in seeking the whereabouts of the debtor, nor may they fail to identify themselves in telephoning a consumer, according to the Fair Debt Collection Practices Act. 15 U.S.C. 1692.

Intentionally accessing a computer without authority and thereby obtaining information from a consumer reporting agency is a crime. 18 U.S.C. 1030. See **Computer Crime**.

The Fair Credit Reporting Act says that credit bureaus must provide a credit report to a consumer without charge once a year. The law pre-empts stronger state laws. Retailers and lenders must now notify customers before reporting negative information to credit bureaus. Consumers may have access to their credit scores. Credit reports may be used in insurance underwriting. The major credit bureaus are required to respond to victims of identity theft with a "fraud alert." Retailers may print only the last five digits of a credit-card number on receipts. Ads for "free credit reports" must disclose that the government provides a free Web site for this purpose. 15 U.S.C. 1681.

CRIMINAL JUSTICE INFORMATION SYSTEMS

Alabama–Release of records in the criminal justice information system is limited by "the right to privacy." There may be no release of records without convictions to outsiders and no release of other information to those with no "need to know." Ala. Code 41-9-636.

Alaska–The Governor's Commission on the Administration of Justice is authorized to establish rules, regulations, and procedures to insure the privacy and security of criminal justice information systems. Alaska Stat. sec. 12.62.010. The law gives a person the right to inspect information on him or her, and limits access to other parties. Regulations published at 6 AAC 10.010. Criminal information, with exceptions, is available only to law enforcement with a need to know. A victim of unauthorized disclosure may sue the state. 12.62.030(a).

Arizona–Conviction information may be shared with non-law enforcement agencies of government; and arrest and/or conviction data may be given to the individual involved. Ariz. Rev. Stat. sec. 41-1750.

Arkansas–The Criminal Justice and Highway Safety Information Center within the state administration department has been authorized by statute. The personal data it may keep is proscribed by statute. Ark. Code Ann. sec. 12-12-201. A supervisory board is responsible for monitoring the system, including its privacy and security aspects. Sec. 12-12-213 says, "Nothing in this act shall be construed so as to give authority to any person, agency or corporation or other legal entity to invade the privacy of any citizen... other than to the extent provided in this act." Individuals who have been charged with a crime may inspect their

own files. Sec. 12-12-207 requires the Center to purge its files of all records of persons acquitted or whose charges were dropped.

California–Cal. Penal Code sec. 11075-81 restricts dissemination of criminal offender records to those authorized by statute and allows an individual to challenge his or her own file. Secs. 13100 to 13202 regulate criminal justice systems. Sec. 11105 regulates dissemination of criminal histories by the state attorney general. Secs. 296, 299.5, and 299.6 governs collection of DNA samples by law enforcement.

Penal Code sec. 11121-26 affects the individual's correction of his or her own record.

Colorado–State law requires that certain criminal justice information be kept confidential to comply with federal rules. Colo. Rev. Stat. sec. 24-72-301.

Connecticut–Managers of the state's criminal history system have an obligation of accuracy and may disclose only to authorized persons. Conviction information is open to all; non-conviction information is open to the subject of the record or his or her attorney. There is a right of correction by the record subject. Conn. Gen. Stat. Ann. sec. 54-142g-p.

Delaware–There are provisions for individual access, for limiting disclosure, and for sealing information in criminal information systems. Del. Code title 11, sec. 8513.

Florida–An individual may inspect and challenge criminal history records and have all recipients of the original data informed of changes. Certain records are expunged. Fla. Stat. Ann. sec. 943.056.

Georgia–The Georgia Crime Information Center is required to make a person's records available for inspection, allow him or her to challenge their accuracy and have items expunged. If a dispute remains, the county court may resolve it. Ga. Code Ann. sec. 35-3-37 and 38. The Center is authorized to disclose criminal information for certain purposes. 35-3-34.

Hawaii–State law limits disclosure of, and allows individual access to, criminal history records information. Haw. Rev. Stat. sec. 846.1.

Idaho–Exchanges of criminal justice data, with no limitations on further dissemination, is authorized. An individual cleared of charges is entitled to the return of fingerprints taken. Idaho Code sec. 67-3008.

Illinois–"Photographs, fingerprints, or other records of identification so taken, shall upon acquittal of the person charged... be returned to him" by the Department of Law Enforcement for the state. 20 ILCS 2605/55a.

Criminal justice information system records are confidential. 20 ILCS 2630/7. Law enforcement agencies must include dispositions, including verdicts or dropped charges, in their criminal records in a manner approved by the Illinois Criminal Justice Information Authority. Circuit court clerks must report dispositions to police agencies, 20 ILCS 2630/2.1.

Indiana–Criminal intelligence information may only be disclosed to another law enforcement agency and only if the intended use of the information is reasonable and the data will remain confidential. Information may be collected and kept only if there are grounds for suspecting criminal activity. Information about political, religious, or social views, associations or activities may be collected if relevant to criminal activity. Ind. Code Ann. sec. 5-2-4.

Iowa–The state has one of the nation's most restrictive statutes regulating criminal justice information systems. Iowa Code Ann. sec. 692.1. Subsec. 9 forbids maintenance in either manual or automated police files of any "surveillance data" – defined as "information on individuals pertaining to participation in organizations, groups, meetings or assemblies where there are no reasonable grounds to suspect involvement or participation in criminal activity by any person." Also, "files shall be stored on the computer in such manner as the files cannot be modified, destroyed, accessed, changed or overlaid in any fashion by non-criminal justice agency terminals or personnel."

Data in criminal justice information systems may be disseminated only to law enforcement agencies and to certain others. Local police may redisseminate the data if they keep a log of who receives it. An individual (or his attorney) may inspect his own file in the system and may request elimination or correction of an item. If his request is refused, he may appeal to a court to order the change, which must then be reported to all recipients of the information. Arrest records with no disposition after five years must be eliminated from the system. Sec. 692.5.

Kansas–Security in the state's police information network and individual access to one's own record are governed by Kans. Stat. Ann. 22-4704.

It is unlawful to require an applicant or employee to inspect his or her own criminal history to qualify for employment. 22-4710.

Kentucky–If prosecution is complete, certain information in investigative reports is available to outsiders and certain information must be kept confidential. Ky. Rev. Stat. Ann. sec. 17.150.

Louisiana–La. Rev. Stat. Ann. sec. 15:575 creates the Louisiana Criminal Justice Information System for the storage of offender information, excluding intelligence data. The attorney general is to oversee management of the system, including security protections.

Maine–Dissemination of criminal history record information (acquittal, pardon, dismissal, indictment) is limited to criminal justice agencies, to persons researching criminal justice systems who insure the confidentiality of the data, and to agencies authorized by court order or statute. Me. Rev. Stat. Ann. title 16, sec. 611. Sec. 620 provides a right to any person to inspect his records and request correction.

Maryland–Md. Crim. Law 10-202 creates a state criminal justice information system and advisory board, a central repository; sets limits upon dissemination and provides a right to inspect and challenge. The law on access to criminal justice information systems is similar to Kentucky's. Sec. 13.03(3).

Massachusetts–The Criminal Offender Records Information law establishes a criminal history system board, including state officers and four "persons who have experience in issues relating to personal privacy." It monitors privacy concerns in the criminal history information system and writes regulations. Public access is permitted to offenders' records until three years after release from custody. An offender may copy his or her own record and ask the board for corrections. Mass. Gen. Laws Ann. ch. 6, sec. 167 to 178B. See also Ch. 279, sec. 1.

Michigan–Arrest data in the state system is to be returned to an individual who is not convicted. Mich. Comp. Laws. Ann. sec. 28.243.

Minnesota–The Minnesota Government Data Practices Act governs the collection and dissemination of law enforcement data. Minn. Stat. Ann. sec. 13.82. "No state agency or political subdivision shall transfer or disseminate any private or confidential data on individuals to the private international organization known as Interpol, except through the Interpol-U.S. National Central Bureau, U.S. Department of Justice." Sec. 13.05, subdivision 10.

Mississippi–The justice information center has procedures to contest inaccuracies. Miss. Code Ann. 45-27-11.

Montana–State law regulates the storage of criminal history information and permits the individual to see and challenge the record. Mont. Code Ann. sec. 44-5-101.

Nebraska–There may be no dissemination of criminal justice information without the disposition of the record, except for cases of certain candidates for public office, for active cases, and for records sought by the subject individual. Neb. Rev. Stat. sec. 29-3523.

Nevada–A person may inspect criminal records in the central depository and local police departments. Nev. Rev. Stat. sec. 179A.150.

New Hampshire–Criminal records that may reflect on the loyalty of a resident shall not be divulged except with the permission of the attorney general, for law enforcement purposes. N.H. Rev. Stat. Ann. sec. 648.9.

New Jersey–There is a procedure for expunging and sealing records in the criminal justice system. N.J. Rev. Stat. sec. 2C:52-1.

Disclosure of genetic profiles in criminal justice data bases is regulated by 53:1-20.19.

New Mexico–Employees of the central law enforcement data system face a misdemeanor penalty for disclosure of data outside the data processing division of the originating agency. N.M. Stat. Ann. sec. 15-1A-11. Citizens have a right of access. Sec. 29-10-6.

North Carolina–Investigative files of the state bureau of investigation are considered not public. N.C. Gen. Stat. sec. 114-15.

North Dakota–The attorney general shall adopt rules for individual access. N.D. Cent. Code sec. 12-60-16.3.

Ohio–Criminal histories are not public information, but may be released if authorized by regulation. Ohio Rev. Code sec. 109.57 (D) and (E).

Oklahoma–Law Enforcement Telecommunications Systems Division of the Department of Public Safety was created to maintain on-line, real-time computer system for distribution of information on vehicle registrations, driver records, criminals. Okla. Stat. title 47, sec. 2-124. All department personnel charged with custody of confidential or privileged information are subject to a criminal penalty for divulging it. Sec. 2-129.

Oregon–Dispositions of arrests must be reported by law enforcement. Ore. Rev. Stat. sec. 181.540. And inaccurate criminal data must be purged. Sec. 181.555(4).

Police must not collect political, social, religious, or associational data unless related to a criminal investigation. Sec. 181.575.

Pennsylvania–There is a right of review and correction. Pa. Stat. Ann. title 18, sec. 9151.

South Carolina–The Criminal Information and Communication System was created to prevent disclosure of any information in a manner prohibited by existing law. S.C. Code sec. 53-30.

South Dakota–There is a right of review. S.D. Codified Laws Ann. sec.23-5-12.

Tennessee–Bureau of Criminal Identification investigatory records are to be confidential, unless disclosed under court order, or to the general assembly or the governor, or to those who investigate the bureau. Tenn. Code Ann. sec. 10-7-504.

Texas–There is a right of review. Tex. Gov. Code. Sec. 552.023. See also sec. 411.083 and Tex. Code of Crim. Proc. art. 60.02.

Utah–The state Law Enforcement and Technical Services Division may not disclose criminal data except for criminal justice purposes and as authorized by statute. Utah Code Ann. sec. 53-5-214.

Virginia–The Criminal Justice Information System may purge data. A citizen has the right to inspect and to correct. Va. Code secs. 9-192 and 19.2-389. The law limits dissemination of data in the system.

Washington–Criminal records gathered by state authorities are regarded as privileged. Wash. Rev. Code Ann. sec. 43.43.710. Unauthorized use of information is a criminal offense. 43.43.810.

West Virginia–There is a right of inspection and copying. W. Va. Code 29B-1-3.

Wisconsin–There is a right of inspection and copying. Wis. Stat. Ann. sec. 19.35(1)(a).

Wyoming–There is a right of inspection and purging. Wyo. Stat. sec. 7-19-109.

Federal law–The Office of Justice Programs in the Department of Justice is required to promulgate privacy and security regulations covering federally funded criminal justice information systems. The regulations are published at 28 Code Fed. Reg. 1. Arrest data in such systems must include dispositions of the case "to the maximum extent feasible." The regulations are to assure the privacy and confidentiality of such information. Any individual included in a federally supported criminal justice information system is entitled to a copy of information about him or herself. 42 U.S.C. 3789g (b)&(c). [See 1978-79 book.]

ELECTRONIC SURVEILLANCE
(Including Wiretapping, Telephone Monitoring, Video Voyeurism and Camera Surveillance)

Alabama–Except for law enforcement and telephone employees, whoever overhears or records private communications without the consent of one party while trespassing in a private place commits a misdemeanor. Installing an eavesdropping device is a felony. Divulging the contents of a tapped conversation is a misdemeanor. Ala. Code title 13A, sec. 11-30.

Secret observation or photography while trespassing on private property is "criminal surveillance." Code 13A-11.31.

Alaska–Unlawful to use eavesdropping device to record any oral conversation without consent of a party. To eavesdrop on an oral conversation (whether on a telephone or not) without the consent of one party or to divulge the contents of an intercepted conversation is a misdemeanor. Law enforcement officers are covered by this law also. Alaska Stat. sec. 42.20.310.

"Indecent viewing or photography" is a crime. Stat. sec. 11.61.123.

Arizona–It is a felony to intercept a wire or other oral communication "without consent of a party" or a court order based on probable cause. Also exempt from the ban is providing information requested by subpoena or by demand of lawful authority. Ariz. Rev. Stat. sec. 13-3004.

It is unlawful to film a person without consent in a restroom, locker room, bathroom, or bedroom, or when a person is undressed or engaged in sex. Rev. Stat. sec. 13-3019.

Arkansas–Without the consent of one party to the conversation, "if any person without authority intercepts a dispatch or message transmitted by telegraph or telephone, ... he is guilty of a misdemeanor." Ark. Code Ann. sec. 5-60-120.

Video voyeurism is punished. Code Ann. sec. 5-16-101.

California–It is illegal to tap without consent of **all parties**, except for telephone companies. A person may tap his or her own phone if the conversations are related to commission of a serious felony and the contents are admissible in a trial. California law makes it a felony for anyone, except the parties to a conversation, to disclose contents of a telephone or telegraph message without permission. There is a flat prohibition on tapping privileged conversations. Cal. Penal Code sec. 631 through 637.

Cellular telephone conversations and digital pagers are protected. Sec. 632.5.

Private investigators may have a license suspended or revoked for violation. Cal. Bus. & Prof. Code sec. 7551.

Except for law enforcement, no person or entity may use an electronic tracking device on a vehicle or other moving thing without the consent of the owner. Cal. Penal Code sec. 637.7.

It is a misdemeanor to use a concealed camera to tape or photograph the intimate parts of a person who does not consent. Cal. Penal Code sec. 647. Telephone companies must keep a record of all devices for overhearing conversations that their employees discover, and companies must take "adequate steps to ensure privacy of communications over [their] systems." Cal. Pub. Util. Code sec. 7905.

Using a hidden video camera may violate Penal Code sec. 647.

Colorado–Taps illegal without the consent of at least one party or a court order. Making, possessing or using eavesdropping equipment also illegal; telephone companies excepted. Colo. Rev. Stat. sec. 18-9-301 and 16-15-101.

Connecticut–Wiretapping, including intercepting a cellular telephone conversation without the consent of **both parties**, is prohibited, except for law enforcement. Conn. Gen. Stat. Ann. sec. 53a-187. Application for law enforcement taps must be made to a panel of judges who must agree unanimously that there is probable cause and also that not more than 35 wiretap orders have previously been granted in the past year (unless an emergency). Order expires in 15 days. It is illegal to intercept private conversations or the lines of physicians, attorneys or clergy. Sec. 54-14a through h.

Video surveillance with or without sound and audio surveillance are prohibited in employee locker rooms and rest rooms. Sec. 31-48b(b).

Video voyeurism is punished. Stat. Ann. sec. 53a-189a.

Delaware–Interceptions are prohibited except with consent of **all parties** or under color of law. Tap contents must be retained for ten years. Court order expires in 30 days, with extensions granted. Violation of privacy is a misdemeanor. Del. Code title 11, sec. 2401.

A device for observing, photographing, recording, or amplifying may not be installed in any private place without consent. Title 11, sec. 1335(a)(2).

Law enforcement taps are governed by Code title 11, sec. 2401. The law now requires consent of one party to a conversation in order to intercept or record it. Title 11, sec. 2403(c)(4).

Employers many not monitor or intercept any telephone conversation, email, or Internet access or usage of an employee unless the employer either provides an electronic notice of the monitoring policies at least once during each day the employee accesses employer-provided email or Internet access services, or has first given a one-time notice to the employee of its monitoring policies. Title 19, sec. 705(a).

District of Columbia–Wiretap authorization is intended to "supplement not to limit" federal wiretap authority. U.S. attorney may install a tap if he or she applies for a warrant within 12 hours after. Tapes to be kept until ordered destroyed by a judge. D.C. Code Ann. sec. 23-541.

Florida–Taps permitted only with **two-party** consent, by the phone company or under color of law (based on "reasonable grounds"). Like federal law, there is provision for punitive damages and actual damages of at least $100 a day for illegal taps. Illegal to advertise, mail or possess equipment. No person shall publish or broadcast the identity of persons notified that wiretaps have been placed on themselves until those persons are indicted. Fla. Stat. Ann. sec. 934.01.

It is unlawful for a merchant to observe directly or videotape a person in a changing room where there is a reasonable expectation of privacy. Sec. 877.26.

Secretly videotaping or observing a person with lewd intent is criminal voyeurism. Stat. Ann. sec. 810.14.

Georgia–It is illegal to surreptitiously "observe, photograph or record the activities of another which occur in any private place and out of public view" without consent of one party. Law enforcement taps permissible with a warrant. Ga. Code Ann. sec. 16-11-62. Telephone companies must keep a public list of all subscribers using phone monitoring equipment. Such subscribers must have a license from the public service commission for electronic surveillance for business improvement. Sec. 16-11-66.

Use of a hidden camera without consent to record activities in any private place or out of public view is illegal. It is illegal to record a private conversation in any private place. Code Ann. sec. 16-11-62(2).

Hawaii–Interception without consent of **both sender and recipient** by any person, acting under color of law or otherwise, or disclosure of information so obtained is unlawful. Haw. Rev. Stat. sec. 803.42(8)(b)(3) (A). Possession of materials collected in this way is punishable. The law on video voyeurism is similar to Arizona's. Sec. 711-1110.9. Law enforcement is governed by a law similar to the federal statute. Sec. 803.41 through 48.

"Any person who intentionally installs or uses a mobile tracking device without a search warrant or other order or consent of the owner of the property shall be guilty of a felony." Sec. 803-42(a).

Idaho–Like the federal wiretap law. Idaho Code sec. 18-6701. The law makes illicit videotaping a crime. Sec. 18-6609.

Illinois–Anyone who taps or makes any connection with telegraph or telephone line is guilty of a misdemeanor. 720 ILCS 360/1.

Consent of **all parties** is required when an "eavesdropping device" is used by telephone or in person. 720 ILCS 5/14-1.

Monitoring of employees' phone calls by any business dealing with the public is permitted for quality control, training, or research, but not if the conversation is personal and so long as notice and a place for confidential personal calls are provided. 720 ILCS 5/14-3.

The law on videotaping is similar to Tennessee's. 720 ILCS 5/26-4.

Indiana–The contents of wiretapped conversations must be disclosed to the subject prior to trial. Except for law enforcement, disclosure of the contents of taps is limited. Ind. Code Ann. sec. 35-33.5-5-1.

Video voyeurism is a crime. Code Ann. 35-45-4-5.

Iowa–Tapping telephone or telegraph line is punishable by five years and/or $500. Iowa Code Ann. sec. 716.7-8. One-party consent is required. Sec. 727.8.

Law enforcement electronic installations are governed by sec. 808B.3.

Kansas–Comparable to the federal wiretap statute. Kans. Stat. Ann. sec. 22-2514. See also sec. 21-4001.

It is a misdemeanor to use a hidden camera without consent to photograph a person who is nude in a place where there is a reasonable expectation of privacy. Stat. Ann. 21-4001(a)(4).

Kentucky–Illegal to eavesdrop, except on one's own telephone, without the consent of one party. Illegal to divulge contents of illegally obtained information, except for telephone companies and party-line users who mistakenly overhear. Ky. Rev. Stat. Ann. sec. 526.010.

"A person is guilty of video voyeurism when he or she intentionally: (a) Uses or causes the use of any camera, videotape, photo-optical, photoelectric, or other image recording device for the purpose of observing, viewing, photographing, filming, or videotaping the sexual conduct, genitals, or nipple of the female breast of another person without that person's consent; or (b) Uses or divulges any image so obtained for consideration; or (c) Distributes any image so obtained by live or recorded visual medium, electronic mail, the Internet, or a commercial on-line service." Images used as evidence in a prosecution of this crime are to be destroyed or sealed. Rev. Stat. 531.100 and 110.

Louisiana–A telephone company may intercept obscene calls. La. Rev. Stat. Ann. sec. 45:1166.

It is illegal to wiretap without the consent of a party to the conversation, except for law enforcement "obtaining information to detect crime." Sec. 14:322. Police authorization to wiretap is similar to federal law. State law requires the consent of only one party to intercept or record a conversation. Sec. 15:1303(4).

No person shall use a tracking device to determine the location or movement of another person without the consent of that person. Tracking device means any device that reveals its location or movement by transmission of electronic signals. Sec. 14:323.

Surreptitious **videotaping** for a lewd purpose – "video voyeurism" – is a crime. A court may destroy the evidence. Sec. 14:283.

Maine–Wiretapping is prohibited except when one is acting under color of law, where such person is a party to a conversation or where one of the parties gives prior consent. Me. Rev. Stat. Ann. title 15. See also title 17-A, sec. 511.

The law punishes public video "upskirting" and use of a covert camera in a private place. Rev. Stat. Ann. title 17-A, sec. 511.

Maryland–Wiretaps are "contrary to public policy of this state and shall not be permitted except by court orders in unusual circumstances." There must be prior court approval, based on reasonable grounds. To wiretap without court approval, the consent of "participants" to a conversation is required. (The case law says this means **all parties**.) Md. Cts. & Jud. Proc. Code Ann. sec. 10-402.

Massachusetts–Wiretaps "under strict judicial supervision... should be limited to the investigation of organized crime." The consent of **all parties** is necessary to intercept. Mass. Gen. Laws Ann. ch. 272, sec. 99.

"No person who owns or operates a retail establishment selling clothing shall maintain in a dressing room a two-way mirror or electronic **video** camera or similar device capable of filming or projecting an image of a person inside... ." Ch. 93, sec. 89.

Michigan–It is illegal for a telephone company to divulge the contents of a telephone conversation. Mich. Comp. Laws Ann. sec. 750.539.

It is illegal to use any **audio or video** device to eavesdrop or to photograph in a private place, except for peace officers. The law has been interpreted as requiring a warrant for law enforcement wiretaps and as allowing legal eavesdropping when one party to a conversation consents. Sec. 750.539d.

Minnesota–The state wiretap authority sets a penalty of $500 for intercepting a conversation between a cordless telephone handset and the base unit. Minn. Stat. Ann. sec. 626A.01. Providers of phone service may not divulge the content of conversations. 626A.27.

It is illegal to observe or photograph through an opening to a private place any person exposing one's body or undergarments. Stat. Ann. sec. 609.746.

Mississippi–Interception is permitted with the consent of one party to the conversation. Miss. Code Ann. 41-29-531. Otherwise only the Bureau of Nar-cotics with a court order may install a wiretap. Information collected in violation of this law is inadmissible. 41-29-501. Pen registers or Caller ID may be installed with a court order in felony investigations. 41-29-701.

Videotaping in a place where a person may be undressed and expects privacy is illegal. 97-29-63.

Missouri–It is an invasion of privacy to film a person without consent in a state of full or partial nudity in a place where there is an expectation of privacy. Mo. Ann. Stat. sec. 565.253.

Law enforcement taps are covered by Ann. Stat. sec. 542.400.

Montana–It is a misdemeanor to record a conversation or to intercept it without the consent of **all parties** or to intercept it. Mont. Code Ann. sec. 45-8-213.

Nebraska–State law on electronic surveillance is comparable to the federal statute. Neb. Rev. Stat. sec. 86-701.

Nevada–State law allows wiretaps by law enforcement for up to 72 hours prior to getting ratification of a court; or by court order or consent. The state law is comparable to the federal act, although the law has been interpreted as requiring two-party consent. Nev. Rev. Stat. sec. 200.610. See also sec. 179.410.

New Hampshire–Comparable to the federal wiretap law, except that consent of **both parties** appears to be required. N.H. Rev. Stat. Ann. sec. 570-A:1.

Use of a hidden camera in a private place without consent is a misdemeanor. Rev. Stat. Ann. sec. 644:9.

New Jersey–Judges may grant 48-hour verbal approval for a tap based on oral statements. A law enforcement officer who is party to the conversation or has the consent of one party need not have a warrant, with a prosecutor's approval. A warrant for a tap will be issued in investigations of major crimes, based on probable cause and a showing that evidentiary conversations will in fact be overheard. Applicants for a tap warrant must show a *special need* if they intend to overhear public phones or news reporters, clergy, psychologists, physicians or spouses and they must show that such a person is involved in criminal activity. Cordless telephone communications are included in the protections. N.J. Rev. Stat. sec. 2A:156A-1.

The law punishes covert videotaping for a lewd purpose. Rev. Stat. sec. 2C:14-9.

New Mexico–Comparable to the federal wiretap statute. N.M. Stat. Ann. sec. 30-12-2.

New York–Similar to the federal law. N.Y. Crim. Proc. Law sec. 700.05 (McKinney) covers law enforcement surveillance; taps with one-party consent are legal, according to court decisions. Cordless conversations are protected. N.Y. Penal Law 250.000 covers eavesdropping by private parties.

It is illegal to install a camera, two-way mirror, or viewing device in a bathroom, fitting room, or hotel room. N.Y. Gen. Bus. Law 395-b.

"Unlawful surveillance" and dissemination of the images are felonies (video voyeurism). A person is guilty if for no legitimate purpose he or she surreptitiously installs an imaging device to view or record another in a bedroom, bathroom, changing room, or other room: or for sexual arousal or gratification: or covertly to view a person dressing or undressing when the person has a reasonable expectation of privacy; or under the clothing of a person ("upskirting"). Penal Law sec. 250.040 through 65.

North Carolina–Unlawful to tap telephone or telegraph lines. N.C. Gen. Stat. sec. 14-155.

Law enforcement taps are covered by Gen. Stat. secs. 15A-260 through 265 and 15A-286 through 298542.400. Video voyeurism is covered by 14.202.

North Dakota–It is a felony to intercept wire or oral communications or intentionally to disclose them.

26

Interceptions with one-party consent are permissible, according to state courts. N.D. Cent. Code sec. 12.1-15-02.

Ohio–Ohio Rev. Code Ann. sec. 2933.51 through .66 prohibits wiretapping except to prevent a crime (and with the consent of one party to the conversation). Breaking or tapping a line is illegal. Sec. 4931.28.

State law prohibits "upskirting," "downblousing," and similar types of covert **videotaping** under or through clothing to view the undergarments or body. Sec. 2907.08.

The law prohibits covert videotaping for a sexual purpose. Rev. Code sec. 2907-08.

Oklahoma–Disclosing contents of telegraph or telephone communications except upon lawful court order is a misdemeanor, except for public officers in the discharge of their duties. Okla Stat. Ann. title 21, sec. 1782. Interception of a phone call with consent of one party is permissible. Title 13, sec. 176.1. The same provision covers law enforcement taps.

Using video equipment in a clandestine manner for an illegitimate or prurient purpose when the targeted person has an expectation of privacy is a crime, as is publishing such images. Stat. Ann. 21-1171.

Oregon–The contents of a tapped conversation are confidential. An application for a warrant must show probable cause that a crime "directly and immediately affecting the safety of human life or the national security has been committed or is about to be committed." Court approval good for 60 days. Otherwise consent of **all parties** is necessary. Violation is a felony. Or. Rev. Stat. sec. 133.721 and 165.540.

A person commits the misdemeanor of invasion of personal privacy by videotaping another person in a state of nudity or partial nudity without consent in a place where there is a reasonable expectation of privacy. Sec. 163.700.

The law has been interpreted as permitting electronic surveillance when one party to a conversation consents. Rev. Stat. sec. 165.540.

Pennsylvania–Perhaps the nation's strongest, Pennsylvania law forbids any wiretapping or eavesdropping even by law enforcement, without consent of **both parties**. Police may get a court order to wiretap only for the protection of a police officer, but then may not record the conversation. Telephone company and national security wiretaps not prohibited. Pa. Stat. Ann. title 18, sec. 5701. [See 1978-79 book.]

Rhode Island–A court may approve wiretapping after a law enforcement official has justified his or her belief that criminal activity of occurring and that other means of investigation have failed. Warrant expires in 30 days with one 30-day extension possible. R.I. Gen. Laws Ann. sec. 12-5.1-1. Sec. 11-35-21 governs monitoring by private parties.

"No employer may cause an audio or video recording to be made of an employee in a restroom, locker room, or room designated by an employer for employees to change their clothes, unless authorized by court order." Gen. Laws Ann. 28-6.12-1.

South Carolina–A pen register or a trap and trace device requires a court order, except for telephone companies. S.C. Code sec. 46-740.33. See also sec. 16-17-470.

The law on videotaping is similar to Washington's. Code sec. 16-3-17-470.

South Dakota–All wiretapping authorizations must "conform to federal standards." S.D. Codified Laws Ann. sec. 23A-35A-1.

The law on hidden cameras is similar to New Hampshire's. Codified Laws Ann. sec. 22-21-1 and 2.

Tennessee–Illegal to tap a telephone line. But permissible to record a phone conversation with one-party consent. Tenn. Code Ann. sec. 65-21-110.

It is a misdemeanor to use a hidden camera to photograph a person who is nude without consent in a place whether there is a reasonable expectation of privacy, if the viewing would offend an ordinary person and is done for sexual purposes. Code Ann. 39-13-605 and 607.

Law enforcement taps are covered by Secs. 39-13-600 and 40-6-304.

Texas–It is illegal to wiretap or try to tape or disclose contents of a conversation without one-party consent, except that law enforcement may do so with one-party consent and the approval of a magistrate. Tex. Penal Code Ann. sec. 16.02.

Court approval is required for police use of a pen register, a device that attaches to a telephone to log incoming or outgoing telephone numbers. Tex. Rev. Stat. Code of Crim. Proc. sec. 18.21.

A judge may authorize the state Department of Public Safety to install a wiretap, using "covert entry" if necessary, for evidence of violation of the state laws on controlled drugs. Sec. 18.20.[See 1987 book.]

"Improper photography or visual recording" violates the law. Penal Code Ann. sec. 21.15.

A person commits an offense if the person knowingly installs an electronic or mechanical tracking device on a motor vehicle owned or leased by another person. Penal Code Ann. sec. 16.06.

Utah–Law on electronic surveillance is virtually identical to federal law. Utah Code Ann. sec. 77-23a-1. See also sec. 76-9-401.

The law on hidden cameras is similar to New Hampshire's. Code Ann. sec. 76-9-401.

Virginia–Like the federal wiretap statute. Va. Code sec. 19.2-61. The law on covert videotaping is similar to Missouri's, and applies also to hotels, locker rooms, and tanning booths. Sec. 18.2-386.

Peeping or spying into a dwelling or private enclosure, in a hotel room or tanning salon or other places, for the purpose of viewing someone fully or partially nude is illegal. Code sec. 18.2-130.

Washington–Electronic interception of communications is permitted if **all parties** to the conservation consent. An announcement by one party that the call is being recorded complies with the two-party consent requirement. Calls to police emergency number 911 may be recorded (but not admitted into evidence), as well as calls involving harassment or criminal activity if one party consents. Law enforcement may wiretap with the consent of one party and a court authorization based on probable cause of a felony. Since 1989, state law has permitted the police to use wiretapping with one-party consent. Wash. Rev. Code Ann. sec. 9.73.030.

The anti-voyeurism statute prohibits photographing a person without that person's knowledge and consent in "a place where he or she would have a reasonable expectation of privacy [defined as a] place where one may reasonably expect to be safe from... hostile intrusion." Rev. Code 9A.44.115(1)(b)(ii).

West Virginia–Virtually identical to the federal wiretap law. W. Va. Code 62-1D-1.
It is illegal to monitor telephone service unless the telephone is so marked and a warning appears in the telephone book. Sec. 61-3-24c.
Covert videotaping is a criminal invasion of privacy. Code Ann. 61-8.28.

Wisconsin–The state wiretap law is like the federal statute. Wis. Stat. Ann. sec. 968.27. State agencies may not discipline state employees based on electronic surveillance or one-way mirrors except for evidence of a crime or the monitoring is approved by an agency head. Sec. 230.86.

Making, possessing, or distributing videotapes that depict someone in the nude when that person has a reasonable expectation of privacy is prohibited. Sec. 942.09.

Wyoming–The state wiretap law is similar to federal law; interception with one-party consent is legal. Wyo. Stat. sec. 7-3-601 through 611.

Federal law–"To safeguard the privacy of innocent persons, the interception of wire or oral communications where none of the parties to the communication has consented to the interception should be allowed only when authorized by a court of competent jurisdiction and should remain under the control and supervision of the authorizing court." Court warrants must be based on probable cause. Private parties that wiretap without one-party consent are subject to damages of at least $100 per day. The exceptions to the warrant requirement are (1) telephone companies and the Federal Communications Commission, (2) police officers who are a party to the communication, and (3) taps with the consent of one party. 18 U.S.C. 2510. [See 2002 book.] Federal law enforcement need not be specific in identifying the telephone or the premises to be targeted if the suspect's "actions could have the effect of thwarting interception." 18 U.S.C. 2518(11)(b).

Internet service providers may authorize the government to intercept a trespasser's communications for an extended period of time at the premises of the Internet provider in the event of a digital attack. 18 U.S.C. 2511(2). Police may rely on "consent" provided by employers, libraries, schools, and others to monitor an individual's e-mail or Internet browsing, without a court warrant. 18 U.S.C. 2511(2).

The federal law extends to cellular telephones, cordless phones, electronic mail, paging devices, and electronic data transmissions. Interception of such communications by a private party or the government is a crime, unless a law enforcement authority has a court warrant based on probable cause. Radio transmissions "readily accessible to the general public" (like cordless telephone calls between the receiver and the station) are not protected. Electronic Communications Privacy Act of 1986, amending 18 U.S.C. 2511, 3117, 2701, 3121, and other sections.
"A telecommunications carrier shall ensure that its equipment, facilities, or services... are capable of expeditiously isolating and enabling the government, pursuant to a court order or other lawful authorization, to intercept, to the exclusion of other communications, all wire and electronic communications carried by the carrier within a service area to or from equipment [and] to access call-identifying information." This particular requirement excludes electronic messaging services, electronic publishing, and on-line Internet providers. It requires law enforcement, in order to get access to customer information in such on-line services, to procure an administrative subpoena or comparable legal process based on "specific and articulable facts" showing relevance to a criminal investigation. 18 U.S.C. 2522.
It is illegal to manufacture or import devices that scan for cellular signals. 47 U.S.C. 302(d).
The law on electronic surveillance to gather foreign intelligence, the Foreign Intelligence Surveillance Act of 1978, was extended in 2012 to 2017. It removes the necessity to have the approval of the FISA court in order to install such surveillance. The court apparently may review such installations. Providers of phone services must cooperate. 50 U. S. C. 1801 et seq.
It is a federal crime, in certain jurisdictions, to videotape or photograph the naked or underwear-covered private parts of a person without consent when the person has a reasonable expectation of privacy. Penalties can be up to $100,000 or imprisonment for one year. 18 U. S. C. 1801.

EMPLOYMENT
(Including Demands for Social-Media Passwords)

Alaska–Employees or former employees have the **right to inspect** and copy their personnel files at their cost during business hours. Alaska Stat. sec. 23.10.430.
California–Public and private employers are required to permit an employee **to inspect** all records and personnel files concerning the employee, at reasonable times, upon request. Letters of reference and criminal investigation records excluded. Records must be made available where the employee reports to work. Cal. Labor Code sec. 1198.5 and Cal. Educ. Code sec. 24317 and 92612.

There are limits on employers' use of applicants' medical histories. Cal. Civ. Code 56.05(b) and 56.20(a).

There may be no "spotters" monitoring employees in a "public service corporation." Cal. Pub. Util. Code sec. 8251.

The law prohibits an employer from demanding that a person disclose a username or password for the purpose of accessing personal social media like Facebook, that he or she access personal social media in the presence of the employer or divulge any personal social media. Labor Code sec. 980.

An employer may not inquire into certain arrest and certain conviction information. See **Arrest Records**.

See **Insurance Records** for the California Genetic Information Nondiscrimination Act (CalGINA). See also **Credit Reporting.**

Colorado–No blacklists may be maintained but an employer may give a fair and unbiased opinion. The employee is entitled to a copy at the time a job reference is sent to another person. Colo. Rev. Stat. sec. 8-2-114.

Connecticut–Private and public employees have a right **to inspect** their own personnel files, after a written request. The company must correct inaccuracies or include an employee's rebuttal. There are limits on disclosures to outsiders. Conn. Gen. Stat. Ann. sec. 31-128a.

An employer may not inquire into applicants' or employees' erased arrests, with exceptions. Sec. 31-51i.

A firm may not "blacklist" an employee so as to prevent him or her from getting another job, but may give "a truthful statement" about a present or former employee. Sec. 31-51.

Camera surveillance is prohibited in employee health areas, locker rooms and lounges, and an employer may not audio- or video-tape contract negotiations. Employers engaged in electronic monitoring are required to give prior notice to employees, informing them of types of monitoring which may occur, except where reasonable grounds to believe employee is engaged in illegality. Sec. 31-48d.

See also **Credit Reporting.**

Delaware–On his or her own time, an employee may **inspect** his or her files in the presence of a company official, once a year. He or she may take notes, but no copies. If disputing the information, the employee may submit a written rebuttal, to be inserted in the personnel file and sent to third parties requested by the employee. A $200 fine for violations. Del. Code title 19, sec. 719, 723.

It is "unlawful for employers to mandate that an employee or applicant disclose password or account information that would grant the employer access the employee's or applicant's social networking profile or account. The law also prohibits employers from requesting that employees or applicants log onto their respective social networking site profiles or account to provide the employer direct access. Title 19, sec. 710.

District of Columbia–Records of the district government must be maintained "to ensure the greatest degree of applicant or employee privacy." D.C. Code Ann. sec. 1-632.1.

Florida–No derogatory or anonymous information may be kept in files of school employees; there is a right of access and amplification. Records are confidential, with exceptions. Fla. Stat. Ann. sec. 231.291.

A locality may not require itinerant workers to be registered and to submit to a background check and carry an identity card. Fla. Stat. Ann. sec 125.58(1).

Hawaii–Refusal to hire on the basis of an "arrest or court record which does not have a substantial relationship to the job" is prohibited. Haw. Rev. Stat. sec. 378.1

See also **Credit Reporting**.

Illinois–An employee may sue a company for denial of **access to and copying of** personnel records, except for letters of reference, management documents, or security investigative files. Disciplinary reports may not be released to outsiders. No irrelevant data on off-hours activity may be collected. 820 ILCS 40/1. [See 1984-85 book.]

It is illegal for employers to inquire into social-media passwords or contents. Email is not covered. 820 ILCS 55/10.

See also **Credit Reporting**.

Iowa–Public and private employees may **view and copy** their own personnel files, except for performance evaluations, disciplinary records, and information on "employer-employee relations." Iowa Code Ann. sec. 91B.1.

Disclosure of personal information from public employees' records is limited. Iowa Code Ann. sec. 68A.7(10)-(11).

See also **Testing in Employment**.

Kansas–See **Criminal Justice Information Systems.**

Maine–Employer must, upon written request from an employee or former employee, provide opportunity to **review one's personnel file**. "File" includes any formal or informal evaluations, reports relating to character, credit, work habits, compensation and benefits. Me. Rev. Stat. title 26, sec. 631. Public employees have rights of access. Title 5, sec. 7071.

Maryland–The state law, the nation's first, bars employers from requesting or requiring that an employee or applicant disclose any user name, password or other means to access a "personal account or service" through an electronic communications device. Md. Labor and Emp. Code sec. 3-712.

See also **Credit Reporting.**

Massachusetts–In addition to limits in its arrest records law, Massachusetts prohibits employment discrimination based on an arrest with no conviction or on certain misdemeanor convictions. An employment applicant has the right to withhold such criminal history information. Mass. Gen. Laws Ann. ch. 151B, sec. 4, para. 9.

Upon written request, a private or public employee **may have a copy** of personnel records and may put a rebuttal in the record if employer and employee do not mutually agree to correct the record. An employer is liable for information it should have known was false. Ch. 149, sec. 52C.

Taking a test for HIV may not be a condition of employment. Ch. 111, sec. 70F enacted in 2012.

Michigan–Public and private employees **may have copies** of their own personnel files, except for references, comparative evaluations, medical reports, personal information about a co-worker, investigative and grievance files, and notes kept by an individual executive or supervisor. There is a right to correct information. The law prohibits employers from collecting information about off-duty political activities. Mich. Comp. Laws Ann. sec. 423.501.

Either after two years or the completion of an internal investigation, an employee may inspect an investigatory file. An employer may not request or file records of arrests without convictions. Sec. 37.2205a.

The law on access to social-media passwords and content applies to employers and to public and private universities and schools. It protects applicants. Secs. 37.272 thru 278

Minnesota–Employees **may have copies** of their personnel records, as defined by state statute, once every six months and may include in the record a five-page rebuttal if the employer does not agree to revise or remove disputed information. Minn. Rev. Stat. 181.960.

Nevada–Employers, labor organizations, and employment agencies must give persons a "reasonable opportunity" to **inspect** records about themselves within 60 days of their employment, except for confidential reports or investigatory records on violations of law. Nev. Rev. Stat. sec. 613.075. An employer may not discriminate because an "employee uses a lawful product outside the premises of the employer. Sec. 613.333. An employee may not be dismissed on information from a "spotter" without a hearing or without an opportunity to confront the spotter. Sec. 613.160.

New Hampshire–Public and private employees may **see and copy** their own personnel files. N.H. Rev. Stat. Ann. sec. 275.56.

New Jersey–A person may not be fired for smoking off the job. N.J. Rev. Stat. sec. 34:6B-1.

New York–Employment and medical information in public records may not be released without consent. Pub. Off. Law sec. 89(2)(b)(i). Fingerprints may not be required as a condition of employment. Labor Law sec. 201-a.

Surveillance of employees is prohibited. Labor Law sec. 704(1).

North Carolina–State employment records containing name, age, date of employment, position title, salary, most recent promotion and demotion are open to any person. All other information is confidential. A **public employee** may supplement or seek removal of material in file considered inaccurate or misleading. N.C. Gen. Stat. sec. 126-22. Sec. 153A-98 and 160A-168 extend these provisions to county and local employees' records, respectively.

North Dakota–Public employees may see their own personnel files. N.D. Cent. Code sec. 54-06-21.

Ohio–"No employer or physician, other health-care professional, hospital, or laboratory that contracts with the employer to provide *medical* information pertaining to employees shall refuse upon written request of an employee to furnish to the employee or former employee or their designated representative a copy of any medical report pertaining to the employee." If the physician feels that release of medical information will result in serious medical harm, he or she may disclose to a doctor chosen by the employee. Ohio Rev. Code Ann. sec. 4113.23. [See 1981 book.]

Oregon–An employer shall provide a reasonable opportunity for an employee or former employee within 60 days of termination to **see and copy** his or her own personnel records, except for criminal information and confidential reports from previous employers. Or. Rev. St3 at. sec. 652.750. [See 1981 book.] See also **Credit Reporting**.

Pennsylvania–An employer is required to let a worker **inspect** his or her "personnel files used to determine his or her own qualifications for employment, promotion, additional compensation, termination or disciplinary action." An employee is not able to take copies, unless the employer consents, but he may take notes and be accompanied by a person of his choice. The employer may choose to require a written request for access and to require that the worker use his or her free time, not company time, to inspect the record. Pa. Stat. Ann. title 43, sec. 1321. [See 1981 book.] If an applicant is rejected on the basis of an arrest record, he or she must be so informed. Title 18, sec. 9125.

Rhode Island–Public and private employees have **a right to review** their personnel files, on their own time, in the presence of a company official. There are exceptions: letters of recommendation, medical information, grievance records, and certain managerial records. R.I. Gen. Laws sec. 28-6.4-1. An employer may not inquire into an applicant's arrests (as opposed to convictions). 28-5-7(7). Surveillance in the workplace is prohibited. Sec. 28-7-13.

South Dakota–State employees have a right of inspection. S.D. Codified Laws Ann. sec. 3-6A-31.

Tennessee–State employees may have access, and may make copies at cost. Tenn. Code Ann. sec. 8-50-108.

Utah–Employees of the state and its subdivisions have rights to examine and copy their own files if the request is in writing. They may not see information classified as confidential under the Information Practices Act. Utah Code Ann. sec. 67-18-1.

Vermont–State personnel files are exempt from Freedom of Information disclosure, but **a state employee,** or his or her representative, may inspect his or her own file. Vt. Stat. Ann. title 1, sec. 317(b)(7).

See also **Credit Reporting**.

Washington–Employers must permit **inspection** locally within a reasonable time after a request, except for criminal investigatory information and information that is part of pending litigation if protected by court rule. Personnel records are defined as files maintained as regular business records and any information that would be disclosed in response to requests outside the company for references. Access is permitted for two years after one leaves a company. An employee may place a rebuttal in the file. Wash. Rev. Code Ann. sec. 49.12.250.

Sec. 162-12-140 governs employers inquiries about arrests and other information about applicants.

See also **Credit Reporting**.

Wisconsin–State law permits present and former employees **to see their own personnel files** and to insert their side of the story into the files. Wis. Stat. Ann. sec. 103.13.

Employers must inform new employees of their hairstyle, facial hair, and clothing requirements, if any. Sec. 103.14.

Covert surveillance of state health workers is limited. Sec. 230.86.

Federal law–Regulations under the Occupational Health and Safety Act, 29 U.S.C. 657, require employers to disclose certain occupational medical records on workers to the federal government on demand. The regulations also permit workers to **inspect** their own *occupational medical records*. 29 Code of Federal Regulations 1910.21(e)(1)(i).

Employers who are covered by the Rehabilitation Act, 29 U.S.C. 793, 794 or the Vietnam Era Veterans Readjustment Act, 38 U.S.C. 2012, because they receive government assistance or contracts, are limited in the extent to which they may disclose medical information they receive from employees.

Employers in some states must check the immigrant status and Social Security numbers of applicants for employment. 42 U.S.C. 653(j).

See also **Credit Reporting**, see also **Medical Records** and see also **Testing in Employment**.

GOVERNMENT INFORMATION ON INDIVIDUALS

Alaska–The state **fair information practices law** creates a process for a citizen to challenge the accuracy or completeness of personal information maintained by a state agency and subject to public disclosure. Each state agency must notify applicants of (1) the law that permits information collection, (2) the consequences of not providing information, (3) the anticipated use and disclosure of the data, and (4) instructions in how to challenge the accuracy of information later. Criminal-investigatory and personnel records are exempted. Alaska Stat. sec. 44.99.300.

Arizona–Persons or organizations requesting motor vehicle division information must identify selves and give reasons for request; the division shall verify the requester's identity. Ariz. Rev. Stat. 28-210E.

All state Web sites must post a privacy policy. Rev. Stat. sec. 41-4152.

California–The state's **Fair Information Practices Act**, which is similar to those in other states, gives citizens the right to see and correct state files about themselves. State agencies may disclose personal information only in limited circumstances. The state university system and police are exempt. Unlike other states, California permits invasion-of-privacy lawsuits against a person who intentionally discloses personal information that he or she should have known came from a state or federal agency in violation of law. Cal. Civil Code sec. 1798. [See 1978-79 book.]

Motor vehicle registration information may be sold at cost, but the buyer must identify itself and the reason for the request. Data is freely available to the press and an attorney for pending litigation. There is a ten-day wait for a person requesting access to another person's motor vehicle records. Cal. Civ. Code sec. 1798.26. Certain persons including some police officers may give an alternative address for motor vehicle registration so that one's true home address is not publicly released. Cal. Health & Safety Code sec. 1808.1.

The home address, telephone number, occupation, precinct number, and prior registration number provided by people who register to vote may not be released to the public. Journalists, scholars, political researchers, and other government officials may still get the information. Cal. Election Code 2194. Upon a showing of good cause a person may petition the Superior Court to make all voter information confidential. 2166.

The Department of Motor Vehicles may not sell photos or personal descriptors of individuals to businesses. Cal. Vehicle Code sec. 12800.5(a)(2).

Santa Clara County government data banks are regulated by Ordinance No. NS-300.288, Div. A16, Santa Clara Co. Ordinance Code.

There are limits on disclosure of state information concerning children. Pen. Code sec. 637.9.

A prisoner may not be employed to perform a function that provides access to personal information. Pen. Code sec. 4017.1, 5071 and Wel. and Inst. Code sec. 219.5.

Colorado–State officials must keep the following records confidential but permit the individual to see his or her own file: medical and personnel files, library material and the address and phone number of a public school student. Letters of reference are confidential, and not available to the subject of the letters. Colo. Rev. Stat. sec. 24-72-204(3)(a) and 24-90-119.

Connecticut–Cities, towns, and state agencies are to maintain only relevant and necessary information and provide **individual access to and correction** of such information. Agencies must keep a record of disclosures of personal information. Conn. Gen. Stat. Ann. sec. 4-190. [See 1978-79 book.]

"Any person in possession of personal information of another person shall safeguard the data, computer files and documents containing the information from misuse by third parties, and shall destroy, erase or make unreadable such data, computer files and documents prior to disposal." Gen. Stat. sec. 42-470.

Florida–Each department in state government must have an information security manager, who shall conduct regular risk analyses, draft policies, do security audits, and assure that there are security precautions for data processing operations. Fla. Stat. Ann. sec. 282.318.

Georgia–Much of the personal information in the Department of Motor Vehicles is confidential Ga. Code Ann. secs. 40-2-130, 40-3-23.

Hawaii–The **Uniform Information Practices Act** permits individuals to have access to "personal records" about themselves in state agencies. Privacy interests of the individual must be balanced against the public interest in disclosure of medical, social-service, financial, or performance-evaluation information. An individual may correct factual errors. An Office of Information Practices within the Department of Attorney General enforces the law. Haw. Rev. Stat. 92F. [See 1992 book.]

There may be no release of motor vehicle records except to "a person having a legitimate reason" with an affidavit stating the reasons and affirming that the information will not be used for commercial sales. Sec. 286-172.

Illinois–The state's public records law says: "Nothing in this section shall require the Secretary [of State] to invade or assist in the invasion of any person's right to privacy." The secretary of state must observe state confidentiality laws, including requirements for mental disability records confidentiality and "**shall furnish** upon demand" copies of records to an individual who is the subject of the records. Most state records are public, others may be disclosed if the requester signs an affidavit "that the information... shall not be made available to other persons." 5 ILCS 160/2.

Motor-vehicle and driver-license information may not be released to persons without a specific business reason and there is a ten-day waiting period. Home addresses may not be released if a person has a court order of protection. The law also allows a person to "opt-out" of rentals of DMV lists for commercial mailings and requires mailing firms to disclose how they will use the lists they procure. 625 ILCS 5/2-123.

Indiana–The **Fair Information Practices Act**, Ind. Code 4-1-6, is administered in conjunction with the Access to Public Records Act, Ind. Code 5-14-3-1. State agencies may determine themselves when personal information may be exchanged.

A citizen has a right to inspect personal information in state files, except medical records, according to 4-1-6-3. The person may challenge the accuracy of the information. If the agency refuses access, a citizen may seek reversal in circuit or superior court, where the state has the burden of sustaining its denial. State agencies define personal data as confidential or public.

Individual records in Bureau of Motor Vehicle files are available for $1. Lists of drivers and their addresses are available only when the purchaser certifies that the information will be used only to notify vehicle owners of defects or to compile statistics with individual identities concealed. 9-1-1-8.

Kansas–Most sales of state lists, including motor vehicle records, are prohibited. Kans. Stat. Ann. sec. 21-3914 and 74-2012.

Kentucky–The state open records law mandates access to any and all records of public agencies except records of a personal nature, certain law enforcement records, and a few other categories. Specific provision is made, however, that any person shall have **access to any public record relating to him or her** or in which he or she is mentioned by name. Ky. Rev. Stat. Ann. sec. 61.870 through 61.884.

Maine–The Bureau of Central Computer Services was established to effect the consolidation of existing data processing equipment; the bureau is required to develop rules to safeguard and maintain confidentiality of the information files. Me. Rev. Stat. Ann. title 5, sec. 1851.

Massachusetts–Each agency must designate an individual responsible for its personal data system and must enact regulations governing outside **access and individual challenge and correction**. Each automated or manual personal data system must be registered with the secretary of state. A court may enjoin actual or potential violations of the statute. Mass. Gen. Laws Ann. ch. 66A. [See 1978-79 book.]

If a report of child abuse can not be proven within 90 days or when the family involved no longer has children younger than 18 years old, the case must be expunged from the commonwealth's central registry of child abuse cases. Ch. 119, sec. 51E. Department of Public Welfare records of child abuse are to be disclosed only to the agency making the report and those directly involved in the case.

Welfare records are available to the individual recipient at the discretion of the case worker. Members of the legislature, federal officials and state welfare officials have access. Welfare records are to be destroyed ten years after aid is discontinued. Ch. 66, sec. 17A.

Minnesota–The **Data Practices Act**, codified at Minn. Stat. sec. 13.01, has been amended regularly since it was enacted.

This, the nation's first privacy act, covers the state university, state agencies, school boards, local commissions and authorities, but not townships. It codifies the accepted principles of data privacy and defines confidential personal data (which is not available to the individual). Each agency must designate a person to be responsible for its data banks and report yearly to the state department of administration. Sample forms used for collecting personal data must also be filed.

An individual must be told the purpose and intended use of information he or she supplies, and the consequences of providing or not providing it.

Individuals have a right to contest personal information before action is taken against them as the result of "computer matching." Minn. Stat. sec. 13B.01.

There must be notification of security breaches by government agencies. Stat. Ann. 13.055.

Mississippi–If "confidential information" is wrongfully released to a state agency, the aggrieved person may complain to the central data processing authority and get the government employee fired, and perhaps fined or jailed. Miss. Code Ann. sec. 25-53-53 and 55.

New Hampshire–The Information Practices Act requires that data banks maintained by state agencies be registered with the state department of administration. N.H. Rev. Stat. Ann. sec. 7-A.

New Jersey–Motor vehicle records may be released in certain circumstances, except that Social Security numbers may be released by the motor vehicles agency only "in accordance with an applicable federal or state law." N.J. Rev. Stat. sec. 39:2-3.3.

Emergency responders may not photograph victims or disclose such photographs. Sec. 2A:58D-2.

New York–"Each [state] agency that maintains a system of records shall [prepare] a notice describing each of its systems of records," including the uses made of each category of records and the disclosures of personal information that the agency regularly makes. The Committee on Public Access to Records is responsible for registering all state agency data banks, to take citizen complaints, and to issue advisory opinions. Citizens have **a right to see and correct** their own files. N.Y. Pub. Off. Law sec. 91. [See 1981 and 1984-85 books]. The freedom of information act says that disclosure of state mailing lists to be used commercially is an "unwarranted invasion of personal privacy." Pub. Off. Law sec. 89(2)(b)(iii).

Ohio–Notices stating the nature and character of any personal information system – and name of individual directly responsible for it – must be filed with the director of administrative services. Agencies maintaining these systems must inform persons whether the information they are asked to provide is legally required and must collect only personal information necessary and relevant to the functions of that agency. With certain specific exemptions, personal information may not be disclosed without the consent of the individual. The law provides for **accessing, challenging and amending one's own record**. Ohio Rev. Code sec. 1347.01. [See 1978-79 book.]

An ordinance in the city of Dayton provides for accessing and challenging information in its system. The ordinance specifically protects privacy rights of persons listed in the municipal information systems. Ordinance No. 24963, 1977. Secs. 45.10-45.15 of the City of Dayton Rev. Code of Gen. Ordinances.

Oklahoma–Data Processing Planning and Management Act provides that storage of confidential data in the state's centralized data processing center shall be accomplished so as to preclude access without express authorization. Okla. Stat. title 74, sec. 118.17.

Oregon–"Any person that owns, maintains or otherwise possesses data that includes a consumer's personal information that is used in the course of the person's business, vocation, occupation or volunteer activities must develop, implement and maintain reasonable safeguards to protect the security, confidentiality and integrity of the personal information, including disposal of the data." Implementation of an "information security program" complies with this law. The Department of Consumer and Business Services is responsible for compliance. Or. Rev. Stat. 646A.622.

Rhode Island–The Department of Motor Vehicles shall require identification from persons requesting DMV information about others, a ten-day period to fulfill the request, and notification to individuals. This does not apply to a business with a "requester code" R.I. Gen. Laws 11-49.2.5.

South Carolina–The sale of digital photographs and other information from driver's licenses is prohibited. S.C. Code sec. 30-4-160.

Utah–The Government Records Access and Management Act includes the principles of **fair information practices** found in the federal privacy act. The Department of Administrative Services is to draft regulations and to report each December on the types of data collected by state agencies. There are four categories of personal information in state files – "public," "private" (concerning individuals), "confidential" (medical and psychiatric), and "protected" (trade secrets of businesses). An individual has the right to contest the accuracy or completeness of his or her own data. Local government is not affected. Utah Code Ann. sec. 63G-2-101.

Virginia–The **Government Data Collection and Discrimination Practices Act** prohibits secret personal information systems and collection of unneeded, inappropriate, inaccurate information. The law provides for access and correction. Va. Code sec. 2.2-3800. [See 1978-79 book.]

Washington–The state information review board sets policy for state government data processing. "Confidential or privileged information shall not be subject to submittal to the common data bank" except in cumulative form. Wash. Rev. Code Ann. sec. 43.105.070.

"The work and home addresses, other than the city of residence, of a person shall remain undisclosed" by state agencies if a person certifies that this would endanger his or her safety. Wash. Rev. Code Ann. sec. 42.17.310 (1) (BB).

Wisconsin–State agencies must register their records files and develop rules of conduct for the handling of personal data. An individual may **copy and challenge any record** about himself or herself in a state or local government agency. An agency must correct the information or include a concise statement from the individual. Investigatory or archives records are excluded. An individual must be notified before adverse action is taken as the result of computer matching unless the state or local agency finds the information used "sufficiently reliable." Wis. Stat. Ann. 19.365 and 19.69.

Federal law–The Privacy Act of 1974 adopts the accepted **fair information principles** as policy for federal agencies, including the right of the individual to see his or her own federal files. Outside disclosures are limited, but not for "routine uses of information." Some files, notably national security and law enforcement records, are exempt. Benefits may not be denied (by federal, state, or local agencies) for refusal to provide a Social Security number unless there was a pre-1975 authority to demand it. 5 U.S.C. 552a. [See 1992 book.] The Department of Veterans Affairs is exempt from certain provisions, but has certain other requirements for confidentiality. 38 U.S.C. 5701.

Federal agencies must provide information to the Parent Locator Service in the Department of Health and Human Services, which tracks down parents not supporting their children. 42 U.S.C. 653.

HHS employees may not disclose a "file, record, report or other paper, or information, obtained at any time by any person," for administering the Social Security Act. 42 U.S.C. 1306.

HHS is also authorized to conduct computer "matches," comparing welfare rolls to payroll lists to discover persons claiming improper or duplicate benefits. 42 U.S.C. 611.

Federal agency Web sites may not deposit "cookies" on a user's computer or exploit personal information provided on a Web site, unless it is done so voluntarily. P.L. 107-67, sec. 639a.

It is a criminal offense to fail to answer most surveys conducted by the Bureau of the Census. A refusal to answer a question about your religion is not an offense. Copies of Census reports about an individual, a business or the Census itself are immune to legal process, without the individual's consent. Nor may Census records be used in the Parent Locator search. 13 U.S.C. 221.

The Paperwork Reduction Act of 1980 requires the Office of Management and Budget to create an Office of Information and Regulatory Affairs to "provide overall direction in the development and regulation of Federal information policies" including records management, privacy of records, interagency sharing of information, and acquisition and use of automatic data processing. The office is to establish privacy guidelines, provide agencies with advice and monitor compliance with the Privacy Act. 44 U.S.C. 3501.

State agencies have access to earnings records maintained by the Social Security Administration, 26 U.S.C. 6103(7), and state unemployment agencies, 25 U.S.C. 3304(a)(16).

States must conduct computer matches to eliminate fraud and duplication in federal entitlement programs – and in the process to verify any computer "hits," promptly inform an individual of the findings, and permit him or her to contest the findings. 42 U.S.C. 1320b-7 (a) and (c).

No federal agency and no state agency using federal records may suspend, terminate, reduce, or deny payments to an individual, based on a "computer match," until the individual receives notice and 60 days in which to challenge the computer "hit" in a hearing and appeal. There must be human intervention and confirmation before computer matches are used to deny benefits, computer matching must be pursuant to a public written agreement between agencies, and agencies must establish "data integrity boards" to oversee matches and make annual reports. 5 U.S.C. 552a.

Any foreigner, upon request, may get a review of an entry in the Immigration and Naturalization Service's National Automated Immigration Lookout System, a listing of visitors regarded as undesirable (the "Lookout Book"). The Departments of State and Justice must have guidelines for updating the list. 8 U.S.C. 1182.

Under federal law, state departments of motor vehicles must provide a citizen the means for prohibiting the disclosure of name, address, telephone number, Social Security number, medical information, or photograph on lists that are (1) rented for marketing purposes or (2) provided to other individuals. *Consent* is required before motor vehicle information may be disclosed. Businesses may still receive such information (without any consent) for certain purposes: safety, insurance, uses by licensed investigators, auto alterations or recalls, or to verify information previously supplied. 18 U.S.C. 2721-2725. [See 1997 book.]

In order to be acceptable "for federal purposes," all state driver's licenses must include date of birth, gender, driver's license number, digital photo, physical address and signature, with waivers granted to some states by the U.S. Department of Homeland Security. The license number may not be the Social Security number (but an SSN is still required on the license application). Data must be machine readable and compatible with a nationwide database of information, but states' procedures "shall include procedures and requirements to protect the privacy rights of individuals," according to the REAL ID Act. 49 USC 30301 note. The law has not been enforced pending regulations. Judges on federal courts (including the U.S. Supreme Court) may provide the address of the courthouse where they work, not their home addresses. 49 U.S.C. 30301 ("update"). "The Secretary of Homeland Security, in consultation with the Administrator of Social Security, shall consider and address the needs of victims, including victims of battery, extreme cruelty, domestic violence, dating violence, sexual assault, stalking or trafficking, who are entitled to enroll in state address confidentiality programs, whose addresses are entitled to be suppressed under state or federal law or suppressed by a court order, or who are protected from disclosure of information pursuant to [certain immigration laws]." 49 U.S.C. 30301 note.

Federal agencies must conduct "a privacy impact assessment" each time before "developing or procuring information technology that collects, maintains, or disseminates information that is in an identifiable form; or initiating a new collection of information using information technology and includes any information in an identifiable form permitting the physical or on-line contacting of a specific individual, if identical questions have been posed to, or identical reporting requirements imposed on, 10 or more persons." In addition, all federal Web sites must include a privacy notice similar to what is required under the Privacy Act. 44 U.S.C. 3601, P.L. 107-347, sec 208. See also 44 U.S.C. 3501.

The Office of Information and Regulatory Affairs in the Office of Management and Budget is responsible for overseeing privacy policies and practices of federal agencies. 44 U.S.C. 3503 and 3504.

Development of a national ID system or card is not authorized under the 2002 law creating the Department of Homeland Security. 6 U.S. C. 554. The Department of Homeland Security privacy officer shall have primary responsibility for "evaluating legislative and regulatory proposals involving collection, use, and disclosure of personal information by the Federal Government." 6 U.S.C. 142.

IDENTITY THEFT

Alabama–Theft of another's identity is a crime. Ala. Code 13A-8-190 through 13A-8-201.

Alaska–It is a crime to possess or use an identity document of another to open an account and damage the financial reputation of the victim. Alaska Stat. sec. 11.46.565.

Arizona–A person knowingly taking the identity of another person or using the identity of another person without consent with intent to obtain or use the other person's identity for any unlawful purpose or to cause loss commits a felony. Ariz. Rev. Stat. sec. 13-2708. Or to assume a false identity with the intent to defraud, commit a crime or obtain benefit. Sec. 11.46.570.

Arkansas–Identity theft is a crime. Ark. Code Ann. 5-37-227.

California–Using another's identity to purchase services or get medical information is a crime, as is the use of another's identity to commit a crime. Cal. Penal Code sec. 530.5. Knowingly impersonating another person on the Internet with malicious intent to harm is a misdemeanor. Sec 528.5. Credit-card issuers must confirm changes of address involving offers by mail. Cal. Civ. Code sec. 1747.06 and 1747.9. Financial institutions, credit-card issuers, and utilities must provide information to victims about fraudulent applications using their identities. Sec. 1748.95.

Victims may have a freeze put on their credit files. Sec. 1785.15. Others are prohibited from using an individual's Social Security number to get services. Sec. 1798.85.

ID theft can be a felony offense. Penal Code sec. 530.5 et seq. Conspiring to deprive a person of assets by false pretenses is a crime. Penal Code sec. 182. The statute of limitations for filing a report commences when the crime is discovered, not necessarily when it was committed. Penal Code sec. 803. A debt collector must stop collection when an alleged debtor furnishes a police report of identity theft and other information on his status as an identity-theft victim. Debt collectors who cease collection activities must notify creditors and consumer credit reporting agencies to which the collector previously provided adverse information. Civ. Code sec. 1788.18.

Victims whose "business identity" has been co-opted have rights and may have access to fraudulent accounts opened in their names. Penal Code sec. 530.8.

Victims may submit fingerprints to clear themselves of crimes possibly committed by strangers using their identities. Penal Code sec. 853.5 and Veh. Code sec. 40303, 40305, and 40504.

"A business shall take all reasonable steps to destroy, or arrange for the destruction of a customer's records within its custody or control containing personal information which is no longer to be retained by the business by (1) shredding, (2) erasing, or (3) otherwise modifying the personal information in those records to make it unreadable or undecipherable through any means." Civ. Code sec. 1798.81.

"It shall be unlawful for any person, by means of a Web page, electronic mail message, or otherwise through use of the Internet, to solicit, request, or take any action to induce another person to provide identifying information by representing itself to be a business without the authority or approval of the business [phishing]." Bus. & Prof. Code 22948.

Colorado–Producing a false identification document is forgery. Colo. Rev. Stat. sec. 18-5-102.

Connecticut–"A person is guilty of identity theft when such person intentionally obtains personal identifying information of another person without the authorization of such other person and uses that information for any unlawful purpose including, but not limited to, obtaining, or attempting to obtain, credit, goods, services or medical information in the name of such other person without the consent of such other person. As used in this section, "personal identifying information" means a motor vehicle operator's license number, Social Security number, employee identification number, mother's maiden name, demand deposit number, savings account number or credit card number." Conn. Stat. Ann. Sec. 53a-129a.

See also **Computer Crime.**

Delaware–Identity theft is a crime. Del. Code title 11, sec. 854.

Florida–"Any person who willfully and without authorization fraudulently uses, or possesses with intent to fraudulently use, personal identification information concerning an individual without first obtaining that individual's consent, commits the offense of fraudulent use of personal identification information, which is a felony." Fla. Stat. Ann. sec. 817.568.

Georgia–A person commits the offense of financial identity fraud when without the authorization or permission of another person and with the intent unlawfully to appropriate financial resources of that other person to his or her own use or to the use of a third party he or she obtains or records identifying information which would assist in accessing the financial resources of the other person. Ga. Code Ann. Sec. 16-9-121 G. [See 2002 book.]

"A business may not discard a record containing personal information unless it: (1) Shreds the customer's record before discarding the record; (2) Erases the personal information contained in the customer's record before discarding the record; (3) Modifies the customer's record to make the personal information unreadable before discarding the record; or (4) Takes actions that it reasonably believes will ensure that no unauthorized person will have access to the personal information contained in the customer's record for the period between the record's disposal and the record's destruction." Code Ann. 10-15-2.

Hawaii–Identity theft is a crime. Haw. Rev. Stat. sec. 708-810z.

Idaho–It is an unlawful misappropriation of personal identifying information for any person to obtain or record personal identifying information of another person without the authorization of that person, with the intent that the information be used to obtain, or attempt to obtain, credit, money, goods or services in the name of the other person without the consent of that person. Idaho Code 18-3126.

Credit bureaus must block information when informed of an incidence of identity theft by the victim. 28-51-102.

Illinois–A person commits the offense of financial identity theft when he or she knowingly uses any personal identifying information or personal identification document of another person fraudulently to obtain credit, money, goods, services, or other property in the name of the other person. 720 ILCS 5/16G.

Indiana–It is illegal for a person to obtain property by:

(A) using a credit card, knowing that the credit card was unlawfully obtained or retained;

(B) using a credit card, knowing that the credit card is forged, revoked, or expired;

(C) using, without consent, a credit card that was issued to another person;

(D) representing, without the consent of the credit card holder, that the person is the authorized holder of the credit card. Ind. Code Ann. sec. 35-43-5-4.

Iowa–Similar to Kentucky's criminal law. Iowa Code Ann. sec. 715A.8.

Kansas–"Knowingly and with intent to defraud for economic benefit, obtaining, possessing, transferring, using, one or more identification documents or personal identification number of another person other than that issued lawfully for the use of the possessor" is a crime. Kans. Stat. sec. 21-4018.

Kentucky–A person is guilty of identity theft who without consent possesses or uses any identification information such as Social Security number, date of birth, driver's license number in order to represent that he is that other person. Ky. Rev. Stat. Sec. 514.160

Louisiana–Identity theft is defined as the use or attempted use of personal identifying information (including Social Security number, driver's license number, check or credit-card number, digital signature or birth certificate) in order to obtain credit, money, goods or services or anything else of value. La. Rev. Stat. Ann. Sec. 14: 67.16.

Maine–It is illegal to create a false impression as to identity to deprive someone of property. Me. Rev. Stat. Ann. tit 17-A, sec. 354 (2A).

Maryland–A person may not knowingly and willingly assume the identity of another to obtain benefit, credit, goods, services or any item of value or use the assumed identity to avoid debt or other legal obligation. Md. Crim. Law 8-301. [See 2002 book.]

Massachusetts–Getting someone else's identity and posing as that person is a crime punishable by prison and restitution. Mass. Gen. Laws Ann. ch. 266, sec. 37E.

See also **Computer Crime**, for the law on encryption and security of personal information.

Michigan–It is illegal to forward a credit application in another person's name. Mich. Comp. Laws Ann. sec. 750.219e and f.

The Identity Theft Protection Act of 2005 prohibits identity theft. It requires destruction of personal information (by shredding, erasing, or otherwise modifying the data so that they cannot be read) before documents or electronic media are disposed of. Comp. Laws Ann. sec. 445.72a. The act includes other precautions and remedies for ID theft. To "obtain or possess, or attempt to obtain or possess, personal identifying information of another person with the intent to use that information to commit identity theft or another crime" is punishable. Secs. 445.61 through 445-73.

Minnesota–A person who possesses, transfers or uses an ID not his own with the intent of engaging in an unlawful activity is guilty of theft of identity. Minn. Stat. Ann. sec. 609.527.

Mississippi–Anyone who makes a false statement or representation as to his Social Security number, credit-card number, or other identifying information in order to obtain goods, services or other items of worth is guilty of fraudulent use of an ID Miss. Code Ann. sec. 97-19-85.

Missouri–The law requires restitution to the victim including the costs of correcting credit records. Mo. Ann. Stat. sec. 570.223.

Montana–Theft of identity is a crime. Mont. Code Ann. sec. 45-6-3.

A company must notify individuals when their Social Security numbers are disclosed as part of a breach of security, and certain records must be destroyed. Credit bureaus must block disclosure of certain ID theft-generated data. Code Ann. 33-19-321 and 30-14-1704.

Nebraska–ID theft is a crime. Neb. Rev. Stat. sec.

28-608 and 620.

Nevada–It is unlawful to use another's ID to hurt that person or to obtain goods, services or other benefit or to avoid prosecution. Nev. Rev. Stat. sec. 205.465.

Theft of identity is a crime. Rev. Stat. sec. 205.463 through 465.

New Hampshire–It is a felony to pose as another to obtain goods or services or to obtain records or confidential information not available to the general public. N.H. Rev. Stat. Ann. sec. 638:26.

New Jersey–It is illegal to impersonate another person or to obtain and use another person's ID for benefit. N.J. Rev. Stat. sec. 2C:21-17.

Theft of identity is a crime. Rev. Stat. sec. 2C:21-1. See also **Credit Reporting**.

New Mexico–Theft of identity is a misdemeanor. N.M. Stat. Ann. sec. 30-16-24.1.

New York–ID theft is a crime. N.Y. Penal Law secs. 190.77 through 190.84.

North Carolina–It is a felony to obtain, possess or use another person's personal identifying information (including Social Security number, driver's license number, check or credit-card number, digital signature or birth certificate) for gain. N.C. Gen Stat. 14-113.20.

There must be proper destruction of personal information in trashed records. Gen. Stat. sec. 75-64.

North Dakota–It is a felony to obtain or use another person's ID to obtain anything of value. N.D. Cent. Code sec. 12.1-23-11.

The security-breach notification law includes ID-theft protections. Cent. Code sec. 12.1-23-11.

Ohio–A person may not obtain, possess, or use the identifying information of another person (living or dead) in order to obtain goods, services or other items of value. Ohio Rev. Code Ann. sec. 2913.49.

Oklahoma–Same as Ohio. Okla. Stat. title 21, sec. 1533.1.

Oregon–A person commits the crime of identity theft if with intent to defraud he obtains, possesses, creates or converts to his own use the identifying information of another. Or. Rev. Stat. 165.800.

"Any person that owns, maintains or otherwise possesses data that includes a consumer's personal information that is used in the course of the person's business, vocation, occupation or volunteer activities must develop, implement and maintain reasonable safeguards to protect the security, confidentiality and integrity of the personal information, including disposal of the data." Implementation of an "information security program" complies with this law. Rev. Stat. 646A.622.

Pennsylvania–It is unlawful for anyone to possess the ID of another for any unlawful purpose. Pa. Stat. Ann. title 18, sec. 4120.

Rhode Island–"Identity fraud. – (a) Any person who knowingly and without lawful authority produces an identification document or a false identification document; knowingly transfers an identification document or a false identification document knowing that the document was stolen or produced without lawful authority; knowingly possesses a false identification document that is or appears to be a genuine identification document of the United States, the state of Rhode Island, any political subdivision of them, or any public or private entity, which is stolen or produced without lawful authority knowing that the document was stolen or produced without lawful authority; or knowingly transfers or uses with intent to defraud, without lawful authority, a means of identification of another person with the intent to commit, or to aid or abet, any unlawful activity that constitutes a violation of federal, state or local law; is guilty of a felony." RI Gen. Laws 11-49.1-3.

South Carolina–It is a felony to appropriate the financial resources of another by using identifying information of that person (Financial ID Fraud). S.C. Code sec. 16-13-510.

Identity-theft protections are found at Code Ann. sec. 37-20-180.

South Dakota–Using another's identity without authorization is a misdemeanor. S.D. Codified Laws Ann. sec. 22-30A-3.1.

Tennessee–Similar to Pennsylvania's criminal law. Tenn. Code Ann. sec. 39-14-150. There is a private right of action for victims. 47-18-2101

Texas–Fraudulent use of another's identity is a crime. Tex. Rev. Penal Code 32.51.

A business must take special precautions when discarding documents with personal information on or in them. Bus. and Com. Law sec. 48.102.

Obtaining someone else's personal information to procure a transaction is illegal. Bus. and Com. Law sec. 48.002.

Utah–It is a felony knowingly to obtain identifying information in order to obtain credit, goods and services, or medical information of another person. Utah Code Ann. sec. 76-6-1102.

Vermont–The law punishes identity theft. 13 Vt. Stat. Ann. 2030.

Virginia–It is unlawful for a person to obtain or use the ID of another to obtain credit, goods, services, or any item of value or use the assumed identity to avoid debt or other legal obligation. Va. Code sec. 18.2-186.3.

Washington–It is a felony to transfer a means of identification of another with the intent to harm that person. Wash. Rev. Code Ann. sec. 9.35.020.

"An entity must take all reasonable steps to destroy, or arrange for the destruction of, personal financial and health information and personal identification numbers issued by government entities in an individual's records within its custody or control when the entity is disposing of records that it will no longer retain." Victims of violations may sue for damages. Rev. Code 19.215.020. See also **Credit Reporting**; see also **Tracking Technologies**.

West Virginia–Any person who knowingly takes the name, birth date, Social Security number or other identifying information of another person, without the consent of that other person, with the intent to represent fraudulently that he or she is the other person for the purpose of making financial or credit transactions in the other person's name, is guilty of a felony, and upon conviction, shall be punished by confinement in the penitentiary not more than five years, or fined not more than $1000, or both. W. Va. Code sec. 61-3-54.

Wisconsin–Before they dispose of documents, financial institutions, tax preparers, and entities with medical information must obliterate data from documents or shred documents with Social Security or credit card numbers on them. The law is intended to combat theft of identity. Wisc. Stat. Ann. sec. 895. 505."Whoever intentionally uses or attempts to use any personal identifying information or personal identification document of an individual to obtain credit, money, goods, services or anything else of value without the authorization or consent of the individual and by representing that he or she is the individual or is acting with the authorization or consent of the individual is guilty of a Class D felony." Sec. 943.201.

Wyoming–Theft of identity is a crime. Wyo. Stat. Ann. sec. 6-3-901.

Federal law–Theft of identity to obtain credit is a federal crime. A victim has standing to seek prosecution and restitution. The Federal Trade Commission is obligated by law to assist complainants and to establish a clearinghouse of information on the subject. 18 U.S.C. 1028(a)(7).

Criminal restitution is available in identity-theft cases to compensate victims for the time spent to remediate the resulting harm. Certain offenses for identity theft have increased penalties. 18 U.S.C. 1028A.

The Fair Credit Reporting Act requires the major credit bureaus to respond to victims of identity theft with a "fraud alert" and with a single toll-free phone line. Credit bureaus may not post fraud-generated information in a credit report once it has been deleted because it was reported by the consumer to be inaccurate. Consumers may demand that credit bureaus truncate a Social Security number on file. 15 U.S.C. 1681 et seq.

See also **Social Security Numbers**.

See the section on **Computer Crime** for security breach laws. See the section on **Credit** for "credit freeze" laws.

INSURANCE RECORDS
(Including Use of Genetic Information in Insurance)

Alabama–Health insurers may not require **genetic tests** nor discriminate based on genetic information. Ala. Code 27-53-2). Another law prohibits denial of health or disability coverage because of a diagnosis of sickle cell anemia.

Arizona–The law on insurance record keeping is similar to that in Kansas. Ariz. Rev. Stat. Ann. 20-2110.A **genetic test** may not be required without consent, and health insurers may not discriminate based on genetic profiles. Sec. 20-1379.

California–The Insurance Information and Privacy Protection Act requires insurance companies and agents to give a policyholder or applicant notice regarding the types of personal information that may be collected about him or her from third parties, as well as the individual's rights to access and correction of files held by insurance companies. The individual is entitled to know the reasons for an adverse decision, and such a decision may not be based solely on the fact that another company rejected coverage. The individual must be informed of the opportunity to be interviewed when a consumer investigation is conducted at the request of the insurer. The law prohibits pretext interviews (which use pretense or misrepresentation or misidentity) by insurance companies, their representatives or "insurance support organizations" (like a consumer reporting firm, the Medical Information Bureau, or various clearinghouses). Cal. Ins. Code sec. 791. [See 1981 book.]

The civil rights law prohibits discrimination based on **genetic characteristics**. Health insurers may not solicit genetic information or discriminate in

underwriting. Health & Safety Code sec. 1374.7. Life and disability insurers may use genetic information to establish premiums but may not deny applicants based on asymptomatic genetic characteristics. Insurance Code sec. 10140, 10147.

Insurors may not discriminate based on **genetic information**. Health & Safety Code sec. 1374.7.

See also **Medical Records**.

There are limits on disclosures of individually identifiable medical information by health care providers and health plans. Civ. Code secs. 56.05, .10, .11, .17, and .21.

The California Genetic Information Nondiscrimination Act (CalGINA) extends non-discrimination areas beyond the federal law (which covers employment and insurance only) to housing, mortgage lending, education, access to the facilities of a business, emergency medical care, participation in state-funded programs, and public accommodations. Chap 261, Laws of 2011, Cal. Civ. Code sec. 51(e)(2) (A) through (C).

Colorado–Health insurers may not reject applicants or alter rates based on **genetic-test results**. There must be consent before testing, and test results must be confidential, except as authorized by the person. Colo. Rev. Stat. sec. 10-3-1104.7 and 10-3-1108.

Connecticut–The law on confidentiality and access to **insurance records** is similar to California's. Conn. Gen. Stat. Ann. sec. 38-501.

Health insurers may not use **genetic information** in insurance decisions. Sec. 38a-816(19).

Delaware–It is unlawful to discriminate based on **genetic information**. Del. Code Ann. title 18 sec. 2317. No person shall obtain genetic information about an individual without first obtaining informed consent from the individual. Title 16, sec. 1221.

District of Columbia–There are prohibitions against breaches of confidentiality of AIDS information by insurance companies. D.C. Code Ann. sec. 35-226.

Florida–Insurance companies may inquire about positive HIV test results, but not disclose the information. Group policies may not exclude coverage of AIDS treatment unless the individual had symptoms before getting coverage. Fla. Stat. Ann. sec. 627.429.

Genetic information may not be used in disability insurance. Sec. 760.40. Or in group-health coverage. Sec. 641.31073. Another law says that health insurers may not discriminate based on DNA information. Sec. 627.65625

See also **Medical Records**.

Georgia–The law prohibits pretext interviews by investigators. An application form must clearly label information that is *required* for coverage, as opposed to information that is desired for marketing. Insurance companies must follow certain procedures of notification and fairness when they gather information about individuals. Authorization forms must be clearly stated. Ga. Code Ann. sec. 33-39-2.

State law seems to authorize HIV testing by insurance companies. Sec. 31-22-9.1. Test results are confidential. Sec. 24-9-47.

The law on **genetic tests** is similar to Colorado's, except that disability coverage is included in the protections. 33-54.1.

See also **Social Security Numbers**.

Hawaii–Health insurers may not use **genetic information**. Haw. Rev. Stat. 431:10a-118.

Discrimination based on genetics is prohibited in health insurance. Rev. Stat. 432:1-607.

Illinois–The state's **insurance privacy law** is nearly identical to California's; it requires that authorization forms used by insurance companies to obtain personal information be written in plain language, dated, specific as to the types of persons who may disclose information about the applicant or policyholder and the types of information that may be disclosed. The form must have an expiration date. Illinois' and California's laws were drafted by the National Association of State Insurance Commissioners. 215 ILCS 5/1001 - 1024.

Information from **genetic testing** is confidential, and health insurers may not use it. 410 ILCS 513/20.

Insurance companies may test for AIDS only with consent; results must be kept confidential. 410 ILCS 50/3 (3.b). See also **Medical Records**.

Indiana–Insurers, other than life insurers, may not use genetic materials, nor inquiry into **genetic test results**. Ind. Code Ann. sec. 27-8-26-5. See also **Medical Records**.

Kansas–An **insurance company** or agent must inform an applicant or policyholder of the reasons for an adverse decision to insure or pay a claim, plus the names of institution sources of information used by the company. A company may comply by simply telling the individual that this information is available upon written request. Kans. Stat. Ann. sec. 40-2111.

An insurer or HMO may not seek or use **genetic information** to discriminate against an applicant. Sec. 40-2259.

Kentucky–Health insurers may not deny, vary premiums, terms or conditions on the basis of a **genetic test**. Also they may not require an applicant to disclose any genetic test results. Ky. Rev. Stat. sec. 304.12-090.

Louisiana–State law requires that the patient be entitled to receive any information sent to a company by a health care provider. La. Rev. Stat. Ann. sec. 40:1299.96.

State law prohibits the use of **genetic information** to terminate, cancel, deny, exclude coverage or benefits or set premiums. Sec. 22:213.7.

Maine–Insurance companies are barred from asking applicants to reveal whether they have been tested for the AIDS virus. An insurer may not require an applicant to disclose the results of a test. Test results are to remain confidential except for health purposes. Me. Rev. Stat. Ann. title 5, sec. 19203 and 19204.

An insurer may not discriminate based on genetic information or refusal to take a **genetic test**. Title 24-A sec. 2159-C.

Maryland–Medical files compiled by insurance companies under life or health policies on applicants and claimants shall be made **available for inspection** upon request of the applicant, claimant, or his agent. Information provided by a physician shall be available upon request after a period of five years from the date of the medical examination or sooner upon written authorization of the physician." Md. Ins. Code sec. 4-402. The company may not reveal medical information except with the individual's authorization, to a medical review or accreditation group, in response to legal process, for coordination of benefits, for fraud investigation, or for auditing and processing. Ins. Code sec. 4-402 and 403.

A health insurer may not "use a **genetic test** to reject, deny, limit, cancel, refuse to renew, increase the rates of, affect the terms or conditions of, or otherwise affect a health insurance policy or contract." Genetic information may not be disclosed without consent. Ins. Code sec. 27-909.

Massachusetts–The **Insurance Information and Privacy Act** of 1991 requires applicants and policyholders to be told what information will be collected and how it will be used, to be assured that collection will go no further, to have a copy of personal information held by an insurer (including medical information), to have erroneous information reinvestigated, to be given the reasons for a denial of insurance, and to be able to sue companies for violations. The Commissioner of Insurance will resolve disputes over accuracy. Insurers must adopt policies limiting disclosure of personal information to outsiders. Information about sexual orientation may not be collected nor used for adverse decisions. The law covers "insurance-support organizations" like MIB Inc. Mass. Gen. Laws Ann. ch. 175-I, sec. 1-22. [See 1992 book.]

It is unlawful to discriminate based on **genetic information**. Ch. 175 sec. 108H.

Michigan–Insurers may not require **genetic testing** or disclose results. Mich. Comp Laws Ann. secs. 550.1401(e), 333.21072a, and 500.3407b. Physicians need consent to conduct a genetic test. Sec. 333.16226

Minnesota–The **Insurance Fair Information Reporting Act** limits disclosure of personal information and provides for individual access to information. Minn. Stat. Ann. 72A-499.

The law on **genetic tests** is similar to Colorado's. 72A-139.

Genetics information may be collected and used only for purposes consented to by the individual. Stat. Ann. 13.386. sec. 4.

Missouri–Insurers may test for HIV virus but may not refuse to renew a policy solely because a person has been diagnosed as having AIDS. Test results must remain confidential. Mo. Ann. Stat. sec. 191.671.

An insurer may not require a **genetic test** nor use genetic information in making decisions concerning an applicant. Sec. 375.1303.

Montana–The law on **insurance record keeping** is similar to that in Kansas. Mont. Code Ann. sec. 33-19-303.

Nevada–An insurer may not use **genetic information** of a person or family member to deny, set rates or benefits. Exemption for long-term care. Nev. Rev. Stat. sec. 689A.417.

New Hampshire–**Genetic tests** may not be used to determine health insurance, but life coverage is not affected by the law. N.H. Rev. Stat. Ann. sec. 141-H:4 through 5.

Health insurers and third-party payers may not display SSNs on documents provided for claim payment. Rev. Stat. Ann. sec. 400-A:15-b.

New Jersey–The nation's most far-reaching limitation on use of **genetic-test** results by insurance companies and employers establishes genetic information in one's family history as confidential. Insurance companies need consent to get this information, and then may use it to alter premiums or deny coverage, but not in a discriminatory way. Employers may not screen employees or applicants based on genetic information. N.J. Rev. Stat. 17B:30-12.

State law gives complete authority for a hospital "utilization review committee" to provide any patient information to an insurance company so long as the terms of the policy "authorize the carrier to request and be given such information and data." Sec. 2A:84A-22.8.

New Mexico–No one may obtain **genetic information** without consent. N.M. Stat. Ann. sec. 24-21-3. And health insurers may not discriminate based on it. N.M. Stat. Ann. sec. 24-21-4.

All insurance companies must receive permission ("opt-in") from customers before disclosing account information to unaffiliated entities. Customer information may be disclosed to process a transaction or to comply with legal processes. This is pursuant to a rule issued by the Public Regulation Commission under the authority of Stat. Ann. sec. 59A-4-3.

New York–Insurers may not require **genetic testing** without informed written consent. N.Y. Ins. Code sec. 2612.

North Carolina–The law on **insurance record keeping** is similar to that in Kansas. N.C. Gen. Stat. sec. 58-39-55.

A health insurer may not issue a policy based on **genetic information**. Sec. 58-3-215.

Ohio–The nation's first law on **genetic profiles** prevents health insurers from requiring genetic tests or using test results in underwriting. Life and disability insurers are not covered by the law. Although tests of genes and chromosomes are covered, more superficial tests (like those for PKU in infants or for cystic fibrosis) are not. Ohio Rev. Code Ann. sec. 1742 and 3901.49.

Oklahoma–Like New York's law on **genetic testing**. Okla. Stat. title 36 sec. 3614-1.

Oregon–The law on **insurance record keeping** is similar to that in Kansas. Or. Rev. Stat. sec. 746.650.

The law on **genetic tests** is similar to Colorado's. Sec. 659.036.

Rhode Island–The state's comprehensive HIV testing law permits life and health insurers to require tests, with consent, and to deny or alter coverage accordingly. Current coverage may not be canceled because of a positive test result. HIV test results must be kept "secure," but physicians may inform sex partners of test results. R.I. Gen. Laws sec. 23-6-11 through 24.

South Carolina–An insurance company must specify reasons for cancellation of auto liability insurance upon request. Such notice is deemed a privileged communication and so a defense in a lawsuit for libel. S.C. Code sec. 46-750.33.

South Dakota–Health insurers may not use the results of **genes tests**. S.D. Codified Laws Ann. 58-1-25.

Tennessee–State law prohibits insurers from altering terms based on **genetic information**. Tenn. Code Ann. sec. 56-7-2703.

Texas–**Genetic information** is confidential unless specifically authorized by the individual, there are procedures that must be followed by health insurers using genetic tests. DNA test results may not be used for adverse decisions nor to determine eligibility for group coverage. Tex. Ins. Code Ann. art 21.73.

Utah–Insurers are prohibited from publicly display of an SSN, or printing SSNs on any card required for accessing services. Utah Code Ann. sec. 31A-22-634.

Vermont–No policy shall be conditioned on the basis of any requirement or agreement of the individual to undergo **genetic testing** or the results of genetic testing of an individual's family. Vt. Stat. Ann. title 18 sec. 9334.

Virginia–An insurance company must notify an applicant that he or she may have reasons for an adverse decision stated in writing and may have access to information used in making that decision. The company **must disclose the nature and substance** of all information, including medical information but, if it prefers, may disclose specific medical facts to the customer's physician. Names of private citizens who are sources of information need not be disclosed. An individual may get these materials by mail or in person. Va. Code sec. 38.1-52(11). [See 1981 book.]

A physician is limited in what he or she may disclose to a third-party payor regarding "mental health, mental retardation, substance abuse or emotional condition." The third-party payor may not further disclose such information without the specific written consent of the patient (except for coordination of benefits or for studies when the identity of patients will be protected). Sec. 37.1-225.

The law on **genetic tests** is similar to Colorado's. Insurance companies are limited in disclosing genetic information. Sec. 38.2-613.

West Virginia–Insurance may not be canceled when a policyholder gets AIDS. W. Va. Code sec. 33-15-13 and 33-16-9.

Wisconsin–Health insurers may not require **genetic tests** or ask about previous test results. Life and disability insurers may require applicants to disclose previous test results and may use the information in underwriting. Sec. 631.89.

Federal law–Group health plans may not use genetic information or medical histories to determine eligibility. 26 U.S.C. 9802.

See the Fair Credit Reporting Act described under **Credit Reporting** for the obligations of an insurance company that uses consumer reporting companies.

See also **Medical Records**, Florida, Massachusetts, and Wisconsin.

Access to and use of genetic information about individuals in group health-insurance coverage is restricted. 29 U.S.C. 1182(b)(A). (Also in employment.) The law does not preempt stricter state laws. It does not: (1) limit the authority of a health-care professional to request an individual to undergo a genetic test, or (2) preclude a group health plan from obtaining or using the results of a genetic test in making a determination regarding payment.

LIBRARY RECORDS

Alabama–Library records are confidential. Ala. Code 41-8-10.

Alaska–Public library records that identify patrons are confidential, except that they may be disclosed by court order. Alaska Stat. sec. 09.25.140.

Arizona–It is a misdemeanor to disclose library records about users without consent, a court order, or "for reasonable operation of the library." Ariz. Rev. Stat. 41-1354.

Arkansas–Library records are confidential. Ark. Code Ann. sec. 13-2-701.

California–Library records are exempt under the state public records law. Cal. Govt. Code sec. 6254(j).

Government agencies and other third parties may not access private reading records including electronic materials from libraries, booksellers and commercial providers of a book service, without proper justification. Demands for disclosure would have to be publicized by libraries and others. Civ. Code sec. 1798.90.

Colorado–State agencies must keep library material confidential. Colo. Rev. Stat. secs. 24-72-204(3)(a) and 24-90-119.

Connecticut–Library records shall be confidential. Conn. Gen. Stat. Ann. sec. 11-25.

Delaware–Library borrowers' records are not public. Del. Code title 29, sec. 10002d(12).

District of Columbia–Library records shall be kept confidential, except by court order. The procedure for obtaining a court order is spelled out; patrons must be notified when a subpoena is issued for their records. D.C. Code Ann. sec. 37-108.

Florida–Library records are confidential except by court order. Fla. Stat. Ann. sec. 257.261.

Georgia–Library records are confidential. Ga. Code Ann. 24-9-46.

Idaho–Library records are exempt from public disclosure. Idaho Code sec. 9-340(9)

Illinois–Library circulation records are confidential. 75 ILCS 70/2.

Indiana–Library records are not releasable. Ind. Code 5-14-3-4(16).

Iowa–Library patron records are listed as confidential in the state's records law, except in criminal investigations. Iowa Code Ann. sec. 22.7(13).

Kansas–Libraries are not required to disclose records about borrowers. Kans. Stat. Ann. sec. 45-221(a)(23).

Louisiana–Libraries shall not disclose records about borrowers, except by court order. La. Rev. Stat. Ann. sec. 44:13.

Maine–Library records are confidential, except by court order. Me. Rev. Stat. Ann. title 27, sec. 121.

Maryland–The custodian of public library records about individuals shall deny access to others, under the public records act. Md. State Govt. Code Ann. sec. 10-616. There are restrictions on releasing borrowers records at public university and school libraries. Md. Educ. Code Ann. sec. 23-107.

Massachusetts–Library records are not public records. Ch. 4, sec. 7 (definition 26th, subsec. K).

Michigan–Library patron records are confidential, not subject to the open records law, unless a court orders them disclosed. Mich. Comp. Laws Ann. sec. 397.601.

Minnesota–Library records are private, under the state Data Practices Act. Minn. Stat. sec. 13.40.

Mississippi–Library records are confidential, with an exception for minor children. Miss. Code Ann. sec. 39-3-365.

Missouri–No library is required to release information about individuals, except to the individual, or by order of a court for law enforcement purposes. Mo. Ann. Stat. sec. 182.817.

Montana–The law on library records is similar to Alaska's. Mont. Code Ann. sec. 22-1-1103.

Nebraska–Library records are confidential. Neb. Rev. Stat. 84-712.05.

Nevada–The law on library confidentiality is similar to Missouri's. Nev. Rev. Stat. Ann. sec. 239.013.

New Hampshire–Public-library borrowers' records are not subject to mandatory disclosure under the open records law. N.H. Rev. Stat. Ann. sec. 91-A:5. Borrowers' records in all libraries are confidential, except as requested by the user or by subpoena, court order, or "where otherwise required by statute." 201-D:11.

New Jersey– Identities of borrowers are confidential. N.J. Rev. Stat. sec. 18A:73-43.2.

New Mexico–Library records are confidential, except for children. N.M. Stat. Ann. sec. 18-9-3 through 5.

New York–"Computer database searches, inter-library loan transactions, reference queries, requests for photocopies of library materials, title reserve requests, or the use of audio-visual materials, film, or records" are included in the state's library confidentiality law. Public and private libraries are covered. N.Y. Civ. Prac. Law and Rules 4509.

North Carolina–Librarians may not disclose borrowers' information without consent or legal process. N.C. Gen. Stat. sec. 125-19.

North Dakota–Library patrons' records are private, exempt from disclosure under the public records law. N.D. Cent. Code sec. 40-38-12.

Oklahoma–Libraries "shall not disclose" records about borrowers. Okla. Stat. title 65, Sec. 1-105.

Oregon–Identity of specific library materials used by a named person is not subject to freedom of information law. Or. Rev. Stat. sec. 192.500(i)(j).

Pennsylvania–Public libraries, school libraries, and university libraries shall not disclose information about users, except under court order. Pa. Stat. Ann. title 24, sec. 4428.

Rhode Island–Library records concerning borrowers are exempt from the public records act. Public library records that identify a borrower are not public. R.I. Gen. Laws sec. 38-2-2(U).

It is unlawful to disclose names and addresses with titles of videos, records, cassettes or the like borrowed or purchased from a library, book store, or rental shop. Sec. 11-18-32.

South Carolina–It is a crime to disclose the records of a library borrower, without authorization of the individual or order of the court. S.C. Code 60-4-10.

South Dakota–Library records are confidential except by court order or, in the case of minors, consent of a parent. S.D. Codified Laws Ann. sec. 14-2-51.

Tennessee–Borrowers' records may not be disclosed by private or public libraries except with consent, by court order, or when used to seek reimbursement for missing materials. Tenn. Code Ann. sec. 10-8-101.

Vermont–Library records are exempt from public records disclosure act. Vt. Stat. Ann. title 1, sec. 317(b)(19).

Virginia–Library records are excluded from the public records law. Va. Code sec. 2.1-342(b)(8).

Washington–Library records are exempt from the state public records law. Wash. Rev. Code Ann. sec. 42.17.310(1).

West Virginia–Library records are protected. Parents may authorize release. W.Va. Code sec. 10-1-22.

Wisconsin–Library records may not be disclosed without a court order or consent of the patron. Wisc. Stat. Ann. sec. 43.30.

Wyoming–Library records are not open to inspection. Wyo. Stat. sec. 16-4-203(d).

Federal law–See **Mailing Lists** for the law on video rentals.

MAILING LISTS
(Including Electronic Mail Advertising, 'Spam,' and Information About Video Rentals)

Alaska–Unsolicited electronic mail advertising ("spam") must be labeled as such. Alaska Stat. sec. 45.50.479.

Arizona–Copies of precinct registers shall be on individual cards or magnetic computer tape or both to be furnished to any person at 2¢ per name. Ariz. Stat. Ann. sec. 16-154.

The law on unsolicited email is similar to Alaska's law. Rev. Stat. 44-1372.

Arkansas–The law on unsolicited email is similar to the one in Alaska. Ark. Code Ann. sec. 4-88-601.

California–Personal information, including sales and rental information, may not be disclosed by **video-rental** stores, except by consent; by court order or search warrant or civil discovery; or for tax administration or to law enforcement. Individuals' names and addresses may only be disclosed for use in commercial mailing lists. Cal. Civ. Code sec. 1799.3.

Telephone companies may not include unlisted telephone numbers on lists they rent, except to collection agencies and law enforcement. Nor may they disclose certain subscriber information. Pub. Util. Code sec.

2891.1.

The home address, telephone number, occupation, precinct number, and prior registration number provided by people who register to vote may not be released to the public. Journalists, scholars, political researchers, and other government officials may still get the information. Election Code 2194. Upon a showing of good cause a person may petition the Superior Court to make all voter information confidential. Election Code 2166.

Anybody renting or distributing a mailing or telephone list must obtain the user's identity and a sample of the solicitation and verify the legitimacy of the business. Users or renters of lists with children's names on them must take special precautions. If a parent requests removal of a child's name from a list, the user must comply within 20 days. Penal Code sec. 637.9.

It is a misdemeanor to use an Internet service provider to hide the origins of bulk electronic-mail advertising ("spam"), and the provider may sue anyone sending spam e-mail. Bus. Code sec. 17511.1. Unsolicited e-mail ads must include in the subject line the labels ADV or ADV:ADLT. Senders of bulk e-mail must provide a toll-free number or e-mail address so that recipients may get themselves removed from lists. 17538.4.

Grocery stores may not sell lists of frequent-shopper cardholders, nor may they demand Social Security numbers pr drivers' license numbers as a condition of receiving a card. Civ. Code sec. 1749.60.

State agencies' Web sites must disclose the existence of "cookies" on a user's computer. Civ. Code sec. 1798.16. Anybody who communicates electronically to obtain by false pretenses "from a public utility, confidential, privileged, or proprietary information, trade secrets, trade lists, customer records, billing records, customer credit data, or accounting data" is guilty of a crime. Penal Code sec. 538.5.

See Cal. Civil Code 1785.1 under **Credit Reporting** for the "opt-out" law on rental of credit-bureau lists.

The law on unsolicited email prohibits the sending of "spam" to or from a California email address, unless the recipient consents or has a preexisting business relationship with the sender. The law prohibits the collection of email addresses and sending commercial email with deceptive return addresses. Email ads to existing customers must include a chance to opt-out. The recipient, an email service provider, or the attorney general may bring an action for actual damages and liquidated damages of $1000 per email ad sent in violation. Bus. and Prof. Code secs. 17529 et seq.

A subscriber must give express permission before a cell phone service provider may list the subscriber's number in a directory. Pub. Util. Code sec. 2891.1.

See also **Miscellaneous**.

Web sites or on-line services that collect personal data from Californians must post a conspicuous privacy policy indicating what information they collect and what they will do with it. Deviations from the policy could be considered unfair competition under existing state law. Bus. and Prof. Code sec. 22575.

Colorado–Senders of bulk e-mail advertising must label them ADV and disclose the true sender's identity. Col. Rev. Stat. sec. 6-2.5-103.

Connecticut–"All personally identifiable information contained in the circulation records of any person renting **videotape** cassettes shall be confidential." Conn. Gen. Stat. Ann. sec. 53-450.

The computer-crime law says that it is unlawful to falsify a return address on unsolicited bulk email. Gen. Stat. Ann. sec. 53-451.

Delaware–"Wrongful disclosure" of information about **videotapes** purchased or rented is illegal, except for use in commercial mailing lists. Del. Code. title 11, sec. 925.

"A person is guilty of the computer crime of unrequested or unauthorized electronic mail when that person, without authorization, intentionally or recklessly distributes any unsolicited bulk commercial electronic mail (commercial E-mail) to any receiving address" except for mail sent between human beings or when requested. Title 11 sec. 937.

Florida–Every state agency must audit and purge its publication mailing lists biennially by giving addressees the opportunity to continue or to stop receipt of the publications. Fla. Stat. Ann. sec. 283.28.

Hawaii–Unsolicited advertising may be sent by fax or e-mail only under certain conditions. Haw. Rev. Stat. sec. 481B.

Idaho–A sender of bulk e-mail must provide an opportunity for the receiver to decline it. Idaho Code sec. 48-603E.

Illinois–Residents of the state may sue if someone sends e-mail ads that are falsely labeled or misidentify the source. 815 ILCS 511/10. See also **Government Information**.

Indiana–Each state agency is required to "refrain from preparing lists of the names and addresses of individuals for commercial or charitable solicitation purposes except as expressly authorized by law or [the public records] committee." Ind. Code Ann. 4-1-6.2.

It is unlawful to send commercial email to an Indiana resident or from the state if it is deceptive in its origination or in its subject line. IC 24-5-22-1.

Iowa–Records of **videotape-rentals** may not be disclosed, except with consent, or to a law enforcement agency with court approval, or for marketing purposes if the individual does not "opt out" of the list. Iowa Code Ann. sec. 727.11.

Senders of bulk e-mail must make certain disclosures about its origin. Sending unsolicited e-mail to someone who has previously opted out is prohibited. Sec. 714E.1.

Kansas–Most sales of state lists, including motor vehicle records, are prohibited. Kans. Stat. Ann. sec. 21-3914 and 74-2012.

Unsolicited email must be labeled and must not use deceptive or misleading materials. Stat. sec. 50-6, 107.

Louisiana–Video rental records are confidential. La. Rev. Stat. Ann. sec. 37:1746.

It is unlawful to send bulk email ads contrary to the policies of the receiver's Internet service provider. Rev. Stat. Ann. sec. 14:73.1.

Maine–The law on labeling email ads is similar to California's. Me. Rev. Stat. Ann. title 10, sec. 1497.

Maryland–Video rental stores may not disclose the identity of customers and their choices of video tapes. Md. Crim. Law sec. 3-907.

A licensed driver or car owner may prevent the Department of Transportation from releasing data on mailing lists by submitting a written request. The DMV may refuse to rent lists if it disapproves of the purpose. Trans. Code Ann. sec. 12-112.

It is unlawful to send commercial electronic mail advertising if it is deceptively labeled. Ann. Code 14-3002.

Michigan–Anyone selling, renting or lending books, recordings or videos shall not disclose the identity of the customer. Mich. Comp Laws Ann. sec. 445.1712.

The law against unsolicited email is similar to Colorado's. Mich. Comp. Laws Ann. sec. 445. 2501. A law similar to Utah's prohibits sending ad messages to children's electronic addresses. Sec 752.1061.

Minnesota–No charitable organization may use the name of a person other than an officer in solicitation literature without the written consent of the person. Minn. Stat. Ann. sec. 309.55.

Voter registration lists are not to be used for commercial purposes. Sec. 201.091.

Unsolicited email must be labeled, similar to the requirement in California. Internet service providers doing business in the state may not disclose personal information about subscribers. Stat. Ann. sec. 325M.02.

Missouri–The law on unsolicited ads by e-mail is similar to Hawaii's. Mo. Ann. Stat. sec. 407.1123.

Montana–State agencies may not rent or exchange mailing lists without the consent of the persons on the lists, except to other state agencies. Voting and motor vehicle records not included. Law enforcement not included. Individuals may compile their own lists from publicly available documents, and certain schools may use lists of license applicants. Mont. Code Ann. sec. 2-6-109.

Nevada–E-mail ads must be labeled and not sent to anyone who has opted-out. Nev. Rev. Stat. sec. 41.730. It is illegal to send e-mail that is falsely labeled. Sec. 205.492.

New Hampshire–See **Credit Reporting** for the "opt-out" law on rental of credit-bureau lists.

New Mexico–Anyone sending unsolicited email ads must provide a toll-free number or other means for the recipient to decline further messages, and the sender must abide by the request. N.M. Stat. Ann. sec. 57-12-23.

New York–Personal information about **video renters** is confidential. N.Y. Gen. Bus. Law 670.

Gas, electric and water utilities may not "sell or offer for sale" lists of their customers. N.Y. Pub. Svc. Law sec. 65(7). Telegraph or telephone companies may not sell lists of persons who are unlisted in phone directories. Sec. 91.

The freedom of information act says that disclosure of state mailing lists to be used commercially is an "unwarranted invasion of personal privacy." Pub. Off. Law sec. 89(2)(b)(iii).

"No credit card registration service shall rent, sell, exchange, or otherwise make available the names, addresses and account numbers of cardholders or owners of access devices entrusted to it by a credit card... issuer or other financial institution to any other person for use in direct mail marketing or solicitation without prior written approval of the cardholder." Gen Bus. Law sec. 521-c.

North Carolina–The computer crime law addresses unsolicited email advertising transmitted in violation of an Internet service provider's policies. N.C. Stat. sec. 14.453.

North Dakota–Sending deceptively labeled email ads violates the consumer-protection law. Ads must be labels and provide a toll-free number or other easy method to decline further mailings. N.D. Cent. Code sec. 51-27-01.

Ohio–Email ads must be labeled with the true name of the sender and with an easy method to get off the mailing list. Ohio Rev. Code Ann. sec. 2307.64.

Oklahoma–The law is similar to Iowa's and provides a civil penalty. Okla. Stat. title 15 sec. 776.

Pennsylvania–Sending deceptively labeled "spam" is a crime. Pa. Stat. Ann. title 18, sec. 7661. It is also an illegal trade practice. Title 73, sec. 2250.1.

Rhode Island–It is unlawful to disclose names and addresses with titles of videos, records, cassettes or the like purchased, leased, rented or borrowed from a library, bookstore or record shop. RI Gen Laws sec. 11-18-32.

It is unlawful to forge a return e-mail address for the purpose of sending bulk unsolicited e-mail. Sec. 11-52-4.

A business disclosing customer information in the past year for direct marketing by others must upon request tell individual about the disclosure. A company must maintain information about this entitlement on its Web site. A business is exempt if it earlier had offered a chance to opt out. Gen. Laws 11-49.2-8.

See also **Government Information**.

South Dakota–The law punishes the use of deception to send email commercial messages. S.D. Codified Laws. Ann. 37-24-6.

Tennessee–The law on unsolicited faxes covers e-mail. Tenn. Code Ann. Sec. 47-18-2501.

Utah–The Unsolicited Commercial and Sexually Explicit Email Act prohibits mislabeled "spam." Utah Code Ann. sec. 13-36-101.

Businesses shall not send certain messages to children's instant messaging, email, wireless phones, and fax machines, if the messages advertise "a product or service that a minor is prohibited by law from purchasing, viewing, possessing, participating in, or otherwise receiving." Businesses must pay a fee to consult a database of off-limits addresses and filter their advertising lists. Sec. 13-39-102.

Vermont–Lists compiled by public agencies, with exceptions, may not be disclosed if that would violate a person's right to privacy or would produce private gain. Vt. Stat. Ann. title 1, sec. 317(10).

Virginia–Sending unsolicited electronic mail advertising ("spamming") by use of an Internet provider based in Virginia is a crime, and a recipient of unwanted electronic-mail advertising may sue the sender, but not the Internet service provider. Va. Code sec. 18.2-152.2 It is a misdemeanor to send an e-mail ad "containing material harmful to juveniles and may be examined by a juvenile." 18.2-391.

See **Credit Reporting** for the law on disclosure of retailing information.

Sending spam via deceptive means is a felony. Code sec. 18.2-152.2.

Washington–State residents may add their e-mail addresses to a list maintained by the attorney general so that Internet service providers with policies against unsolicited e-mail advertising ("spam") may restrict such transmissions. The true identity of a sender of Spam must be included in the message. Wash. Rev. Code Ann. sec. 19.190.

Voter registration lists are not to be used for commercial purposes. Sec. 29.04.100.

The work and home addresses of a person shall not be disclosed by state agencies if a person says in writing that disclosure would endanger life, physical safety, or property. Sec. 41.17.310(bb).

West Virginia–Bulk e-mail sent fraudulently or with sexually explicit material is banned. W. VA Code sec. 46A-6G-2.

Wisconsin–A state or local agency may not sell or rent lists with home addresses unless specifically authorized by statute. Wisc. Stat. Ann. Subch. IV, Ch. 19.

"Whoever sends an unsolicited electronic mail solicitation to a person that contains obscene material or a depiction of sexually explicit conduct without including the words "ADULT ADVERTISEMENT" in the subject line of the electronic mail solicitation is guilty of a Class A misdemeanor." Sec. 944.25.

Wyoming–Email ads must be properly labeled, and Internet service providers may block them. Wyo. Stat. sec.40-12-401.

Federal law–World Wide Web sites appealing to children must get permission of parents before collecting personal information on-line from children under age 13. Parents may have access to any family information provided by children and the opportunity to prevent further use of it. 15 U.S.C. 6501 note.

An individual may have the Postal Service prohibit a particular mailer from sending him or her advertisements considered by the recipient to be erotically arousing or sexually provocative. 39 U.S.C. 3008. An individual may direct the Postal Service not to deliver sexually oriented advertisements through the mail. Sec. 3010.

The Federal Election Campaign Act requires political candidates federal office to record one's name and address with any contribution for $50 or more, and occupation and principal place of business once contributions to any one campaign exceed $100. This information is available for public inspection, although the law prohibits use of the information by others for fund-raising or commercial purposes. 2 U.S.C. 438.

Federal agencies may not sell or rent mailing lists unless authorized by law or obligated to release them under the Freedom of Information Act. 5 U.S.C. 552a(n). [See 1992 book.]

A **video**-rental store may rent customer lists if the customer has a chance to prohibit such disclosure and if the list does not reveal the titles or descriptions of tapes used. Customer lists must be destroyed within one year after they are no longer needed. The Video Privacy Protection Act permits a customer to sue a rental or sales outlet that discloses what tapes a person borrows or buys, or releases other "personally identifiable information." 18 U.S.C. 2710.

Multiple electronic mail advertising is permitted. To send bulk email ads with headers that are deceptive or do not include the true physical address of the sender, that are deceptive in identifying the sender, or that do not include a means for the recipient to decline to receive further ads from that originator is an unfair or deceptive business practice. Most state laws like California's limiting "spam" are preempted; some laws punishing deceptive spamming are not preempted. 15 U.S.C. 7701.

For laws on disclosure of mailing lists in state agencies and federal law on disclosure of motor-vehicle records, see **Government Information**.

MEDICAL RECORDS
(Including AIDS Testing)

Alabama–Ala. Code secs. 22-16-2 and 4 require physicians to file with the state confidential reports on sexually transmitted disease.

Alaska–Alaska Stat. sec. 47.30.590 governs the confidentiality of medical records in state files. Physicians and surgeons are subject to privilege except in child abuse cases. Alaska R. Civ. P. 43(h)4 and 8. Mental health records may be disclosed only as patient consents or court orders. Alaska Stat. sec. 47.30.260.

Arizona–Health providers may release patient records only with a patient's consent, or in instances authorized by law. Ariz. Rev. Stat. sec. 12-2292 and 12-2294. A patient may have access to his or her own record unless a physician or psychologist indicates this is "contraindicated due to treatment of the patient for a mental disorder." Sec. 12-2293.

Physicians and surgeons are subject to privilege in most instances. Sec. 12-2235.

Arkansas–Psychologists are subject to a privilege. Ark. Code Ann. sec. 17-96-105. And so are psychotherapists and physicians. Sec. 16-14-101.

See also **Computer Crime**.

California–Every person has the ultimate responsibility for decisions respecting his or her health care and therefore has a right of access to complete information respecting his or her condition and care provided. A health provider must disclose patient records to an individual who is the subject of the records. A mental health professional may refuse, if disclosure would have an adverse effect; but in that case, the patient may designate another professional to inspect on the patient's behalf. A doctor may prepare a summary of the record, but this does not alter the obligation to disclose the full record, with exceptions. Cal. Health & Safety Code sec. 1795.

Any patient is entitled to access his or her own records from a health provider. Health & Safety Code 123110. A patient is entitled to lab test results, even electronically if requested. Sec. 123148.

Individually identifiable information about birth defects or cancer must be treated by state agencies as confidential. Health & Safety Code 103850 and 103885.

Health maintenance organizations and prescription drug companies may not use patient information without prior authorization of the patient. The attorney general and district attorneys have powers to enforce compliance. HMOs may not force patients to waive their privacy rights. Civ. Code sec. 56.05. Employers may not see certain underlying workers compensation medical data. Sec. 56.31. Psychotherapists' records may not be released. Secs. 56.35 and 56.104

Cal. Evid. Code sec. 1010 recognizes the doctor-patient privilege, and includes psychiatrists. Sec. 1016 requires a patient to waive the privilege of confidentiality when he or she is the plaintiff in a civil suit. Eavesdropping in a conversation between a

physician and patient is a felony. Sec. 636. Identity of methadone drug patients or former patients is not to be disclosed, except with consent, or between professionals involved in treatment, or upon a court order, or for protection of state elected officials. Disclosures must be logged in a patient's file. Cal. Wel. and Inst. Code sec. 4353.

"No requester shall acquire medical information regarding a patient without first obtaining [written] authorization from that patient," nor may a user of medical information further disclose it unless specific permission is included on the patient's authorization form. By law, the authorization must be in at least eight-point type, clearly separate from other language on an authorization form, and signed by the patient or a relative. It must state the types of medical information authorized to be disclosed, who may disclose and who may acquire the information, and the purposes of the disclosure. The authorization must include an expiration date. The patient is entitled to a copy.

There are exceptions to the requirement, including disclosures in legal proceedings and law enforcement investigations, medical research and peer review. If a patient or next of kin does not object, a health facility may release the name and address of the patient, as well as gender, age, reason for admission, and general condition. Also, medical information may not be disclosed to an employer unless the individual authorizes the disclosure. Cal. Civ. Code sec. 56. [See 1981 book.]

A doctor, dentist, nurse, psychologist, laboratory or pharmacy must give a copy of an individual's medical record to an attorney for an individual who plans to file a legal action. Cal. Evid. Code sec. 1158.

Blood testing for the AIDS (acquired immune deficiency syndrome) virus (HIV) must be anonymous, and test results may not disclose identities of persons tested, even through subpoena. Cal. Health & Safety Code sec. 199.20.

Patients' Social Security numbers and other identifying information that health facilities file with the state are exempt from the Public Records Act. Health & Safety Code sec. 128735.

"Every provider of health care shall establish and implement appropriate administrative, technical, and physical safeguards to protect the privacy of a patient's medical information [and] reasonably safeguard confidential medical information from any unauthorized access or unlawful access, use, or disclosure." An Office of Health Information Integrity is established to ensure the enforcement of state law mandating the confidentiality of medical information. Health and Safety Code sec. 130200-130203. There are penalties for unauthorized disclosure of patient data. Sec. 1280.15. A health plan may disclose summary health information to the health plan's third party administrator or to another health plan in a manner consistent with the federal HIPAA rule. Civ. Code secs. 56.10 and 56.11.

A business may not seek to obtain medical information from an individual for direct-marketing purposes without clearly disclosing how it will use and share that information and getting the individual's consent. Civ. Code sec. 1798.91.

Colorado–Patient records in the custody of a health care facility are available to the patient except for psychiatric records that would have a significant negative psychological impact–then a summary may be made available. Colo. Rev. Stat. sec. 25-1-801.

Physicians who diagnose sexually transmitted disease shall report it; the name and address of the person is not required unless the doctor believes such person to be a menace, in which case the person's name is to be reported to a health officer and the diagnosis may also be disclosed to a person's spouse, fiancé, or parent (if minor). Sec. 25-4-402.

The state criminal theft statute makes clear that "confidential information, medical records information" is considered a "thing of value" under the statute. Sec. 18-1-901.

The criminal code also states, "Any person who, without proper authorization, knowingly obtains a medical record or medical information with the intent to appropriate [it] to his own use or the use of another, who steals or discloses to an unauthorized person a medical record or medical information, or who, without authority, makes or causes to be made a copy of a medical record or medical information commits theft." Sec. 18-4-412.

See also **Social Security Numbers**.

Connecticut–A patient has the right to see and copy his or her hospital records, including charts and pictures, after discharge. Conn. Gen. Stat. Ann. sec. 4-105.

State law limits the disclosure of mental health data about a patient by name or other identifier (like Social Security number). Identifiable data is intended for use within a mental health facility, although anonymous data may be disclosed for research and the state commissioner of mental health is authorized to enter into intrastate and interstate agreements "for efficient storage and retrieval of such information and records," if each patient is not identified. Sec. 52-146h. State institutions may release to third parties only that patient information necessary to determine appropriate funding. Sec. 17-295c.

Testing for the HIV virus must be done with consent, and results kept confidential. Sec. 19A-581.

See also **Student Records**.

Delaware–Sexually transmitted disease reports are to be treated with strict confidentiality. Del. Code title 16, sec. 711.

Informed consent is required to test for HIV virus, most of the time; results must be confidential. Title 16, sec. 1204.

The physician-patient privilege does not apply in child-abuse cases. Title 16, sec. 907.

District of Columbia–D.C. Code Ann. sec. 14-307 recognizes privileged communications in medical practice with exceptions. Also, a public mental health facility must make patient records available to the patient's attorney or personal physician. Sec. 21-562.

Florida–A licensed health-care provider must furnish copies of patient records to the patient or his or her legal representative, upon request, and may not disclose them to others without consent of the patient, except by subpoena. Fla. Stat. Ann. sec. 455.241 and 395.017.

A hospital must furnish a copy of all treatment records, except for certain psychiatric files, upon the request of a patient after discharge. Sec. 395.202. [See 1981 book.] Each hospital must report details about any cases of cervical or breast cancer it treats. Sec. 395.25.

A psychiatrist-patient privilege is recognized. Sec. 456.059.

HIV test results must remain anonymous and confidential, except that they may be disclosed with consent, or "pursuant to standard practice of medicine or public health." Individuals tested are entitled to have the results, at least after 120 days. Sec. 381.606. HIV tests must be with consent. Results are confidential. All test results must be confirmed before disclosure to the individual. Sec. 381.609. See also **Insurance Records**.

Georgia–A health provider shall provide a complete and current copy of a patient record upon request. Ga. Code Ann. sec. 31-33-2.

There must be written consent to release prescription information to a third party. Sec. 29-9-49.

A privilege for psychiatrists is recognized. Sec. 24-9-21. Sexually transmitted disease and suspected child abuse cases must be reported. Sec. 31-7-2 and 19-7-5. Disclosures of medical records in court or as required by statute does not destroy the confidential nature of the records. Sec. 24-9-42.

Hawaii–Health-care providers, employers, health plans, data providers, educational institutions, and insurers may release patient data only under limited circumstances. Haw. Rev. Stat. 323C and 334-5.

A patient is entitled to copy doctor's and hospital records about himself or herself. Sec. 622-57.

A privilege is recognized in civil cases. Haw. Rev. Stat. sec. 621-20. Medical records in court are governed by sec. 622-51. The identity of individuals in the tumor registry is confidential; no person providing such information is liable for it. Sec. 324-11 and 324-12.

HIV test results are to be confidential. Sec. 325-101.

Idaho–Idaho Code sec. 54-1810(h)(2) provides possible revocation of medical license for betrayal of a professional secret. Child abuse cases must be reported. Sec. 16-1619. Any hospital patient whose records are subpoenaed or any physician or nurse responsible for entries in that record has standing to request a protective order to deny access. Sec. 9-420.

Sec. 9-203(4) recognizes a physician privilege.

Illinois–Among the rights of patients is that **confidentiality** in health care is required unless the patient consents to disclosure, or where authorized by law. 410 ILCS 50/3.

A doctor or attorney may get a **copy** of a patient's hospital record, upon demand of the patient. 735 ILCS 5/8-2001.

The law recognizes a privilege for physicians and psychiatrists. 735 ILCS 5/8-802. Child abuse cases must be reported. 325 ILCS 5/4.

HIV tests may be administered only with consent, and persons may be tested anonymously. There may be no disclosure outside of the health-service community, without consent or a court order. Insurers may test with consent and must keep the information confidential. 410 ILCS 305/1.

Physicians may test for HIV without specific consent if the patient has authorized general medical treatment. 410 ILCS 305/7.

Mental health records are to be kept confidential and may be inspected by a patient or his or her proxy. 740 ILCS 110/1.

See also **Insurance Records**.

Indiana–The patient's consent is required for outsiders to get access to patient records. Ind. Code Ann. sec. IC 16-39-5. All medical records including mental-health records must be made available to the patient and the patient's attorney upon written request. 16-39-2-3. Patient records are the property of the patient and the provider and subject to limits on disclosure. IC 16-39-5-3. Child abuse (31-33-5-1), HIV (16-41-7-3), and certain communicable diseases (16-41-2-2) must be reported. See also 16-41-8-1. Insurance companies may obtain records with written consent. Sec. 16-39-5-2. Automated hospital records must be available to authorized persons only, including the patient. Sec. 34-43-1-3. Sec. 34-46-3-1 recognizes the doctor-patient privilege.

Iowa–Iowa Code Ann. sec. 622.10 recognizes doctor-patient privilege except when a patient files suit. Confidential reports of sexually transmitted disease must be filed. Sec. 140.1-4.

HIV test results must be anonymous, and employers may not require testing. Sec. 441.10 and 216.6.

Kansas–*Mental health* records may not be disclosed except with the patient's consent or a court order. Kans. Stat. sec. 59-2931.

A doctor-patient privilege is recognized. sec. 60-427, 65-2837(f) and 74-5323. Child abuse cases must be reported. Sec. 38-717.

One may not use HIV test results so as to discriminate against a person. Sec. 65-108.

Kentucky–A narrow physician-client privilege and a psychiatrist privilege are recognized. Ky. Rev. Stat. sec. 213.200 and 421.215.

Collection of data about individual (public health) patients shall be in a non-identifying numeric form without a patient's name or SSN. Any person who receives information identifying a patient through error or any other means shall return all copies of the information immediately. Rev. Stat. 216.2927.

Louisiana–La. Rev. Stat. Ann. sec. 15:476 recognizes a physician-patient privilege, interpreted only to apply in criminal proceedings. *State hospitals* must provide **copies** of records upon a patient's request. Sec. 40:2014.1

Maine–The law on confidentiality is similar to Hawaii's. A patient has a right to see one's own files and to add a statement of correction to the patient record. Me. Rev. Stat. Ann. title 22, sec. 1711.

Me. Rev. Stat. Ann. tit 32, sec. 3153 recognizes the doctor-patient privilege.

"A carrier or prescription drug information intermediary may not license, use, sell, transfer or exchange for value, for any marketing purpose, prescription drug information that identifies directly or indirectly the individual." Tit. 22, sec. 1711-E. The law prohibits the collection and use of personal information collected on the Internet from a minor who is at least 13 years of age and under 17 years of age for the purposes of pharmaceutical marketing. Title 10, sec. 9561.

AIDS blood tests may not be conducted without consent, and results must be kept confidential within the health community. Title 5, secs. 19203 and 19204.

Maryland–Md. Cts. & Jud. Proc. Code Ann. sec. 9-109 recognizes a privilege between patient and psychiatrist. Md. Health Gen. Code Ann. sec. 4-102 requires the records of the secretary of health and mental hygiene be kept confidential. It is unlawful to disclose them except for research purposes. To ensure the confidentiality of sexually transmitted disease lab reports, only a case number is assigned. Sec. 18-205.

The state collects data statewide on medical patients' identity, demographics, diagnoses, procedures, fees, and prescriptions, and is required to keep the data confidential. Sec. 19-134.

Md. Trans. Code Ann. sec. 16-119 allows doctors to report to the state motor vehicle administration any data on patients whose driving may be impaired for medical reasons. When an insurance company compiles a medical file, the company must permit a claimant or applicant to inspect his or her file. Information provided by a doctor is not, however, available for five years unless the doctor authorizes its release. Ins. Code 4-402. See also **Insurance Records**.

Massachusetts–A Patient's Bill of Rights provides among other things a right to **"confidentiality** of all records and communications to the extent provided by law; ... to inspect his medical records and to receive a copy; ... to refuse to be examined, observed, or treated; ... to refuse to serve as a research subject; ... to privacy during medical treatment or other rendering of care within the capacity of the facility; ... to informed consent" when hospitalized. The confidentiality provision does not apply to copying by third-party reimbursers under an insurance policy, nor to peer reviews. Mass. Gen. Laws Ann. ch. 111, sec. 70E. [See 1981 book.]

No privilege is recognized. Ch. 111, sec. 70 permits medical records kept by hospitals or clinics to be destroyed after 30 years. Records may be inspected by a patient or his attorney and a copy furnished for a reasonable fee. Ch. 123, sec. 36 states that at the discretion of the mental health commissioner, attorneys for mental patients, and in some cases the patients themselves, may see their medical records. "Any employer requiring a physical examination of any employee shall, upon request, cause said person to be furnished a copy of the medical report following." Ch. 149, sec. 19A.

Labs and hospitals that conduct blood tests for AIDS virus must not disclose the results to outsiders without the consent of the patient. Physicians may test for HIV with verbal consent. Taking a test may not be a condition of employment or of taking a medical exam. Ch. 111, sec. 70F, amended in 2012.

Michigan–A privilege is recognized. Mich. Comp. Laws Ann. sec. 600.2157. Sexually transmitted diseases, tuberculosis, and child abuse must be reported. Sec. 329.152-202, 329.401 and 722.571.

Physicians need consent to conduct a genetic test. Sec. 333.16226.

Minnesota–A physician may not disclose confidential information acquired in his or her professional capacity. Minn. Stat. Ann. sec. 595-02(4). Child abuse and tuberculosis cases must be reported. Sec. 626.554 and 144.42. A medical bill of rights states that patients have a right to every consideration of their privacy and individuality. Sec. 144.651. Further, patients have a right to copy doctors' and hospital records about themselves. Sec. 144.335.

Genetic information may be collected and used only for purposes consented to by the individual. Stat. Ann. 13.386. sec. 4.

Mississippi–A doctor-patient privilege is recognized. Miss. Code Ann. sec. 13-1-21.

Missouri–Physicians and surgeons are covered by a privilege. Mo. Ann. Stat. sec. 491.060.

Montana–Physicians are subject to a privilege. Mont. Code Ann. Sec. 93-70104(4). Physicians must report suspected cases of child abuse and cases of sexually transmitted disease. Sec. 10-902 and 69-4604. See **Testing in Employment**.

Nevada–A patient may refuse to disclose or forbid any other person from disclosing medical information. Nev. Rev. Stat. sec. 49.215-245. A patient has the right to inspect and copy both doctor's and hospital records. Sec. 629.061.

New Hampshire–A physician's privilege to keep patient information confidential is recognized. N.H. Rev. Stat. Ann. sec. 329:26 and 330-A:19.

Unauthorized disclosure of results of HIV tests submitted to state labs is prohibited. Sec. 141-F:7-8. Generally consent is required to test for HIV.

Hospital patients "shall be ensured confidential treatment of all information contained in the patient's personal and clinical record, including that stored in an automatic databank, and the patient's written consent shall be required for the release of information to anyone not otherwise authorized by law to receive it. Medical information contained in the medical records at any facility licensed under this chapter shall be deemed to be the property of the patient. The patient shall be entitled to a copy of such records

upon request." Rev. Stat. Ann. sec. 151. 21. "Medical information in the possession of any health care provider shall be deemed to be the property of the patient. The patient shall be entitled to a copy [at a cost not exceeding $15]. Release or use of patient identifiable medical information for the purpose of sales or marketing of services or products shall be prohibited without written authorization." Sec. 332-1:1.

"Records relative to prescription information containing patient-identifiable and prescriber-identifiable data shall not be licensed, transferred, used, or sold." Sec. 318:47-f.

New Jersey–N.J. Rev. Stat. sec. 2A:84A-22.2-9 recognizes a privilege, with subsequent limitation. There is a limited right of access for attorneys and next-of-kin of *mental patients in state institutions* and for attorneys handling personal injury cases. Sec. 30:4-24.3 and 2A:82-42.

New Mexico–*Mental health* records are confidential except may be shared with another doctor treating the patient, to protect a client from harm, or with a parent if necessary for treatment. N.M. Stat. Ann. sec. 43-1-19

Test results for HIV must be confidential. Sec. 24-2B-6. See also **Testing in Employment**.

New York–Patients have a right of access to medical files. N.Y. Pub. Health Law sec. 18. A physician or hospital must release an individual medical file (except for personal notes of the doctor) to another physician or hospital designated by the individual. Sec. 17. Records concerning sexually transmitted disease treatment or abortion for a minor may not be released, even to the parent.

N.Y. Pub. Health Law, sec. 17. N.Y. Civ. Prac. Law sec. 4504 (McKinney) recognizes privileged communications with regard to doctors and nurses.

See also **Computer Crime**.

North Dakota–Communications with a physician are privileged. N.D. Cent. Code sec. 31-01-06(3). Cases of sexually transmitted disease and child abuse or neglect must be reported. Sec. 23-07-02 and 50-25-01 to 05.

Ohio–A hospital must furnish a copy of a patient's record upon request. Ohio Rev. Code Ann. sec. 3701.74.

Sec. 2317-02(A) recognizes doctor-patient privilege. Child abuse cases must be reported. Sec. 2151-42.1.

"No person shall be liable for any harm that results to any other person as a result of failing to disclose any confidential information about a mental health client, or failing to otherwise attempt to protect such other person from harm by such client." Sec. 5122.34.

See also **Employment Records, Insurance Records**.

Oklahoma–It is a misdemeanor to deny a patient access to all non-psychiatric files. Okla. Stat. title 76, sec. 19.

A doctor's privilege is recognized. Title 12, sec. 385(6). Physicians must report cases of child abuse and make confidential reports on sexually transmitted disease. Title 21, sec. 846 and title 63, sec. 1-528(b).

A health professional may disclose to parents treatment needed by or provided to a minor; such disclosure shall not constitute a breach of the right to privacy. Title 63, sec. 2601.

Oregon–It is the policy of the state to protect the confidentiality of patient records in a private or public facility and to permit a patient to copy a doctor's and hospital's records. Or. Rev. Stat. sec. 192.525.

A physician privilege is recognized. Sec. 44.040(1)(d). Physicians are required to report, in confidence, cases of suspected violence. Sec. 146-750. Sexually transmitted disease data may be disclosed with consent or in the public interest. Sec. 44-040.

State law governs consent and confidentiality in HIV testing. Ore. Rev. Stat. sec. 433.075.

Pennsylvania–A privilege is recognized only as to derogatory information in civil cases. Pa. Stat. Ann. title 28, sec. 328.

Mental health records in state agencies must be kept confidential. Title 50, sec. 7111.

Rhode Island–Organizations that keep medical information must adopt policies to assure confidentiality. Individuals have a right to inspect medical records about themselves, and to amend them if necessary. R.I. Gen. Laws. sec. 5-37.3-3.

Patients have a right of access to their own files. 5-37-22.

Disclosure of prescription information to any other persons other than agents of properly licensed pharmacies is prohibited. Sec. 5-19-28.

See **Insurance Records** for HIV testing law.

South Dakota–A privilege for doctor's and hospital records is recognized. S.D. Codified Laws Ann. sec. 19-2-3. Sexually transmitted disease, tuberculosis, and child abuse must be reported.

Tennessee–Hospital records are the property of the hospital; upon "good cause" access will be provided to the patient. Tenn. Code Ann. sec. 53-1322. Medical records of patients *in state facilities* and those whose care is paid for by state funds are confidential. Sec. 10-7-504.

A privilege exists for psychiatrists. Sec. 24-1-207. And for psychologists. Sec. 63-117.

Texas–Medical information identifiable as to individuals is to be kept confidential *in state files*. Tex. Health & Safety Code Ann. sec. 161.0213.

State law spells out when AIDS blood tests may be conducted, including when an employer can show a necessity to test based on a bona fide occupational qualification. Results must be kept confidential. Health & Safety Code Ann. sec.81-102.

Utah–Utah Code Ann. sec. 78-24-8(4) recognizes a doctor-patient privilege. Suspected child abuse cases must be reported. Sec. 55-16-2 and 78-3b-3. A patient's attorney is entitled to a copy of all medical information. Sec. 78-25-25.

Vermont–A physician, dentist, or nurse is not allowed to testify on information acquired in attending a patient. Vt. Stat. Ann. title 12, sec. 1608.

"Records relative to prescription information containing patient-identifiable and prescriber-identifiable data shall not be licensed, transferred, used, or sold" without consent of the prescribing professional. Vt. Stat. Ann. title 18, sec. 4631.

See **Testing In Employment** for law on HIV testing.

Virginia–"There is hereby recognized a patient's right of privacy in the content of a patient's medical record. Patient records are the property of the provider maintaining them, and, except when permitted by this section or by another provision of state or federal law, no provider, or other person working in a health care setting, may disclose the records of a patient." Va. Code sec. 32.1-127.1:03.

Copies of hospital records shall be furnished at a reasonable charge to the patient or his or her attorney; except for mental records when the doctor specifically declares that release would be injurious to the patient. Sec. 8.01-413. See sec. 10-413.

HIV testing must be done with consent, and the results kept confidential. Sec. 32.1-36.1.

A privilege for physicians is recognized. Sec. 8.01-399. Individual medical data in state files is exempt from public disclosure. Sec. 2.1-342(b).

See also **Computer Crime** and **Insurance Records**.

Washington–There is a right of confidentiality in patient information, with several exceptions. Wash Rev. Code Ann. 70.02. There is also a right to access, to copy, and to amend or correct one's own medical records. 70.02.080.

Medical data collected in the state's health-care financing system will be used only for that purpose and will be exempt from public disclosure, subject to regulations. Sec. 70.170.

A privilege for physicians is recognized. Sec. 5.60.050. Cases of child abuse must be reported. 26.44.030.

"No person may require an individual to take an HIV (AIDS antivirus) test as a condition of hiring, promotion, or continued employment unless the absence of HIV infection is a bona fide occupational qualification." Sec. 49.60.

West Virginia–A physician may testify only with patient's consent. W. Va. Code sec. 50-6-10. Sexually transmitted disease, communicable disease and tuberculosis must be reported. Sec. 16-4-6, 16-2A-5 and 26-5A-4. Patients may have access to their own psychiatric or psychological treatment. Sec. 16-29-1.

Insurance may not be canceled when a policyholder gets AIDS. Sec. 33-15-13 and 33-16-9. Information about HIV testing is generally confidential. Sec. 16-3C-3.

Wisconsin–Patient records must be kept confidential except for use in health care, for processing payments and claims, and for research. Wisc. Stat. Ann. sec. 146.82.

A patient may inspect and have a copy of records, and must be notified of rights under this law. Sec. 146.83. AIDS test results must remain confidential. 146.025.

Sec. 885.21 recognizes a doctor's privilege. Sexually transmitted diseases, tuberculosis, and child abuse must be reported. Sec. 143.06 and 48.981.

Wyoming–A doctor may testify only with patient's consent or when the patient testifies on medical matters. Wyo. Stat. sec. 1-139(1). Child abuse, sexually transmitted disease and communicable disease must be reported to the state. Sec. 14-28.8, 35-177 and 35-172.

Federal law–Federal law requires the Department of Health and Human Services to publish regulations governing the maintenance and disclosure of personal health information. 42 U.S.C. 1320d-2(b). The regulations, 45 Code of Federal Regulations 164.102, take effect in April 2003. Generally they require consent before medical information may be released, except for exchanges in the treatment of patients. There are other exceptions. Patients have a right to inspect their own medical records.

The Privacy Act of 1974, which requires the release of individual information in federal files to the individual himself or herself upon request, permits federal agencies to establish "a special procedure, if deemed necessary, for the disclosure to an individual of medical records, including psychological records, pertaining to him." 5 U.S.C. 552a(f)(3). [See 1992 book.] Under this authority, most federal agencies have established regulations for the release of medical information to a physician chosen by the person who makes the request.

U.S. Department of Health and Human Service employees may not disclose a "file, record, report or other paper, or information, obtained at any time by any person," except in accord with federal law. 42 U.S.C. 1306.

The Public Health Service may issue certificates of confidentiality, protecting sensitive personally identifiable information in health research projects against compulsory legal process. 42 U.S.C. 241(d), sec 301(d).

Federally funded alcohol and drug treatment programs must maintain confidentiality. 42 U.S.C. 290dd-2.

A federal data bank on malpractice actions filed against physicians is authorized by 42 U.S.C. 11101 et seq.

States receiving grants for AIDS prevention must make sure that HIV testing, counseling, and treatment records are maintained in confidentiality, although state laws authorizing disclosure of this information remain in force. 42 U.S.C. 300ff-61.

Records in Veterans Medical Centers are confidential. 38 U.S.C. 5701.

The Americans with Disabilities Act limits a company's ability to conduct medical exams on *all* job applicants, whether disabled or not. The law prohibits pre-employment inquiries into disabilities or their severity, except to determine ability to perform on the job. A company may require a medical exam only *after an offer of employment has been made* and may make it a condition of employment if all "entering employees" are subjected to the same requirement and information from the exam are segregated from other records and kept confidential (except to supervisors who must make necessary accommodations or first-aid and safety personnel). 42 U.S.C. 12112(d).

Patients must be notified if there is a breach of security of their health information, if it were not encrypted or otherwise made indecipherable to outsiders. Vendors who deal in health information must notify the Federal Trade Commission. The FTC must notify the U.S. Department of Health and Human Services. The act provides transparency to patients by allowing them to request an audit trail showing all disclosures of their health information made through an electronic record in the prior three years, including disclosures to treat a patient. The act seems to allow a patient to bar individually identifiable disclosures to a health network if paying out of pocket for medical services. The act affects the sales and mining of patient information by limiting (but not totally eliminating) the sale of an individual's health information without the individual's authorization. This provision may not cover barter and rental arrangements or use of a third-party for mailings.

The 2009 stimulus law requires that health-care providers like doctors, hospitals, and nursing homes also not use patient information for marketing without consent and not use it for fundraising without an opportunity for individuals to opt-out. The act strengthens enforcement of federal privacy and security rules by increasing penalties for violations, providing greater resources for enforcement and oversight activities, creating new training, enforcement, and monitoring capability in the regional offices of HHS. State attorneys general may pursue HIPAA violations. Those who furnish records or receive them in violation of the law may face criminal prosecution. The act creates an Office of the National Coordinator Health Information Technology (ONCHIT) in DHS. See 42 U.S.C. 300jj–11(c), 42 U.S.C. 17921(11).

For the provision on patients' access to their own records, see 45 Code of Federal Regulations 164.524.

See also **Privileged Communications**. See also **Insurance**, District of Columbia, Maine, and Missouri; and **Employment**, Federal law. For laws on genetic testing and employment, see **Testing in Employment**.

MISCELLANEOUS
(Including Non-Electronic Visual Surveillance and Breast-Feeding Protections)

Alabama–Breast-feeding in public may not be restricted. Ala. Code 22-1-13.

Alaska–Cities and towns may not prohibit breast-feeding in public. Alaska Stat. sec. 01.10.060(b), and 29.25.080.

Arizona–Breast-feeding in public is not indecent exposure. Ariz. Rev. Stat. sec. 13-1402.

Arkansas–Breast-feeding in public is not indecent exposure. Ark. Code Ann. sec. 5-14-112, 20-27-2001.

California–There may be no "two-way mirrors" in rest rooms, locker rooms, showers, fitting rooms, or hotel rooms except for treatment facilities and educational institutions. Cal. Penal Code sec. 653n.

"Looking through a bathroom hole to invade the privacy of persons therein" is disorderly conduct. Penal Code 647.

County welfare departments and district attorneys are prohibited from asking applicants to Aid for Families with Dependent Children about paternity "where paternity is not logically an issue." Wel. & Inst. Code sec. 11477.

Businesses that provide bookkeeping services may not disclose business or personal information without written consent, except under legal process, for tax enforcement or to aid a criminal investigation. Civil Code sec. 1799.

A woman may breast-feed in public or private except someone else's home. Civ. Code sec. 43.3

Consumers have rights over their personal information in the hands of businesses. They may learn what happens with their personal information. The law encourages businesses to let their customers opt-out of sharing that information with third parties. In response to a customer request, businesses must provide either: (1) a list of categories of personal information disclosed to third parties or (2) a privacy statement giving customer a cost-free opportunity to opt-out of information sharing. Consumer requests may be written. Civ. Code sec. 1798.83.

"A business [and its contractor] that owns or licenses personal information about a California resident shall implement and maintain reasonable security procedures and practices appropriate to the nature of the information, to protect the personal information from unauthorized access, destruction, use, modification, or disclosure." Sec. 1798.81.5.

Commercial Web sites, apps, and online services that collect information on Californians must have privacy policies that, among other things, identify the categories of personally identifiable information collected about site visitors and the categories of third parties with whom the operator may share the information. An operator is in violation for failure to post a policy within 30 days of being notified of noncompliance. Bus. and Prof. Code secs. 22575 et seq.

Supermarkets may not require applicants for club cards to provide a driver's license or Social Security number as a condition of obtaining the card. Stores may not sell or share personal information regarding cardholders. Civil Code sec. 1749.60-1749.65.

A person or business may not publicly post or display on the Internet specified personal information of participants in the state's program to protect victims of domestic violence or stalking or their family members with a prescribed intent to cause great bodily harm or place a person in fear for personal safety. Employees and patients of a reproductive health facility are similarly protected. Gov. Code sec. 6208.1.

Localities may not limit persons from authorizing male circumcision procedures. Health & Safety Code sec. 125850.

Colorado–"A mother may breast-feed in any place she has a right to be." Col. Rev. Stat. sec. 25-6-302.

Connecticut–"Two-way mirrors" are prohibited in retail stores. Conn. Stat. Ann. sec. 53-41a.

The right to breast-feed in public and in workplaces is protected. Gen. Stat. Sec. 46a-64, 53-34b, 31-40w.

Delaware–A woman may breast-feed her child anywhere she is otherwise permitted to be. Del. Code title 31, sec. 310.

Florida–Breast-feeding in public does not violate the indecent exposure laws of the state. Fla. Stat. Ann. sec. 383.015.

Georgia–Illegal to invade privacy and illegal to be a "peeping Tom." Ga. Code Ann. sec. 26-3002.

A woman may breast-feed in public provided she does so in a discreet and modest way. Sec. 31-1-9.

Hawaii–Breast-feeding in public is protected. Rev. Stat. sec. 489-21 and 22. And in employment, 378-2.

Illinois–Upon request of a citizen, the secretary of state shall issue an ID card with photograph, Social Security number and date of birth required. 15 ILCS 335/4.

The Right to Breast-feed Act is 740 ILCS 137/10.

A public utility shall not disclose customer-record information, including Social Security numbers, to a law enforcement agency unless the law enforcement agency requests the customer-record information in writing, specifying that the information is necessary for a law enforcement purpose. 220 ILCS 5/5-110.

Indiana–Commissioner of motor vehicles shall issue an identification card for residents not carrying a driver's license. Ind. Code Ann. sec. 9-24-16.1.

Law enforcement authorities may use an electronic device worn by a parolee to track his or her whereabouts if it is "minimally intrusive upon the privacy of the offender or other persons residing in the offender's home" and if the offender and those in the household give written consent. Sec. 35-38-2.5-3.

Breast-feeding in public is protected. Code. Ann. sec. 16-35-6-1.

Iowa–A woman may breast-feed her own child anywhere she is entitled to be. Iowa Code Ann. sec. 135.30A.

Kansas–"A mother may breast-feed in any place she has a right to be." Kans. Stat. sec. 43-158.

Kentucky–Monitoring devices that indicate *only* whether an offender on parole is in the home or not are authorized; devices that provide information as to the activities of an offender inside the home are prohibited. Ky. Rev. Stat. sec. 532.200(5).

Beast-feeding in public is protected. Rev. Stat. sec. 211.755.

Louisiana–It is illegal to be a "Peeping Tom," defined as "one who peeps through windows or doors, or other like places, situated in or about the premises of another for the purpose of spying upon or invading the privacy of persons spied upon." La. Rev. Stat. sec. 14:284.

"Notwithstanding any other provision of law to the contrary, a mother may breast-feed her baby in any place of public accommodation, resort, or amusement." Rev. Stat. sec. 51:2247.1.

Maine–Breast-feeding in public is legal. Me. Rev. Stat. Ann. title 5, sec. 4634.

Maryland–There may be no visual surveillance in the rest rooms and dressing rooms of retail stores without consent. Md. Code Ann. art. 27, sec. 579c. It is a misdemeanor to trespass in order to look into the window of a structure. Art. 27, sec. 580.

No one may restrict a mother's right to breast-feed, including in public. Code sec. 20-801.

Massachusetts–"No person who owns or operates a retail establishment selling clothing shall maintain in a dressing room a two-way mirror or electronic video camera or similar device capable of filming or projecting an image of a person inside..." Mass. Gen. Laws Ann. ch. 93, sec. 89.

Michigan–Prohibited public nudity does not include breast-feeding. Mich. Comp. Laws Ann. sec. 41.181.

Minnesota–Internet service providers doing business in the state may not disclose personal information about subscribers. Minn. Stat. Ann. sec. 325M.02.

Breast-feeding in public is protected Sec. 617.23, 145.905. Employers must provide private accommodations for breast-feeding. Sec. 181.939.

Mississippi–Breast-feeding in public is not a violation. Miss. Code Ann. sec. 17-25-7.

Missouri–"Notwithstanding any other provision of law to the contrary, a mother may, with as much discretion as possible, breast-feed her child in any public or private location where the mother is otherwise authorized to be." Mo. Stat. Ann. sec. 191.918.

Montana–Breast-feeding is permissible in public, and public employers must provide accommodations for it. Mont. Code Ann. sec. 50-19-501.

Nebraska–Pawnbrokers are required to maintain color photo of each person pawning goods, for inspection by police. Neb. Rev. Stat. sec. 69-210.

Nevada–Businesses must use encryption when transferring personal data electronically, except for fax transmission. Nev. Rev. Stat. sec. 597.970.

Breast-feeding in public is not lewd behavior. Sec. 201.210 and 220.

New Hampshire–Breast-feeding does not constitute an act of indecent exposure and to limit or restrict a mother's right to breast feed is discriminatory. N.H. Rev. Stat. Ann. sec. 132:10-d.

New Jersey–It is a crime to invade privacy and peer through the window of a dwelling place knowing that you are not licensed or privileged to do so. N.J. Rev. Stat. sec. 2C:18-3.

No automated toll device may photograph the image of the face of an automobile's occupants. Sec. 27:23-34.2.

School staff may not strip search a pupil or conduct cavity searches. Sec.18A:37-6.

Breast-feeding in permissible in public. Rev. Stat. sec. 26:4B-4.

Emergency responders may not photograph victims or disclose such photographs. Sec. 2A:58D-2.

New Mexico–N.M. Stat. Ann. sec. 28-20-1 protects breast-feeding in public.

New York–It is illegal to install a camera, two-way mirror, or viewing device in a bathroom, fitting room, or hotel room. N.Y. Gen. Bus. Law 395-b. Breast-feeding is permissible wherever a woman is entitled to be. N.Y. Civ. Rts. Law 79-e. Breast-feeding in public is an exception to the restrictions on nudity in public. Penal Law 245.01.

North Carolina–Breast-feeding in public is not indecent. N.C. Gen. Stat. sec. 14-190.9.

North Dakota–Upon proper application, plus production of birth certificate, anyone 18 or older may obtain a photo identification card from the state highway commissioner. Information obtained from the application is confidential. N.D. Cent. Code sec. 39-06-03.

Ohio–Breast-feeding in public is protected. Ohio Rev. Code Ann. sec. 3781.55.

Oklahoma–Breast-feeding is permissible in public. Okla. Stat. title 63, 1-234.1.

Oregon–A woman may breast-feed in public. Or. Rev. Stat. sec. 109.001.

"Any person that owns, maintains or otherwise possesses data that includes a consumer's personal information that is used in the course of the person's business, vocation, occupation or volunteer activities must develop, implement and maintain reasonable safeguards to protect the security, confidentiality and integrity of the personal information, including disposal of the data." Implementation of an "information security program" complies with this law. The Department of Consumer and Business Services is responsible for compliance. Rev. Stat. 646A.622.

Pennsylvania–A woman has "permission," not a right, to breast-feed in public places. Pa. Stat. Ann. title 35, sec. 636.2.

Rhode Island–The laws on breast-feeding in public and at work resemble Minnesota's. R.I. Gen. Laws 11-45-1 and 23-13.2-1

A homeless person "has the right to a reasonable expectation of privacy in his or her personal property to the same extent as personal property in a permanent residence." 34-37.1-3.

South Carolina–It is illegal to be an eavesdropper or a "Peeping Tom." S.C. Code sec. 16-17-470.

Breast-feeding in public is not indecent exposure. Code sec. 20-7-97.

South Dakota–The law on breast-feeding is the same as South Carolina's. S.D. Codified Laws Ann. sec. 22-22-24.1.

Tennessee–The law prohibits nudity in public places (except theaters). Included in the definition of nudity is "the showing of the covered male genitals in a discernibly turgid state." But a person does not violate the law "if the person makes intentional and reasonable attempts to conceal the person from public view while performing an excretory function, and the person performs the function in an unincorporated area of the state."Tenn. Code Ann. sec. 39-13-511.

The law protects breast-feeding in public. Code Ann. sec. 68-58-101. And requires employers to accommodate it. Sec. 50-1-305.

Texas–A woman may breast-feed wherever she otherwise may be allowed to be. Tex. Health & Safety Code Ann. sec. 165.001.

Utah–Breast-feeding is not lewd nor does it not constitute an act of indecent exposure. Utah Code Ann. sec. 10-8-50.

Vermont–The state is not liable for claims arising out of alleged invasion of privacy. Vt. Stat. Ann. title 12, sec. 5602.

Breast-feeding is legal where the mother and child are entitled to be. 9 Vt. Stat. Ann. 4502(j).

Virginia–Breast-feeding is protected in public. Va. Code sec. 8.2-387. And on land owned by the Commonwealth of Virginia, sec. 2.2-1147.1.

Washington–Breast-feeding is protected in public. Wash. Rev. Code Ann. sec. 9A.88.010. And at work. Sec. 3.70.640.

Wisconsin–Ordering a strip search of a school pupil is a misdemeanor. Wisc. Stat. Ann. sec. 942.02.

Breast-feeding in public is not a violation. Stat. Ann. sec. 944.17, 944.20 and 944.10.

Wyoming–Breast-feeding anywhere is not indecency. Wyo. Stat. sec. 6-4-201.

Federal law–Customarily law enforcement notifies a person that he or she has been the target of a search warrant. But federal law permits notice to the targeted individual to be delayed if a court finds reasonable cause to believe that notice may have an adverse impact. A court may delay notice indefinitely. 18 U.S.C. 3103a.

The FBI may seek a court order "requiring the production of any tangible things (including books, records, papers, documents, and other items) for an investigation to protect against international terrorism," but the investigation may not be based solely on activities protected by the First Amendment. 50 U.S.C. 1861 et seq.

Customs officers may stop, search and examine any vehicle, person, trunk or envelope "whenever found" if there is reasonable cause to suspect merchandise that was imported contrary to law or that is subject to duty tax. 19 U.S.C. 482.

"Whoever takes any letter, postal card, or package... before it has been delivered to the person to whom it was directed, with design to obstruct the correspondence, or pry into the business or secrets of another, or opens, secretes, embezzles, or destroys the same, shall be fined not more than $2000 or imprisoned not more than five years, or both." 42 U.S.C. 1702.

Food stamp households are required to produce a photo identification card to obtain food stamps in certain urban areas designated by the U.S. Department of Agriculture. 7 U.S.C. 2020.

Breast-feeding is permissible in any federal facility, including national parks, where the mother and child are entitled to be. Public Law 106-58, sec. 647. Employers must provide accommodations for breast-feeding at work. Public Laws 111-148 & 111-152, 29 U.S.C. 207, Sec. 7, (r)(1).

POLYGRAPHING IN EMPLOYMENT
(Including Honesty Tests)

Alabama–A polygraph examiner may lose a license for failing to inform a person that testing is voluntary, and that the person may have the results of the test. Ala. Code. sec. 34-24-32.

Alaska–Suggesting or requiring a lie-detector test in private or public employment (except for a police department applicant) is prohibited. Maximum penalty: $1000 and one year. Alaska Stat. sec. 23.10.037.

Arizona–License is required; grounds for a refusal, suspension, or revocation of a license include failing to inform a subject that participation is voluntary, making inquiries during pre-employment exam regarding religious, labor or sexual activities or political affiliation, or failing to inform a subject of results if requested. Ariz. Rev. Stat. sec. 32-2701.

Arkansas–Similar to Alabama's. Ark. Code Ann. sec. 17-32-211.

California–Cal. Labor Code sec. 432.2 prohibits mandatory polygraphing or "similar test" in private employment.

Police officers do not have to submit to polygraphing in departmental investigations. Cal. Govt. Code sec. 3307.

Connecticut–Conn. Gen. Stat. Ann. sec. 31-51g prohibits an employer or employment agency from using a polygraph or similar device. Penalty: $250 to $1,000.

Delaware–Use of polygraphs in both public and private employment is prohibited. Del. Code title 19, sec. 704.

District of Columbia–Polygraphs may not be used as a condition of employment. D.C. Code Ann. sec. 36-801 to 803.

Georgia–Polygraph exams are limited to no more than 15 questions (and no fewer than seven), and all questions must be provided in advance in writing. A person examined is entitled to a written copy of the results, and no one else may receive the results without consent of the examined person. No questions may be asked about religion, politics, race and racial opinions, labor organizing, or sexual activities. An examiner may be sued for violations of the act. Ga. Code Ann. sec. 43-36-1.

Hawaii–Haw. Rev. Stat. sec. 378.21 prohibits use in both public and private employment. Maximum penalty: $1,000 and one year.

Idaho–Prohibits polygraphing in private employment; exempts government agencies. Idaho Code sec. 44-903.

Illinois–Polygraph examiners may not ask about religion, beliefs on racial matters, political views, labor organizing or union membership, sexual preferences, or sexual activities unless the inquiry is "directly related to the employment." 225 ILCS 430/14/1.

Iowa–Employers may not require an applicant or employee to take a polygraph test as a condition of employment, except for applicants for law enforcement jobs. Iowa Code Ann. sec. 730.4.

Louisiana–A polygraph examiner can lose a license for failing to inform a person that testing is voluntary and that refusal to take a test may not be grounds for employment termination. La. Stat. Ann. sec. 36-A:2848.

Maine–An employer may not *request* or suggest a polygraph test. Me. Rev. Stat. Ann. title 32, sec. 7166. [See 1984-85 book.] There may be no questions on sex, politics, or religion; and no tests without consent. Title 32, sec. 7154.

Maryland–The law requires private and public employers to include the following language on applications: "Under Maryland law an employer may not require or demand any applicant for employment or prospective employment or any employee to submit to or take a polygraph, lie detector, or similar test or examination as a condition of employment or continued employment. Any employer who violates this provision is guilty of a misdemeanor and subject to a fine not to exceed $100." Md. Ann. Code of Labor and Employ., sec, 3-702. [See 1978-79 book.]

Massachusetts–All employment applications must state: "It is unlawful in Massachusetts to require or administer a lie detector test as a condition of employment or continuous employment. An employer who violates this law shall be subject to criminal penalties and civil liability." A victim may sue for treble damages. Honesty tests in employment are expressly prohibited. Mass. Gen. Laws Ann. ch. 149, sec. 19B.

Michigan–Employers may not require a "lie detector" or similar test of an employee nor discharge an employee for failure to submit to a test or solely for allegedly lying on a test. Employees may not be required to waive their rights and must receive a copy of this law if requested to take a polygraph exam. An employer may not use the results of a polygraph test nor divulge them. Mich. Comp. Laws Ann. sec. 37.201.

Minnesota–An employer may not *request*, require, or coerce an individual to take any test, including voice stress analysis, "purporting to test the honesty of any employee or prospective employee." Even if a person takes such a test at his or her own request, the results may go only to those authorized by the individual tested, and it is a misdemeanor to disclose that another person has taken a polygraph test. Minn. Stat. Ann. sec. 181.75.

Mississippi–Similar to Alabama's. Miss. Code Ann. sec. 73-29-31.

Montana–"No person, firm, or corporation shall require as continuation of employment any person to take a polygraph test or any form of a mechanical lie detector test." Mont. Code Ann. sec. 39.2-304.

Nebraska–Generally no one may require a truth-detection test as a condition of employment, unless (1) there are no questions on sex, politics, labor organizing, religion or marriage; (2) the subject volunteers, in writing; (3) the test is job-related and not selectively administered; (4) it is part of a specific investigation and is not the sole determinant. Neb. Rev. Stat. sec. 81-1932.

Nevada–Written consent to take a test is required, and there is a limit on questions. Nev. Rev. Stat. sec. 648A.190. Polygraph exams by employers are limited to investigations of embezzlement. Sec. 613.480.

Employers may take no adverse action as the result of polygraph results. Rev. Stat. sec. 613.480 (3).

New Jersey–N.J. Stat. Ann. sec. 2C:40A-1 states that any employer who influences or requires a polygraph test is a disorderly person.

New Mexico–License required; may be revoked or refused if examiner asks any question relative to sexual affairs, race, creed, religion, union affiliation, or activity not previously agreed to by written consent. N.M. Stat. Ann. sec. 61-26-9.

New York–No employer may require, *request*, suggest or knowingly permit applicant to take a test with *a psychological stress evaluator*, a machine that purports to detect falsehoods. An employer may not use test results. A practitioner may not administer a test to an employee. An employee may not be discriminated against for complaining about this law. N.Y. Labor Law sec. 733.

Oklahoma–Similar to Alabama's. Okla. Stat. title 36, sec. 1468.

Oregon–Or. Rev. Stat. sec. 659A.300 prohibits use in private and public employment. Maximum penalty $500 and one year.

Pennsylvania–State law prohibits employment polygraphing except for persons in law enforcement or those who have access to narcotics or dangerous drugs. Maximum penalty $500 or one year. Pa. Stat. Ann. title 18, sec. 7321.

Rhode Island–A private or public employer may not *request* an employee or applicant to take a test. *All honesty tests* are prohibited. The penalty is a $1000 fine. R.I. Gen. Laws sec. 28-6.1-1.

South Carolina–Similar to Alabama's. S.C. Code sec. 40-53-180.

Tennessee–"No employer may take any personnel action based solely upon the results of a polygraph examination." No exam, whether for employment or otherwise, may ask about sexual behavior or orientation unless relevant to the exam, unless there is written permission of the examinee, and unless the examinee has an opportunity to explain any "deception." Exams in connection with employment may not ask about religious, political, labor, racial, or sexual activities or beliefs, nor about anything that took place five or more years ago (except for felonies and drug violations).

A polygraph examiner must make an audio tape of the interrogation upon the request of the person examined and, if the test is determined to show honesty, the examiner must keep the tape for one year. If the examined person lodges a complaint about the test and no tape has been kept, the complainant *can force the examiner to undergo a polygraph examination.* An examiner may conduct no more than one exam per hour. Tenn. Code Ann. sec. 62-27-123.

Texas–A test must be voluntary. Tex. Occ. Code Ann. 1703.351(a)(7)(B). The subject must be informed of the results. Sec. 1703.204.

Utah–It shall be unlawful for refusal to submit to a surreptitious exam to be the basis for denying or terminating employment. Utah Code Ann. sec. 34-37-16.

Vermont–It is illegal to *request* or require a polygraph test as a condition for employment, except in jobs involving law enforcement, drugs, or precious metals. Polygraph examiners must provide exams and a copy of this law in advance. Vt. Stat. Ann. title 21, sec. 5a.

Employers may not request or require polygraph examinations. 21 Vt. Stat. Ann. 494a. Certain employers are exempted. Sec. 494b.

Virginia–In employment tests, questions on sex are prohibited. Va. Code sec. 54.1-1806.

Washington–It is a misdemeanor to conduct a polygraph test in employment except for law enforcement *applicants*, persons who dispense narcotic or dangerous drugs, and persons in positions related to national security. Violation is a misdemeanor. There is a private right to sue, for applicants and employees who are subjected to polygraph tests in violation of state law. A victim may be awarded $500 without proving damages and may receive attorney's fees. Employees may not require tests *directly or indirectly*. Wash. Rev. Code Ann. sec. 49.44.120

West Virginia–Employers may not subject employees or applicants to polygraph tests. W. Va. Code sec. 21-5-5a. [See 1984-85 book.]

Wisconsin–Polygraphs are permitted in employment if the person consents in writing, if questions are disclosed in advance, and if there is a chance to retake the test. A person may be fired for the results, but not for refusing to take a test. *Psychological stress evaluators* may not be used. Wisc. Stat. Ann. sec. 111.37. All polygraphs or other honesty tests, whether for employment or other purposes, must have written consent to take the test and to disclose results. Sec. 942.06.

Federal law–The Employee Polygraph Protection Act of 1988 prohibits most polygraph tests by private employers. Tests may be administered (1) when the examinee may terminate the test at any time, (2) when no questions are asked about religion, race, politics, sex, or union activities, (3) when there is no medical reason why the employee should be excused, (4) when the examinee has written notice and the opportunity to hire a lawyer, (5) when the employee is informed in advance of the nature of the test, (6) when the employer or employee has the opportunity to record the session, (7) when the employee receives a statement saying that the test may not be a condition of employment nor contrary to law, and (8) when the examinee is given a copy of all questions asked and of any opinion or conclusion rendered. Companies in the security business and in drug manufacturing or sales may test *applicants*, in some cases, under the conditions described above. An employer may "request" a polygraph test as part of an ongoing investigation based on "a reasonable suspicion that the employee was involved" in misconduct. 29 U.S.C. 2001.

PRIVACY STATUTES/STATE CONSTITUTIONS
(Including the Right to Publicity)

Alaska–"Right of Privacy. The right of the people to privacy is recognized and shall not be infringed. The legislature shall implement this section." Art. 1, sec. 22, Alaska Constitution, 1972.

Arizona–"Right to Privacy. No person shall be disturbed in his private affairs, or his home invaded, without authority of law." Art. II, sec. 8, Ariz. Constitution, 1912, as amended.

California–"All people are by nature free and independent, and have certain inalienable rights, among which are those of enjoying and defending life and liberty; acquiring, possessing, and protecting property; and pursuing and obtaining safety, happiness, and privacy." Art. I, sec. 1, Cal. Constitution, Nov. 1972. State courts thus far have interpreted this state right to privacy as identical to the federal right to privacy recognized by U.S. Supreme Court decisions.

A celebrity or a victim of a crime may sue photographers if they trespass or use telephoto lenses to capture images of persons in personal or family activities. Cal. Civ. Code sec. 1708.8.

Any person who knowingly uses another's name, voice, or likeness in a commercial way, without consent, is liable for damages. Heirs and descendants have property rights in certain commercial uses of a deceased celebrity's name, voice, signature, or likeness for 50 years after death. Civ. Code sec. 990 and 3344.

A person is liable for the tort of physical invasion of privacy when he or she knowingly enters onto the land of another person without permission with intent to capture any type of visual image, sound recording, or other physical impression of the person engaging in a personal or familial activity and the physical invasion occurs in a manner that is offensive to a reasonable person. A person is liable for constructive invasion of privacy when he or she does this under circumstances in which the other person had a reasonable expectation of privacy, through the use of a visual or auditory enhancing device, regardless of whether there is a physical trespass, if this image, sound recording, or other physical impression could not have been achieved without a trespass unless the visual or auditory enhancing device was used. Cal. Civ. Code 1708.8 (a).

Delaware–Violation of privacy is a class A misdemeanor. Del. Code. title 11, sec. 1335.

Florida–"Searches and Seizures. The right of the people to be secure in their persons, houses, papers and effects against unreasonable searches and seizures, and against the unreasonable interception of private communications by any means, shall not be violated. No warrant shall be issued except upon probable cause, supported by affidavit, particularly describing the place or places to be searched, the person or persons, thing or things to be seized, the communication to be intercepted, and the nature of

evidence to be obtained. Articles or information obtained in violation of this right shall not be admissible in evidence." Art. I, sec. 12, Fla. Constitution, 1968.

"Every natural person has a right to be let alone and free from governmental intrusion into his private life except as otherwise provided for herein. This section shall not be construed to limit the public's right of access to public records and meetings as provided by law." Art. I, sec. 23.

A person has a right of action in court for the unauthorized use of his or her name or picture for commercial advantage. Fla. Stat. Ann. sec. 540.08

No person shall have more than one choice of venue for damages for invasion of privacy. Sec. 770.05. Adverse judgment in any jurisdiction bars any other action founded on same publication. Sec. 770.06. Cause of action for damages shall be deemed to have accrued at the time of the first publication. Sec. 770.07.

Georgia–Illegal to invade privacy and illegal to be a "peeping Tom." Ga. Code Ann. sec. 26-3002.

Hawaii–Art. 1, sec. 6 of the constitution provides for a right to privacy. Sec. 7 protects against unreasonable searches and seizures.

Illinois–The provision on "Searches, seizures, privacy and interceptions" provision is similar to Florida's. Art. I, sec. 6, Ill. Constitution, 1970. "Every person shall find a certain remedy in the laws for all injuries and wrongs which he receives to his person, privacy, property or reputation. He shall obtain justice by law, freely, completely, and promptly." Art. I, sec. 6 and 12.

Actions for publication of matter that violates the right to privacy must be commenced within one year. 735 ILCS 5/13-201.

Indiana–Using a person's name, voice, signature, likeness, or mannerisms without consent for a commercial purpose within that person's lifetime or 100 years thereafter commits a tort. Newsworthy and entertainment uses are expressly exempt. Ind. Code Ann. sec. 32-36-1.

Kentucky–"The traditional right of privacy terminates at death but the right of publicity, which is the right of protection from appropriation of some element of an individual's personality from commercial exploitation, does not terminate [until 50 years after] death." Ky. Rev. Stat. sec. 391.170.

Louisiana–"Right to Privacy. Every person shall be secure in his person, property, communications, houses, papers, and effects against unreasonable searches and seizures, or invasions or privacy. No warrant shall issue without probable cause supported by oath or affirmation, and particularly describing the place to be searched, the persons or things to be seized, and the lawful purposes or reason for the search. Any person adversely affected by a search or seizure conducted in violation of this Section shall have standing to raise its illegality in the appropriate court." Art. I, sec. 5, La. Constitution, 1975.

Maine–"1. A person is guilty of violation of privacy if, except in execution of a public duty or as authorized by law, he intentionally:

"A. Commits a civil trespass on a property with intent to overhear or observe any person in a private place; or

"B. Installs or uses in a private place without consent of a person entitled to privacy therein, any device for observing, photographing, recording or broadcasting sounds or events in that place; or

"C. Installs outside a private place without consent, any device for hearing sounds that not ordinarily be audible.

"2. 'Private place' means a place where one may reasonably expect to be safe from surveillance but does not include a place to which the public or a substantial group has access." Me. Rev. Stat. Ann. title 17-A, sec. 511.

Massachusetts–"A person shall have a right against unreasonable, substantial or serious interference with his privacy." Courts may award damages for violations. Mass. Gen. Laws Ann. ch. 214, sec. 1B. State law explicitly recognizes the "misappropriation" right of action. Ch. 214, sec. 3A.

Montana–"Right of Privacy. The right of individual privacy is essential to the well-being of a free society and shall not be infringed without the showing of a compelling state interest." Art. II, sec. 10, Mont. Constitution, 1972.

Nebraska–The state has recognized the traditional rights of action for invasion of privacy: intrusion, portrayal in a false light, and misappropriation of a person's image or name. One-year statute of limitations. Neb. Rev. Stat. sec. 20-201-211.

New York–The first paragraph of the state's constitutional provision on privacy is identical to the Fourth Amendment of the U.S. Constitution. The second paragraph is as follows: "The right of the people to be secure against unreasonable interception of telephone and telegraph communications shall not be violated, and ex parte orders or warrants shall issue only upon oath or affirmation that there is reasonable ground to believe that evidence of a crime may thus be obtained, and identifying the particular means of communication, and particularly describing the person or persons whose communications are to be intercepted and the purpose thereof." Art. I, sec. 12, N.Y. Constitution, 1938.

State law recognizes the "misappropriation" tort (or "right of publicity"). N.Y. Civil Rights Law, sec. 50 (McKinney).

Oklahoma–State law recognizes the "misappropriation" right of action. Okla. Stat. title 21, sec. 839.1.

The right of publicity is extended to 100 years beyond the death of the individual. Title 12, sec. 1448-9.

Pennsylvania–Among the "inherent rights of mankind" is "acquiring, possessing and protecting property and reputation." Pa. Constitution Art. 1, sec. 1.

Rhode Island–"It is the policy of this state that every person in this state shall have a right to privacy," which includes freedom from intrusions, from appropriation of one's name or likeness, from "unreasonable publicity given to one's private life," and from "publicity that reasonably places another in a false light before the public." R.I. Gen. Laws sec. 9-1-28.1.

South Carolina–Art. 1, sec. 10, S.C. Constitution, 1970, prohibits unreasonable searches and "unreasonable invasions of privacy."

Tennessee–The right of publicity extends ten years after the death of an individual "whether or not such rights were commercially exploited by the individual during the individual's lifetime." Tenn. Code Ann. sec. 47-25-1101 to 1108.

Texas–The right of publicity for celebrities extends beyond death. Tex. Stat. title IV, ch. 26, sec. 26.001.

There is a right to sue for misappropriation of one's name, voice, signature, photograph, or likeness, even after death. Prop. Code Ann. sec. 26.001.

Utah–"Offenses against privacy" law resembles Maine's. Utah Code Ann. sec. 76-9-401. Utah recognizes the "misappropriation" tort. Sec. 76-4-8.

Virginia–By statute, the "right of publicity" is recognized. Va. Code sec. 8.01-40.

Washington–Provisions identical to Arizona's. Art. I, sec. 7, Wash. Constitution, 1889, as amended.

Regarding records held by the government, a person's privacy "is violated only if disclosure of information about the person: (1) would be highly offensive to a reasonable person, and (2) is not of legitimate concern to the public." Wash. Rev. Code Ann. sec. 42.56.050.

Wisconsin–The state recognizes the right to sue for an invasion of privacy, except for a disclosure that holds you in a "false light." Wis. Stat. Ann. secs. 893.19(10) and 895.50.

Federal law–The Lanham Act on trademark registration states, "No trademark by which the goods of the application may be distinguished from the goods of others shall be refused registration on account of its nature unless it (a) consists of or comprises immoral, deceptive or scandalous matter, or matter which may disparage or falsely suggest a connection with persons, living or dead, institutions, beliefs, or national symbols, or bring them into contempt or disrepute . . .(c) consists of or comprises a name, portrait or signature identifying a particular living individual except by his written consent." 15 U.S.C. 1052(a). Forty-six states have similar language in trademark laws. These provisions affect registration, but not misuse alone, of another person's name.

PRIVILEGED COMMUNICATIONS

Alabama–Ala. Code sec. 34-26.2 recognizes the psychologist-client privilege, protecting from disclosure confidential communications between the two.

Alaska–Patient conversations with psychologists and psychological associates are privileged by statute. Alaska Stat. sec. 08.86.200. Patient-psychotherapist privilege is recognized in case law.

Arizona–Communications between husband and wife are privileged. Ariz. Rev. Stat. Sec. 12-2232. And clergy, 12-2233. And attorneys, 12-2234.

Colorado–Privilege is established by statute for psychologists, clergy, certified public accountants. Colo. Rev. Stat. sec. 13-90-107.

Connecticut–A limited privilege applies to psychotherapists. Conn. Gen. Stat. Ann. sec. 52-146. There is a privilege for school personnel. 10-154a.

Delaware–Psychologists are covered by privilege. Del. Code title 24, sec. 3518.

Georgia–Psychologists' communications with clients are privileged. Ga. Code Ann. sec. 43-39-16. Accountants are also covered. Sec. 43-3-32. There is a privilege for a pharmacist to refuse to reveal medical information concerning a customer. Sec. 24-9-40.

Idaho–Psychologist-client privilege exists. Idaho Code sec. 54-2314. Clergy conversations are privileged. Sec. 9-203.

Kentucky–Conversations between psychologist and client may not be disclosed. Ky. Rev. Stat. Ann. sec. 319.111. Also attorney-client (sec. 421.210), doctors (sec. 213.200), and psychologists (sec. 421.215).

Louisiana–Psychologist-client communications are secret. La. Rev. Stat. Ann. sec. 37:2366. Also clergy. Sec. 13:3744.

Maryland–There is an attorney-client privilege. Md. Courts Code Ann. 9-108. As well as privileges for mental health professionals (9-109), accountants (9-110), and clergy (9-111).

Massachusetts–A limited psychotherapist-client privilege exists. Mass. Gen. Laws Ann. ch. 233, sec. 20B. Sec. 20A recognizes a privilege for clergy.

Michigan–Mich. Comp. Laws Ann. sec. 338.1018 covers psychologist-client with a privilege. Sec. 600.2156 forbids disclosure of confessions made to clergy.

Minnesota–A privilege is recognized for chiropractors, dentists and psychologists. Minn. Stat. Ann. sec. 595.02.

Mississippi–Psychologist-client communications are privileged. Miss. Code Ann. sec. 73-31-29.

Missouri–Confessions made to ministers are privileged. Mo. Ann. Stat. sec. 491.060.

Montana–Conversations with speech pathologists and audiologists may not be disclosed. Mont. Code Ann. sec. 93-701-4(9). Nor psychologist-client communications. Sec. 66-3212.

Nebraska–Privileges affect attorneys, clergy, physicians, spouse, and one's ballot. Neb. Rev. Stat. sec. 27-503 to 508.

Nevada–Privilege is recognized for psychologists, psychiatric social workers, dentists. Nev. Rev. Stat. sec. 49.215. And for accountants, sec. 49.125, and clergy, 49.255.

New Jersey–Clergy are covered by statute. N.J. Rev. Stat. sec. 2A:84A-23. Marriage counselors are also covered. Sec. 45:8B-29.

New Mexico–N.M. Stat. Ann. sec. 38-6-6 establishes a privilege for accountants and attorneys.

New York–Privileged communications are recognized for dentists, clergy, psychologists and social workers. N.Y. Civil Prac. Law sec. 4504, 4505, 4507, and 4508 respectively.

North Carolina–Christian Science practitioners and communicants and clergy are subject to privilege. N.C. Gen. Stat. sec. 8-53.2. Psychologists are also subject to privilege. Sec. 8-53.3.

Ohio–Communications between psychologist and client may not be disclosed. Ohio Rev. Code Ann. sec. 4732.19. Confessions made to priests may not be disclosed either. Sec. 2317.02(B).

Oklahoma–Okla. Stat. title 12, sec. 385 establishes a privilege for clergy, title 59, sec. 1372 for psychologists.

Oregon–Psychologists' and clergy's communications are confidential. Or. Rev. Stat. sec. 44.040.

Rhode Island–R.I. Gen. Laws. sec. 9-17-23 subjects priests and rabbis to a privilege.

South Carolina–A privilege protects conversations with clergy. S.C. Code sec. 19-11-90.

South Dakota–Psychologist-client and clergy communications are privileged. S.D. Codified Laws Ann. sec. 19-2-3.1 and 19-2-2.

Tennessee–Conversations between accountants and clients may not be disclosed. Tenn. Code Ann. sec. 62-143. Nor may those with clergy. Sec. 24-1-206.

Texas–State law establishes a privilege for clergy-penitents. Tex. Rule of Evidence 505. Communications between a patient/client and a professional licensed to treat mental or emotional conditions are confidential. One exception to this rule is an instance where the professional determines there is a possibility of imminent physical injury. Tex. Health & Safety Code Ann. sec. 611.002.

Utah–Utah Code Ann. sec. 58-25-9 establishes a privilege for psychologists; sec. 58-35-10 for social workers; sec. 58-39-10 for marriage counselors; sec. 58-41-16 for speech pathologists, and sec. 78-24-8 for clergy.

Virginia–A privilege for psychologists is recognized. Va. Code sec. 8.01-399.

Washington–Wash. Rev. Code Ann. sec. 18.83.110 establishes a privilege for psychologists; sec. 18.53.200 for optometrists; sec. 5.60.060 and 10.52.020 for priests.

Wisconsin–Conversations with clergy and psychologists are privileged. Wis. Stat. Ann. sec. 885.20 and 455.09 respectively.

Wyoming–Wyo. Stat. sec. 1-139 covers clergy; and sec. 33-343.4 covers psychologists.

For privileges related to medical care, see **Medical Records**. For privileges related to students and counselors, see **Student Records**.

SOCIAL SECURITY NUMBERS

Alabama–A state agency is prohibited from placing or revealing the Social Security number of a person, on any document that is available for public inspection except for a legitimate government purpose. Ala. Code sec. 41-13-6.

Alaska–Both private parties and government agencies "may not request or collect" SSNs and may not print them on ID cards nor deny services to a person who declines to provide a SSN, except for some uses in insurance, medical services, fraud prevention, or law enforcement, or when required by law. Alaska Stat. sec. 44.48.400. SSNs collected for admission to legal practice may be disclosed for child-support enforcement only. Sec. 08.08.137.

Arizona–State universities and colleges may not assign (nor display) a student identity number that uses all or part of a person's Social Security number, unless the student consents. Ariz. Rev. Stat. Sec. 15-1823.

A person may not intentionally communicate the Social Security number of a resident to the general public, display an individual's number on any card required for the individual to receive products or services, require the transmission of an individual's number on the Internet unless the connection is secure or the number is encrypted, or require a SSN to access a Web site, unless a password or unique personal identification number or other authentication device is also required to access the site; print an individual's number on any materials that are mailed to the individual, unless state or federal law requires the number to be on the document (but this does not prohibit the mailing of documents with SSNs sent as a part of an application or enrollment process or to establish, amend or terminate an account, contract or policy or to confirm the accuracy of the Social Security number). Still, an entity that before 2005 used or displayed an individual's SSN may continue doing so, so long as it doesn't suspend doing so and provides the individual with an annual written disclosure of the individual's right to stop the use of the Social Security number in a manner prohibited by this law. State and municipal agencies shall not use an individual's number on government-issued forms of identification. Rev. Stat. sec. 44-1373.

Information in voter-registration records, including SSNs, shall not be accessible *except* by the voter, by an authorized government official in the scope of his duties, for signature verification on filings, for election purposes, for news gathering, or pursuant to a court order. Sec. 16-168.

SSNs provided to the motor vehicle department shall not appear on a license or permit.

The department may not release this number unless the applicant requests that the number appear on the license or permit. Sec. 28-3158. Nor may it appear on birth certificates. Sec. 36-322.

SSNs provided for marriage licenses shall not be released except for child enforcement purposes. Sec. 25-121. Numbers provided for real-estate licenses are restricted. Sec. 32-2125.03.

Uses of SSNs provided at death are restricted. Sec. 16-165.

Arkansas–See **Computer Crime**.

California–Other persons are prohibited from using an individual's Social Security number to get services. Cal. Civ. Code sec. 1798.85.

An applicant must provide a Social Security number for a driver's license, but it may not appear on the face of the permit nor a magnetic strip. Cal. Vehicle Code sec. 12801.

It must appear on hospital discharge papers if it is in a patient's records. Health & Safety Code sec. 443.31.

See also **Mailing Lists**. See also **Medical Records**.

Uses of Social Security numbers by private entities are limited, in ways similar to those in Arizona's law. Numbers may not appear on the outside of mailing pieces. Civ. Code sec. 1785.11.2.

Banks must cease printing SSNs on account documents mailed to consumers. Civ. Code sec. 1786.60. Employers may not put SSNs on pay stubs, except the last four digits. Labor Code sec. 226.

State agencies and the university system may not use SSNs in public ways similar to those listed in Arizona's law. Nor may they embed the number if they are prohibited from displaying it. Nor may they record any document that includes more than the last four digits of the SSN. Civ. Code sec. 1798.85.

Unwarranted disclosure of the SSNs of applicants for student aid, and their parents and students, reported to the Tax Board, is a misdemeanor. Rev. and Tax Code sec. 19557.

Supermarkets may not require applicants for club cards to provide a driver's license or Social Security number as a condition of obtaining the card. Stores may not sell or share personal information regarding cardholders. Civ. Code sec. 1749.60-1749.65.

The SSNs of people involved in the dissolution of marriage or separation proceedings shall be confidential, and disclosed only on good cause shown to the court. A separate one-page form containing the parties' SSNs is to be placed in the confidential portion of a court file. Parties may redact the SSNs only after the document is placed in the confidential portion of the court file. Fam. Code sec. 2024.5.

A parent is not required to disclose SSN at the birth of a child if "good cause" is shown. Health and Saf. Code sec. 102150. Parents' SSNs registered with live births are confidential. Sec. 102425. But they shall be accessible to agencies in order to operate the Child Support Enforcement Program. Sec. 102447. SSNs will not appear on death certificates for public release. Health and Saf. Code sec. 102231.

Patient SSNs should be exempt from disclosure under the Public Records Act. Health and Saf. Code sec. 128735-7. SSNs used for the purposes of voter identification shall not be disclosed to any person. Elec. Code sec. 2194 and Gov. Code sec. 6254.4.

Colorado–Businesses may not print SSNs on ID documents nor disclose them to the public. Colo. Rev. Stat. sec. 6-1-715.

No registered voter shall be prohibited from voting for failure to provide a SSN, or the last four digits. Any SSN, or its last four digits, obtained by the clerk/recorder shall be confidential. Sec. 1-2-204.

A public entity shall not issue a license, permit, pass or certificate that contains the holder's SSN unless the issuing authority determines that it is necessary or required by federal or state law. A public entity shall not request a SSN over the phone or Internet unless it determines that it is required by federal law or essential to provision of services. Agencies shall make proper disposal of documents with SSNs on them. An insured may require that an insurer not display a SSN on an insurance card. An insurer in Colorado shall not issue an insurance card that displays the insured's SSN. A person shall not possess personal identifying information – including SSNs – of another person with the intent to use the information, or aid another, "to unlawfully gain a benefit" for himself or to injure or defraud someone. Sec. 24-72.3-101.

The SSN required for an application for a driver's license or ID card shall remain confidential and not be placed on the license or card, unless the applicant waives confidentiality (for the license). Confidentiality will not prevent disclosure to the child support enforcement agency or to a court. If federal law is changed to prohibit the collection of SSNs on license applications, the department will cease doing so. Secs. 42-2-107 an d 42-3-302.

The Secretary of State shall remove SSNs from publicly accessible electronic records of financing statements. Sec. 4-9-531. There are restrictions on disclosure of SSNs of mental-health patients. Sec. 27-10-120. And disabled persons. Sec. 27-10.5-120.

A police officer may not require a person to divulge a SSN. Sec. 16-3-103.

A person shall not be required to report a SSN for obtaining health coverage or claiming benefits when "not required by applicable federal statute or regulation." Sec. 10-16-104.

When payment is made by check, a person shall not require the maker of the check to record a SSN for ID or proof of creditworthiness, except for payment of a student loan. Sec. 4-3-506.

Each post-secondary institution (apparently including private institutions) shall take reasonable steps to insure the privacy of a student's SSN, and not use it, or any part of it, as the student's primary identifier. Institutions that are unable to comply because of cost may qualify for permission to phase out the use of SSNs. Sec. 23-5-127.

Connecticut–Businesses may not print SSNs on ID documents nor disclose them to the public. Conn. Gen. Stat. sec. 42-470.

Registrars shall not use SSNs for voter ID numbers. Sec. 9-35. The tax collector shall withhold from disclosure taxpayers' SSNs. Sec. 12-148.

The law penalizes any individual or business that intentionally fails to protect personal information like Social Security numbers. Companies (but not government agencies) that collect SSNs must have privacy policies in place. Sec. 42-471

Delaware–Licenses shall bear the licensee's SSN. Del. Code title 21, sec. 2718(a).

District of Columbia–The SSN may not appear on a driver's license unless licensee requests it. D.C. Code Ann. sec. 50-402.

Florida–A Social Security number may not be used as a customer's personal identifying number by a bank operating an automated funds transfer system. Fla. Stat. Ann. sec. 659.062.

The individual records of students enrolled in school readiness programs, including SSNs, are confidential. Stat. sec. 411.011. A voter's SSN is confidential and may be used only for voter registration purposes. Sec. 97.0585.

Taxpayer's SSNs are confidential, sec. 192.0105, and so are numbers on assessment rolls, sec. 93.114.

The SSNs of certain persons in state files are exempt from mandatory disclosure. Sec. 119.071. SSNs generally may be released but "the display or bulk sale of Social Security numbers to the general public or the distribution of such numbers to any customer that is not identifiable by the distributor" is disallowed. Sec. 119.071(5)5.

Georgia–"Personal identification cards for persons who do not have a driver's license shall bear an identification card number which shall be the same as the Social Security number of the person identified." Ga. Code Ann. sec. 68B-207.

Businesses may not print SSNs on ID documents, disclose them to the public, not demand them unencrypted online. Sec. 10-1-393.8.

News reporters may have access to Social Security numbers in state files, but the public may not. Code Ann. sec. 50-18-72.

The state law on SSNs and voting is identical to Florida's. Sec. 21-2-225.

Department of Motor Vehicles identification cards should not use the SSN as the card number unless someone specifically requests it. Sec. 40-5-100.

The SSN of a juvenile should not be disclosed in connection with court proceedings. Sec. 15-11-114.

"Insurance ID cards shall not use or display the insured's SSN." Sec. 33-24-57.1.

Hawaii–Businesses may not print SSNs on ID documents nor disclose them to the public. Haw. Rev. Stat. sec. 487J-2. Drivers' licenses should not be issued displaying SSNs. Sec. 286-109. A driver's license number should not be the SSN. Sec. 286-239. A poll book shall not contain the SSN of anyone. Sec. 11-136.

Idaho–SSNs received for the college savings program shall be confidential. Idaho Code sec. 33-5404. A SSN in the motor vehicle and driver records shall not be disclosed without the person's consent, except if requested by an agency or for use in matters of motor vehicle or driver safety, or theft. Idaho Code sec. 49-203.

A driver's license, permit or ID card shall not contain an applicant's SSN. Secs. 49-306 and 49-2444. Uses of SSNs at death are restricted. Sec. 67-3007.

Illinois–The Secretary of State may not release Social Security numbers outside of the government. 625 ILCS 5/2-123(h).

A business or government agency may not disclose Social Security numbers, print them on mailings, require a person to send a SSN by Internet unless the connection is secure or the number encrypted, require a SSN to access a Web site. Uses prior to July 2005 are permitted to continue. 815 ILCS 505/2RR. An entity may not print an individual's Social Security number on an insurance card. 815 ILCS 505/2QQ.

SSNs will not be included on the child's birth certificate. The numbers will be used only for "those purposes allowed by federal law." 410 ILCS 535/11. An individual should not be required to give a SSN when applying for a ballot, and a notice stating this should appear on the certificate. 10 ILCS 5/4-22.

There are limits on disclosure of SSNs by the Secretary of State. 625 ILCS 5/2-123.

Indiana–No state agency (except Revenue, Welfare, Employment and State Personnel) may compel a person's Social Security number unless required to do so by federal law. Release of Social Security numbers by state agencies is restricted unless required by state or federal laws. Ind. Code Ann. sec. 4-1-8-1. The motor vehicle department must require a SSN. Sec. 9-24-9-2.

The law also "provides [in state files] that disclosure of the last four digits of a Social Security number is not considered a disclosure of the Social Security number." Ind. Code Ann. sec. 36-2-7.5-3. In the same law, the state is apparently the first to require an individual who prepares a document for recording to: (1) certify that the individual reviewed the entire document and took reasonable care to redact Social Security numbers in the document; and (2) record the certification. Each county will collect $2 for recording a certification and use the money "to search

documents using redacting technology to redact Social Security numbers before the documents are released for public inspection." The law authorizes a pilot project to develop and test technology for scanning recorded documents and redacting Social Security numbers.

A person's SSN shall not be disclosed on a motor vehicle registration, nor disclosed from a marriage license. Sec. 9-14-3.5-7. 31-11-4-4. SSNs on certificates of death will not be disclosed to the public. Sec.16-37-3-9.

When an individual declines to provide a Social Security number to a state agency, the agency is prohibited from obtaining the number from any other source. Sec. 4-1-8-4.

Iowa–The Department of Motor Vehicles "shall advise an applicant that the applicant for a motor vehicle license other than a commercial driver's license may request a number other than a Social Security number as the motor vehicle license number." Iowa Code Ann. sec. 321.182.

A mortgage presented for recording may not disclose a SSN. Code Ann. sec. 36-2-11-26. The county registrar shall take all necessary steps to ensure the confidentiality of the SSN of each applicant for a marriage license. Sec. 595.4. SSNs should not be included on documents prepared for recording in county recorders' offices, with some exceptions. Sec. 331.606A.

Kansas–Both private parties and government agencies may not "solicit, require or use for commercial purposes an individual's SSN" except if necessary for the normal course of business and if no other identifying number may be used. Stat. Ann sec. 75-3520.

Parents' SSNs shall not be recorded on the birth certificate. Sec 65-2409a.

Kentucky–An applicant must submit a Social Security number for a driver's license, but it will not appear on the face of the license. The government must use a number system other than Social Security numbers for management of drivers' licenses. Ky. Rev. Stat. sec. 186.412(2) and (3).

Parents' Social Security numbers are required on birth certificates. Sec. 213.046(14).

The Board of Education shall create a statewide student ID numbering system based on students' SSNs, but for those students whose parents or guardians object, a number similar to the SSN shall be used instead. Rev. Stat. 156.160. See also sec. 197.120.

The SSNs of voters will be redacted before materials are publicly inspected. Sec. 18A.0551.

Drivers' licenses should not contain SSNs. Sec. 186.412. Any SSN recorded on a marriage license shall not be available for public release except for enforcing child support. Sec. 402.100.

Louisiana–The motor vehicles department shall maintain confidentiality of SSNs it obtains. La. Rev. Stat. Ann. sec. 32:409.1. An applicant's driver's license *may* bear his SSN if he chooses. The SSN should not be included on the license's magnetic strip. Sec. 32:410.

The clerk of court shall maintain the confidentiality of a party's SSN in an application for a marriage license, provided a request is made in writing to the clerk at the time of application. Sec. 9:224. Sec. 9:313 covers the same procedure for divorce proceedings.

The information regarding persons who died, including SSNs, shall be confidential (except authorized Employment Security Law personnel). Sec. 23:1671.

No clerk of court or recorder of mortgages shall refuse to accept for recordation any instrument that does not contain the SSN or taxpayer ID. Sec. 9:5141.

Voting officials should not disclose voters' SSNs (except to verifying the number with the Department of Motor Vehicles). Sec. 18:154.

Maine–Display of Social Security numbers is prohibited on credit cards, debit cards, and "customer service cards," except for medical-insurance cards. 10 Me. Rev. Stat. 1271-2.

Title 29, sec. 539-A states that the secretary of state may ask citizens for their Social Security numbers to use as permanent operator's license numbers.

No one may deny goods and services to an individual because he or she refuses to provide a SSN, but exempted are credit reporting, certain lenders and financial organizations, insurance, health-care billing, a background check by landlord, lessor, or employer. Also if the SSN is necessary to verify the identity of the individual for a transaction authorized by the individual, or to prevent fraud. Rev. Stat. Ann. title 10, sec. 1272-B.

SSNs recorded for marriage certificates are not open records. Title 9-A, sec. 651. The Department of Health and Welfare may not use the SSNs gathered for birth certificates except for the purposes of the Social Security Act. Title 22, sec. 2761.

Maryland–It is illegal to display a Social Security number publicly or to require a person to transmit an SSN online or send it or, in most cases, to fax it (with exceptions). Md. Comm. Law 14-3501. Parents' SSNs, recorded at a child's birth, may be disclosed only to the child-support Administration. Sec. 4-208. Pharmacies must keep SSNs confidential. Sec. 12-403.

Massachusetts–A person must submit a Social Security number to secure a driver's license or any other kind of license but may request that it not appear on the face of the license. Mass. Gen. Laws Ann. ch. 30A, sec. 13A.

The university system may not display a student's or employee's Social Security number on identification cards. Sec. 92, Ch. 140, Laws of 2003 (unclear whether this has permanent effect).

The town clerk may not retain SSNs in connection with a marriage license. Gen. Laws Ann. ch. 207, sec. 20. The SSNs provided by parents at birth shall not be open records. Researchers may obtain such information by written request but must keep it confidential. Ch. 111, sec. 24B. The child-support enforcement agency may disclose parents' SSNs only with regard to support enforcement. Ch. 119A, sec. 14.

A consumer's SSN shall not be used as a central information file number by any financial institution. However, it may be used to assist an institution in verifying the identity of a consumer. Ch. 167B, sec. 14.

When information like a SSN is obtained for verification of a customer's decision to switch electricity companies, this information shall not be sold, or used for commercial or marketing purposes. Ch. 164, sec. 1F.

Michigan–SSNs should not be displayed on drivers' licenses; the SSNs obtained for application purposes shall be disclosed only "as required by law." Mich. Comp. Laws Ann. sec. 257.307. SSNs shall not be displayed on a marriage or death certificate. Sec. 333.2813. The display of others' Social Security numbers in government or the private sector is restricted. Entities collecting SSNs must have privacy policies protecting them. Secs. 445.83 through 86.

A public record may be exempt from disclosure under the open-records law if it would disclose the SSN of an individual. Sec. 15.243.

Minnesota–Social Security numbers are required on applications for drivers licenses for heavy vehicles, but not for automobiles or small trucks. Minn. Stat. Ann. sec. 171.06.

Businesses may not publicly display a person's SSN; print it on any card required to access services; require a customer to transmit a SSN online unless the line is secure or the number is encrypted; require an SSN to access a Web site unless an PIN is also used; print a SSN on mailed materials (with exceptions); use the number as a primary account number; or sell a person's SSN. Companies must limit access to SSNs to employees with a need to know. Stat. Ann. 325E.59.

New parents must provide SSNs, but they are not to be used on the birth certificate. The SSNs are considered private, but will be provided to public authorities who request them for the establishment of parentage or enforcement of child support debts. Sec. 144.215.

Mississippi–"When any state agency mails, delivers, circulates, publishes, distributes, transmits, or otherwise disseminates, in any form or manner, information or material that contains the SSN of an individual, the agency shall take such steps as may be reasonably necessary to prevent the inadvertent disclosure of the individual's SSN to members of the general public or to persons other than those persons who, in the performance of their duties and responsibilities, have a lawful and legitimate need to know the individual's SSN." Miss. Code Ann. sec. 25-1-111.

The SSNs of parents shall not appear on the birth certificate and disclosed only to the Division of Child Support Enforcement. Sec. 41-57-14.

SSNs in voter-registration files shall not be public records. Sec. 23-15-165.

Missouri–State law prohibits private entities, but not government agencies, from using SSNs in ways listed in Arizona's law. Mo. Rev. Stat. sec. 407.1355.

No state entity shall publicly disclose any SSN of a living person unless permitted by law, authorized by the holder, for use in civil, criminal or administrative proceedings, or pursuant to a court order. State agencies currently using SSNs in a way that is inconsistent with this law may continue to do so in ways similar to those in Arizona's law. Sec. 610.035. SSNs are used as driver's license numbers. Sec. 302. 181.

The law on SSNs and birth certificates is similar to Mississippi's. Secs. 193.075 and 454.440.

Montana–A SSN may not be used as the distinguishing number on a driver's license unless the individual expressly authorizes it. Sec. 61-5-111(2)(b).

A company must notify individuals when their Social Security numbers are disclosed as part of a breach of security, but only when the breach materially compromises confidentiality, integrity, or security of information *and* is reasonably believed to cause loss or injury. Mont. Code Ann. 33-19-321 and 30-14-1704.

Nevada–A Social Security number may not be the basis for a driver's license number. Nev. Rev. Stat. Ann. 483.345.

New Hampshire–Social Security numbers are required on an application for a driver's license, but an applicant may get a waiver to the requirement. N.H. Rev. Stat. Ann. sec. 263:40-a.

An applicant may request that SSN not be printed on the driver's license. Rev. Stat. Ann. sec. 263:40-a. Parental SSNs may not appear on a birth certificate. Sec. 5-C:10.

Health insurers and third-party payers may not display SSNs on documents provided for claims. Sec. 400-A:15-b. Agencies may not require by rule a submission of a SSN unless mandated by law. Sec. 541-A:22.

New Jersey–Businesses may not publicly display SSNs. N.J. Stat. Ann. Sec. C.56:8-164. Documents filed with county clerks may not display SSNs. Sec. 47: 1-16.

See also **Government Information**.

New Mexico–No business may require a SSN as a condition for doing business, but a customer may consent, and then access to SSNs must be limited to employees who require them to perform their duties. Sec. 57-12B-3. A SSN shall not be used as a PIN or code to activate a remote financial service unit. Sec. 58-16-13.

New York–Public schools and colleges may not use Social Security numbers as student identifiers. N.Y. Educ. Code sec. 2-b.

Employers may not publicly display employees' Social Security numbers, put them on ID badges, store them in unrestricted files, or use them as ID numbers for occupational licensing purposes. Employers may not communicate to the general public an employee's SSN, home address or telephone number, personal email address, Internet identification name or password, parent's surname prior to marriage or driver's license number to the general public. This seems to be the first and only law limiting dis-

closure of employee information. Employers who fail to create or implement policies to prevent prohibited uses of employees' SSNs or disclosure of employees' personal information are presumed to have knowingly violated the law. Without consent and encryption, companies may not require an employee or consumer to disclose all or part of a Social Security number and may not refuse any service, privilege or right for refusing to make that disclosure. If the company possesses an SSN, it must take precautions to prevent disclosure of it. Employers may not hire inmates for any job that would provide them with access to Social Security numbers. Gen. Bus. Law 399-ddd.

Public schools and colleges may not use SSNs as student identifiers. Educ. Code sec. 2-B.

North Carolina–Entities may not make SSNs public in many instances. N.C. Gen. Stat. sec. 75-62.

North Dakota–A driver's license number may not be related to a licensee's SSN or encrypted version of the SSN. N.D. Cent. Code 39-06-14.

A document that includes a SSN may not be filed or recorded with the recorder unless the law otherwise requires. N.D. Cent. Code sec. 11-18-23.

Ohio–A merchant may not record the Social Security number (or address or phone number) of a credit-card holder in credit-card sales, with exceptions. Ohio Rev. Code Ann. 1349.17.

Driver's licenses may not display SSN. Rev. Code Ann. sec. 4501.31.

Oklahoma–State agencies may not require nor use the Social Security number, unless the use is related to Social Security benefits or the use began prior to 1974. Okla. Stat. title 74, sec. 3111. [See 1978-79 book.]

It is illegal "for any person to willfully and with fraudulent intent obtain the name, address, social security number, date of birth... or any other personal identifying information of another person living or dead, with intent to use, sell, or allow any other person to use or sell such personal information to obtain or attempt to obtain money, credit, goods, property, or service in the name of the other person without the consent of that person." Title 21 sec. 15331.1.

Employers may not display or disclose SSNs. Stat. tit. 40, sec. 173.1.

A driver may not request that DMV use the SSN as license number, and upon renewal, any SSN as a license number must be changed. Sec. 6-106.

Oregon–There are restrictions on businesses and government disclosing Social Security numbers, similar to those in Michigan. Or. Rev. Stat. 646A.620.

Pennsylvania–A SSN may not appear on the license. Pa. Stat. Ann. title 75, sec. 1510.

Rhode Island–Except for pharmacies, insurance, and health providers, businesses may not demand all or part of a customer's Social Security number when a purchase is made. Amended in 2011. This is the first law in the nation limiting collection of SSNs by private businesses (aside from an Ohio law prohibiting merchants from recording SSNs in credit-card transactions). Merchants in Rhode Island may not record all of part of SSNs on checks. R.I. Gen. Laws 6-13-17.

The state is authorized to develop a universal student ID number *not* involving Social Security numbers. Sec. 42-72.5-2(6).

Public colleges and universities may not display students' Social Security numbers publicly nor use as an ID. Sec. 16-38-5.1.

Entities may not disclose individuals' SSNs. Sec. 6-48-8.

See also **Credit Reporting**.

South Carolina–Display and disclosure of SSNs is prohibited in the identity-theft law, with exceptions. S.C. 37-20-180, 37-20-310, 320.

The SSN may be used for a driver's license number. S.C. Code Ann. sec. 56-1-90. An application for an absentee ballot does not require SSN. Sec. 7-15-340. The SSN used in voter registration is not open to inspection. Sec. 7-5-170.

Texas–A business may not print a SSN on a card or other device to access a product or service unless the individual requests in writing that such printing be made. A business may not intentionally communicate or make publicly available an individual's SSN, or transmit an unencrypted SSN over the Internet, or require a SSN for Web site access, unless required by law. Bus. and Com. Code sec. 35.58. Social Security numbers in voting files shall be confidential. Tex. Elec. Code sec. 13-004.

The SSN may not be printed on a license. Tex. Trans. Code sec. 521.044.

Tennessee–The driver's license may not display a SSN unless applicant requests so in writing. Tenn. Code Ann. sec. 55-50-331.

No state entity may publicly disclose a person's SSN. Sec. 4-4-125.

Utah–"Except as allowed by other law, a person may not display a Social Security number in a manner or location that is likely to be open to public view." Utah Code Ann. sec. 13-42-301.

Insurers are prohibited from publicly displaying any SSN, or printing SSN on any card required for accessing services. Sec. 31A-22-634.

Vermont–The law prohibits businesses and government from posting or displaying Social Security numbers in public places. 9 Vt. Stat. Ann. 2440.

Prior to circulating documents, government agencies must attempt to redact SSNs. Sec. 2480m.

Virginia–It is unlawful to require a Social Security number for any activity or to refuse service if it is not furnished, unless disclosure is specifically required by federal or state law. Va. Code sec. 2.1-385. State law does require that Social Security number be given in order to receive a driver's license and that it appear on the license. Sec. 46.2-323.

A Social Security number is required to register to vote. Sec. 24.2-418. But "Any person assisting an applicant with the completion or return of a mail voter registration application shall not copy, disclose or make any use of the Social Security number of the applicant except as authorized by law for official use. Sec. 24.2-416.5.

"Each student shall present a federal social security number within 90 days of his enrollment" unless the superintendent waives the requirement because a pupil is ineligible for a number. Sec. 22.1-260.

Drivers are able to choose to have a number other than their Social Security numbers on their licenses. Sec. 46.2-342. The DMV may permit a person not to provide certain personal information "for good cause." Sec. 46.2-323.

Businesses may not display or embed Social Security numbers of individuals, except as authorized by law. Code sec. 59.1-443.2.

ID cards or licenses may not display an entire SSN. Sec. 2.2-3808. Driver's license numbers may not be the SSN. Sec. 46.2-342.

Government agencies may not disclose individual SSNs unless specifically required by law. Sec. 2.2-3808. They may collect them only as authorized by law. 46.2-703.

Universities must report names and Social Security numbers of students to the sex-offender database for cross-checking. Sec. 23-2.2:1.

Washington–The "enrollee identifier" in the state's health-care financing program must meet standards of uniqueness and accuracy above that of the Social Security number. Wash. Rev. Code Ann. sec. 70.170.

The SSN may not be displayed on licenses. SSNs may not be disclosed except as required by state or federal law. Rev. Code sec. 26.23.150. Institutions of higher education may not use SSNs for identification. Sec. 28B.10.042. Health carriers and state health programs may not use SSN on ID cards. Rev. Code secs. 48.43.022 and 74.09.037.

West Virginia–All public and private schools including institutions of higher education are prohibited from using student SSNs for identification. SSNs may be used for internal recordkeeping. W. Va. Code Ann. sec. 18-2-5f. Establishments that scan drivers' licenses may verify age but may not record SSNs. Sec. 60-2-22.

Wisconsin–Public schools may not use a student identity number that includes the Social Security number, but they may collect the number. Wisc. Stat. Ann. Sec. 118.169. Nor may universities. Sec. 36.32(2).

Wyoming–The SSN is not required to appear on license, though a licensee may request it. Wyo. Stat. Ann. sec. 31-7-115.

Federal law–Government benefits may not be denied an individual for failing to provide a Social Security number unless prior to 1975 there was a law or regulation authorizing such a demand. In any case, state, local and federal agencies must notify an individual of the authority that allows them to collect the Social Security number and what uses will be made of it. 5 U.S.C. 552a (note). State welfare, tax, and motor vehicle agencies are exempt from this provision. 42 U.S.C. 405(c)(2)(c)(i).

There are criminal penalties for disclosing or using a person's Social Security number contrary to federal laws. Anyone in a government agency receiving a Social Security number of an individual may not further disseminate it. 42 U.S.C. 405(c)(2) (c)(viii).

A taxpayer claiming a dependent of one year or older must have a Social Security number for that person and report it on Form 1040. 26 U.S.C. 6109(note).

A state must forfeit a portion of federal funds if it does not require all parents to provide their Social Security numbers before a birth certificate will be issued for a newborn, unless the state waives the requirement "for good cause." The law says the SSNs may not be recorded on the birth certificate. 42 U.S.C. 1305, 42 U.S.C. 607, 42 U.S.C. 602.

The Social Security numbers of both parents must be included on any application to issue a Social Security number to a minor child and this information will be reported by the Social Security Administration to the Internal Revenue Service. 42 U.S.C. 405(c)(2).

The "administrative simplification" part of a 1996 law requires a unique identification number for health care. The law does not specify the Social Security number. Congress has suspended the effect of this law. 42 U.S.C. 1320 d-2(b).

All states must collect Social Security numbers when renewing or issuing a professional license, driver's license, occupational license, or marriage license, as well as from a party to a divorce decree, child-support order, or paternity determination. In addition, "If a state allows the use of a number other than the Social Security number, the state shall so advise any applicants." 42 U.S.C. 666(a)(13).

A Social Security number may not be collected, presumably, when a person registers for a federal election through a state motor vehicle form, because the form may not ask for personal data that is also required on the DMV form. 42 U.S.C. 1973gg-3.

Employers in some states must check the immigrant status and Social Security numbers of applicants for employment. This computer screening of Social Security numbers also includes persons delinquent in payment of student loans. 42 U.S.C. 653(j).

The Department of the Treasury must ensure that Social Security numbers are not visible through window envelopes mailed by the federal government. 31 U.S.C. 3327. Nor printed on checks. 42 USC 1305 note.

Financial institutions must meet minimum standards set by the Department of Treasury for identifying any person opening a new bank account. 31 U.S.C. 5318. See also **Government Information** and see also **Student Records**.

A consumer may demand that credit bureaus truncate a SSN in the files. 15 U.S.C. 1681 et seq.

A state may not display a Social Security number on a driver's license, motor vehicle registration, or personal identification card that it issues. 42 U.S.C. 405(c)(2) (C)(vi)(II).

Each state must implement a computerized statewide voter registration list with a unique identifier. Each applicant to vote must submit his or her driver's license number, or, if none has been issued, the last four digits of his or her Social Security number. Some states that currently gather SSNs are exempted from the database requirement. State motor vehicle departments may match the information with data in the files of the Social Security Administration to confirm name, date of birth, Social Security number, and whether the applicant is alive. In exceptional circumstances the Social Security Administration may decline to confirm information. 42 U.S.C. 15483. See also **Credit Reporting**.

STUDENT INFORMATION

Arizona–School records are considered confidential and professional, with access only to parents, professional staff, state and federal agencies (if the information is kept anonymous), colleges, pupils older than 18 and others on the parents' instructions. A parent has the right to attach a written response to any disputed item. Ariz. Rev. Stat. sec. 15-151.

Schools may not use biometric identifying technologies, including fingerprints and facial comparisons, on pupils, with no exceptions. Rev. Stat. Ann. sec.15-203

California–Students in public institutions of higher education are entitled to the state constitutional right of privacy, and limits are placed on the use of evidence seized from student dormitories in violation of constitutional rights. Cal. Penal Code sec. 626.11.

State law on access to and disclosure of student records conforms to federal law. Educ Code (1976) sec. 49060. State law dictates that parents have an absolute right in both private and public schools to see their children's records. Public schools must establish procedures for parental inspection and challenge of records. In public schools, additional access is permitted to school officials, other state officials authorized by law, pupils 16 years or older, courts, financial-aid organizations, accrediting associations, and others in an emergency.

Educ. Code (1976) sec. 76200 conforms state law on student records to federal law as it affects public community colleges. [See 1978-79 book.]

Bullying of pupils committed by means of an electronic act ["cyberbullying"] can result in suspension or expulsion of pupils. Educ. Code secs. 32261, 32265, 32270, and 48900.

Public and private postsecondary educational institutions may not require or request a student, prospective student, or student group to (1) disclose a user name or password for accessing personal social media, (2) access personal social media in the presence of the institution's employee or representative, or (3) divulge any personal social media information. Schools may still guard against and investigate student misconduct. Educ. Code sec. 99120.

See also **Social Security Numbers**.

Colorado–Unless contrary to federal law, schools may allow employers or law enforcement access to pupil records without parental consent. Colo. Rev. Stat. sec. 24-72-204.

Connecticut–Parents have right of access to scholastic and medical information held by a school. Conn. Gen. Stat. Ann. sec. 10-15b.

School personnel are protected from legal redress for statements made. The communications between student and counselor are privileged, even from parents. Sec. 10-154a.

Delaware–The law allows access only to government agencies unless there is parental consent; permits schools to grant parental access to their own children's records; school personnel are protected from suits for record-keeping abuses. Del. Code title 14, sec. 4111.

Public and private institutions may not inquire into passwords or content related to students' use of social media like Facebook. Title 14, sec. 9402.

Florida–Records are open only to parents, to courts, to school staff, to school boards, and to others whom the principal or parents may authorize. Fla. Stat. Ann. sec. 232.23.

See also **Social Security Numbers**.

Idaho–School psychologists and counselors are immune in court from disclosing information without the consent of the pupil. Idaho Code sec. 9-203(6).

Illinois–The school student records act provides safeguards similar to federal law and requires drafting of regulations for public schools. 105 ILCS 10/1.

Written permission of parents is required before public schools gather biometric information (like fingerprints, eye scans, genetic profiles) from pupils. Refusal to give permission may not result in a denial of school services. ILCS 5/10-20.40

"The University [of Illinois] may not provide a student's name, address, telephone number, social security number, email address, or other personal identifying information to a business organization or financial institution that issues credit or debit cards, unless the student is 21 years of age or older." 110 ILCS 305/30. See also 110 ILCS 805/3-60.

Iowa–Records of present and former pupils are regarded as confidential, to be released at the discretion of the county superintendent. Iowa Code Ann. sec. 68A.7.

Kentucky–Counselor-student communications are privileged. Ky. Rev. Stat. sec. 421.216.

The Board of Education shall create a statewide student ID numbering system based on students' SSNs, but for those students whose parents or guardians object, a number similar to the SSN shall be used instead. Rev. Stat. 156.160. See also sec. 197.120.

Louisiana–Attorney General's Opinion, January 31, 1974, proclaims that children have a right to privacy in schools and that their records are confidential.

Maine–Counselor communications are privileged. Me. Rev. Stat. Ann. title 20, sec. 805.

Maryland–Records relating to the biography, family, physiology, religion, academic achievement, and physical or mental ability of any student may be disclosed to the student or to education officials. Md. State Gov't. Code Ann. sec. 10-616.

Any written or oral statement made by a student to a professional educator when the student is seeking information for overcoming any form of drug abuse may not be used as evidence against the student in any proceeding. The teacher's, principal's, or counselor's observations during such consultations are not admissible either. Md. Educ. Code Ann. sec. 7-410.

Massachusetts–A school "shall, upon request of any student or former student, ... furnish to him a written transcript of his record." Mass. Gen. Laws Ann. ch. 71, sec. 34A. Further, "Each school committee shall, at the request of a parent or guardian of a pupil, or at the request of a pupil 18 years of age or older, allow such parent, guardian or pupil to inspect academic, scholastic, or any other records concerning such pupil." Sec. 34E. The state board of education is required to adopt regulations for the storage and destruction of pupil records. Sec. 34D.

Michigan–In legal proceedings, counselors, teachers and school employees may not disclose pupil information received in confidence. Test results are open only to qualified educational personnel. Mich. Comp. Laws Ann. sec. 600.2165.

The law on access to social-media passwords and content applies to employers and to public and private universities and schools. Secs. 37.272 thru 278

Minnesota–Public school and university records on students are governed by the state Data Practices Act. Minn. Stat. Ann. sec. 13.32.

Mississippi–Cumulative records shall not "be available to the general public." Miss. Code Ann. sec. 37-15-3.

Montana–Counselor communications are privileged. Mont. Code Ann. sec. 93-701-4.

Nebraska–Academic and disciplinary records are to be segregated; disciplinary records destroyed at graduation if authorized by the state records board. Teachers, parents and the pupil have access to records. Neb. Rev. Stat. sec. 79-4,157. Local school boards shall set student records policy. Sec. 79-4,158.

Nevada–A privilege is recognized for counselor-pupil communications. Nev. Rev. Stat. sec. 49.290 and 49.291.

New Jersey–The law permits access by outsiders, although regulations may limit somewhat. School personnel are protected from legal action based on statements in the records. N.J. Rev. Stat. sec. 18A:36-19.

State law prohibits requiring that university students disclose social-media passwords or user names or asking students to waive this right. Sec. 18A:3-29.

New York–Commissioner of Education decision, September 20, 1960, permits parental access to records in conference with school officials.

North Carolina–Counselor communications are privileged. N.C. Gen. Stat. sec. 8-53.4.

North Dakota–Counselors are immune from disclosure. N.D. Cent. Code sec. 31-06.1.

Ohio–There may be no release of files for profit-making activities. Disclosure with parental consent or to another school is permissible. Directory-type information may be disclosed. Military recruiters may have mailing lists of high schoolers unless a parent or student objects. Ohio Rev. Code sec. 3319.321.

Oklahoma–It is a misdemeanor for any teacher to reveal any information regarding any child obtained in one's capacity as a teacher except as required in performance of contractual duties or as requested by parents. Okla. Stat. 70-6-115.

Oregon–Parental access allowed; they may see behavioral records only in conference with a professional. Records are regarded as confidential but may be released to anyone with "demonstrated interest in the student." Or. Rev. Stat. sec. 336.195. Elementary and secondary school teachers' communications are privileged. Sec. 44.040.

Rhode Island–State law creates a misdemeanor for circulating a questionnaire, without approval of the state department of education and the local school committee, that is "so framed as to ask the pupils of any school intimate questions about themselves and/or their families, thus trespassing on the pupils' constitutional rights and invading the privacy of the home... ." R.I. Gen. Laws sec. 16-38-5.

South Dakota–Elementary and secondary school counselors' communications are privileged except in cases of child abuse. S.D. Codified Laws Ann. sec. 19-2-5.1. College and university counselor-student communications are also privileged. Sec. 19-2-5.2.

Tennessee–School records are confidential, except when compelled under legal process, or released for the safety of person or property. Outsiders are authorized access to pupil records for research, and a pupil may give consent for others to have access. Tenn. Code Ann. sec. 10-7-504.

Texas–Student records are regarded as confidential, to be released only upon request of educational personnel, a student, parent or spouse. Tex. Gov. Code sec. 552.114.

Vermont–There are limits on the release of school records except as required by federal law. Vt. Stat. Ann. title 1, sec. 317(11).

Virginia–The freedom of information act allows access only to student involved or, if under age 18, his or her parent. Letters of recommendation not included. Va. Code sec. 2.1-342(b)(3).

See also **Social Security Numbers**.

Universities must report names and Social Security numbers of students to the sex-offender database for cross-checking. Code sec. 23-2.2:1.

Washington–Records of students in public schools exempt from public records act of the state. Wash. Rev. Code Ann. sec. 42.17.310. Attorney general's interpretation, March 13, 1974, regards pupil records as open to the parents. Student-counselor communications regarded as privileged.

Wisconsin–Allows access to parents or pupils, courts, school officials and persons designated by parents or pupil. Provides for destruction of old records and mandates that behavioral records be destroyed one year after graduation unless the graduate requests otherwise. Records created before September 1974 are not affected. Wis. Stat. Ann. sec. 118.125. [See 1978-79 book.]

Ordering a strip search of a school pupil is a misdemeanor. Sec. 942.02.

Federal law–Family Education Rights and Privacy Act of 1974, 20 U.S.C. 1232g, provides that, as a condition of receiving federal funds, school districts and colleges must grant students 18 years and older or, in the case of younger students, their parents, access to student records; must limit outside access; and must establish procedures for the parents or students to challenge erroneous records. [See 1997 book.] The law permits wide disclosure to the juvenile justice system, usually pursuant to state laws, and requires school officials not to reveal when student records have been subpoenaed from them.

Statistical student information may be released for purposes of reporting on campus crimes. 20 U.S.C. 1092.

The Department of Education is authorized to exchange information with credit bureaus on student loans in default. 20 U.S.C. 1080. [See listing under **Credit Reporting**.]

"No student shall be required, as part of any [federally funded school] program, to submit to psychiatric... or psychological examination, testing, or treatment, in which the primary purpose is to reveal information concerning (1) political affiliations; (2) mental and psychological problems potentially embarrassing to the student or his family; (3) sex behavior and attitudes; (4) illegal, anti-social, self-incriminating and demeaning behavior; (5) critical appraisals of other individuals... ; (6) legally recognized privileged and analogous relationships, such as those of lawyers, physicians, and ministers; or (7) income (other than that required by law to determine financial aid), without the consent of the student... , or in the case of an unemancipated minor, without the prior written consent of the parent." 20 U.S.C. 1232h(b).

Businesses, including Internet companies and Web sites, may not collect personal information from school pupils without parental consent (magazine subscriptions and student-recognition programs are exempt). Parents may inspect all pupil surveys administered in schools that are written by non-school persons. 20 U.S.C. 1232h(b).

Colleges and universities are required to provide a list to the Internal Revenue Service each year with the name, address, and Social Security number of each student for whom tuition was paid and the same information for any parent who claims the student as a dependent, plus the amounts of tuition paid. 26 U.S.C. 6050S.

TAX RECORDS

Alaska–Information in possession of department of revenue that discloses particulars of the business or affairs of a taxpayer is not a matter of public record except for purposes of investigation and law enforcement. Information to be kept confidential. Alaska Stat. sec. 9.25.100.

Arizona–Except by court order or by request of attorney general or county attorney or on reciprocal basis with other tax officials, it is a misdemeanor to disclose in any manner information on income tax returns. Ariz. Rev. Stat. sec. 42.108. A tax preparer shall not divulge any information except upon express permission. Sec. 43.381.

Colorado–Except with a court order, department of revenue may not divulge any tax return information. Colo. Rev. Stat. sec. 39-21-113(4)(a).

Connecticut–Tax records are confidential, but may be released to other state agencies with a need to know and with a system for security and for logging disclosures. Conn. Gen. Stat. Ann. sec. 12-15.

Delaware–Unlawful for any employee of state tax commission or data processing division to divulge amount of income or any particulars on personal income tax return. Del. Code title 30, sec. 368.

Georgia–Ga. Code Ann. sec. 48-7-60 provides for the confidentiality of information contained within the tax data system. Data processing service organizations may have access to tax information where necessary, provided the state revenue commissioner gives prior approval and provided the organizations are subject "to the direct security control of revenue department personnel during subject periods of access."

Hawaii–Disclosure of tax return information by a return preparer or service agency is prohibited. Haw. Rev. Stat. sec. 231.15.5. Disclosure of tax return information by state employees is prohibited. Sec. 235.116.

Idaho–Idaho Code sec. 63-3076 prohibits the disclosure of income tax information, with exceptions.

Illinois–Tax returns are confidential, with exceptions. 35 ILCS 5/917.

Iowa–Tax information may be used for statistical purposes by the legislative services agency, but shall not include SSNs. Iowa Code Ann. sec. 422.72.

Kansas–Unlawful for any employee of revenue to disclose amount of income or any particulars of income tax returns and reports. The secretary of revenue may make available return information to federal or other states' tax officials provided such information is not used for any other purpose but tax compliance. Kans. Stat. sec. 79-3234.

Kentucky–No employee of department of revenue shall divulge information on returns or reports of any person except for prosecutions for filing false reports. Ky. Rev. Stat. Ann. sec. 131.190.

There is a prohibition against prisoners in jobs with access to taxpayer information, including Social Security numbers. Rev. Stat. 131.191.

Louisiana–Records and files of the collector of revenue shall be considered confidential and privileged. La. Rev. Stat. Ann. sec. 47:1508.

Maine–Tax assessor or any employee of bureau of taxation prohibited from divulging amount of income or particulars on any income tax return. Legislative investigating committees and federal and state tax officers have access. Me. Rev. Stat. Ann. title 36, sec. 191.

Maryland–Unlawful for employee of department of revenue to divulge amount of income or any particulars on any tax return. Md. Tax-Gen. Code Ann. sec. 13-202. Disclosure by persons in business of preparing tax federal or state income tax returns unless authorized by taxpayer or by law or court order is unlawful. Md. Tax-Gen. Code Ann. sec. 13-207.

Massachusetts–Mass. Gen. Laws Ann. ch. 62C, sec. 21 requires the commissioner upon request to tell any citizen of the state whether or not another person filed an income tax return for any year. Disclosure of any other information besides name and address of the taxpayer is prohibited. Ch. 62C, sec. 74.

Minnesota–No private tax preparer nor government tax examiner "shall divulge any particulars" of a tax return, except that government agents may exchange data within state and federal agencies. Preparers may divulge personal information for purposes of obtaining computer services. Violations are misdemeanors. Minn. Stat. Ann. sec. 290-611. [See 1978-79 book.]

Nebraska–Unlawful for any person permitted to inspect any report or return to divulge the amount of income or any particulars. Neb. Rev. Stat. sec. 77-27,119(1)(b) and (c).

New York–Personal income tax return information is not to be released by any employee of the tax commission. N.Y. Tax Law sec. 697 (McKinney).

North Carolina–Employees of the commissioner of revenue may not disclose any information except on reciprocal basis with other state revenue officers or the Internal Revenue Service. N.C. Gen. Stat. sec. 105-259.

North Dakota–Secrecy of income tax returns shall be guarded. N.D. Cent. Code sec. 57-38-57.

Ohio–Income tax information is confidential. Ohio Rev. Code sec. 5101.18.2.

Oklahoma–Records and files of the tax commission regarding any state tax law shall be considered confidential and privileged. Okla. Stat. Ann. title 68, sec. 205.

Oregon–No officer or employee may make known the amount or source of income or any particulars disclosed in any return. Or. Rev. Stat. sec. 314.835.

Rhode Island–Unlawful to reveal information on personal income tax return. The maximum penalty is $1,000 and one year. R.I. Gen. Laws sec. 44-30-95(c).

South Carolina–A state employee shall be dismissed for breaching confidentiality of sales tax information. S.C. Code sec. 12-7-1680.

South Dakota–Tax records are confidential except by "proper judicial order." S.D. Codified Laws Ann. sec. 10-1-28.1.

Tennessee–Records of taxpayers in the department of revenue shall be treated as confidential. Tenn. Code Ann. sec. 67-1-110(5).

Utah–Individual income tax returns are confidential. Utah Code Ann. sec. 59-1-403.

Vermont–An income tax preparer must declare that he or she has not or will not use any information furnished by a taxpayer for any purpose other than to prepare a return. Vt. Stat. Ann. title 32, sec. 5901. Taxpayer information in state government is confidential. Title 32, sec. 3102.

Virginia–State tax information on individuals is exempt from mandatory disclosure, but may be released at discretion of the tax agency. Va. Code sec. 2.1-342(B)(3).

Tax information may not be disclosed except under judicial process. Exceptions: exchanges with out-of-state tax authorities and release of details about real estate. Sec. 58-46.

The freedom of information act exempts personal tax information from mandatory disclosure. Code sec. 2.2-3705.7(1). In addition Sec. 58.1-3 makes it a misdemeanor to release tax information about individuals.

Washington–Information required of any taxpayer in the collection and assessment of any tax, if disclosure of the information to others would violate taxpayer's right to privacy, is exempt from the definition of a public record and therefore not open to the public. Wash. Rev. Code Ann. sec. 42.17.310(1)(c).

West Virginia–The principle of confidentiality is recognized in tax information, with exceptions. W.Va. Code sec. 11-10-5s.

Wisconsin–Tax return information may not be divulged except for "publication in any newspaper of information lawfully derived from income tax or gift tax returns for purposes of argument" and "any public speaker... referring to such information in any address." Residents of the state (and of other states with reciprocal arrangements) may obtain, for $1, the net income tax or gift tax reported by another individual or corporation, provided the taxpayer is informed of this within 24 hours. Legislators, federal and local government officials and persons with court authorization may examine tax returns, but only in the discharge of their duties. The person who submitted a tax return, or his or her attorney, may see it. Each year, localities receive lists of persons and amounts of taxes paid, information that is to be kept confidential. Wis. Stat. Ann. sec. 71.78. [See 1978-79 book.]

Federal law–Federal tax returns are confidential with certain exceptions. They may be disclosed with the consent of the taxpayer or his or her spouse; upon written request of state tax authorities; to the administrator of an estate and a deceased taxpayer's kin; to committees of Congress; to the Departments of Justice or Treasury for tax investigations; to federal investigators in non-tax cases (but only with a court order); for statistical surveys and to track down parents who have failed to meet child support obligations. The President is entitled to see selected individual tax information, but only if the request is in writing from the President himself and only if he reports to Congress each quarter with the names of individuals involved. The President and heads of agencies are also entitled to know whether prospective appointments to major government positions are under suspicion of violating tax laws. 26 U.S.C. 6103. [See 1978-79 book.]

A federal employee may not browse through individual tax return information, even if not disclosing them, without a need to know. If this occurs, the taxpayer will be notified. 26 U.S.C. 6103.

Firms and persons who regularly prepare income tax returns for others may not disclose personal tax information nor use it for other purposes, except for certain exceptions listed in Internal Revenue Service regulations. 42 U.S.C. 7216.

TELEPHONE SERVICES
(Including Telephone Solicitation)

Alabama–Telemarketers must abide by their own do-not-call lists, but there are 25 categories of businesses exempted. Ala. Code 8-19C-2.

Alaska–There may be no telephone solicitation to a person identified in a telephone directory as not wanting it. Phone companies are required to make these notations. There may be no use of automatic dialers and recording devices. Alaska Stat. sec. 45. 50.475. The state runs a do-not call list that telemarketers must consult. Sec. 45.50.475.

Arizona–It is a misdemeanor to use an automated dialing device for commercial sales. Ariz. Rev. Stat. sec. 13-2919. There may be no commercial blocking of caller ID. Telemarketing is restricted. There may be no sales calls once a person has said that he or she does not want them. Sec. 44-1278.

The law punishes obtaining, selling, or soliciting the numbers dialed to or from a person's telephone with pretext and without consent. Rev. Stat. sec. 44-1376.

Arkansas–Automatic dialing and recorded messages for sales calls are illegal. Ark. Code Ann. sec. 5-63-204. There is a state-run do-not-call list, and every telemarketing company must purchase the list from the attorney general's office. Sec. 29-30-178 Solicitors may not block their numbers from a consumer's call-number display. Sec. 4-99-302.

California–State law outlaws automatic recording devices in telephone sales, except with consent and a live operator introducing the message. Cal. Pub. Util. Code sec. 2873 and 2874.

"Caller ID," a service that displays the incoming telephone number on a person's telephone, may be offered by telephone companies only if they also offer a free service whereby callers may block the display ("per-call blocking"). A phone company may not charge for unlisted service. There may be no withholding of the display of an incoming phone number by a company engaged in telemarketing. Pub. Util. Code sec. 2893.

Telemarketers must have a live person available on any sales call, preventing "dead air" calling. Pub. Util. Code sec. 2875.5. Unsolicited fax advertisements are prohibited. Cal. Bus. Code sec. 17538.4.

The attorney general maintains a do-not-call list. 17590. Telephone companies may not include unlisted "telephone access numbers" on lists they rent. Nor may they disclose certain subscriber information. Pub. Util. Code sec. 2891.1. Lists of numbers dialed by customers may not be released to competing phone companies without consent. Pub. Util. Code sec. 2891. Nothing in the law prevents the Public Utilities Commission from protecting customer privacy. Pub. Util. Code sec. 2882.5.

Telemarketers may not conduct "phantom calling" or "dead calls," in which no operator or recording is heard when a person answers (because no one is cur-rently available in the telemarketing operation). Pub. Util. Code sec. 2875.5.

It is a crime punishable by a fine, imprisonment, or both, to purchase, sell, offer to purchase or sell, or conspire to purchase or sell, without the written consent of the subscriber, or to procure through fraud or deceit a telephone-calling pattern record or list. Penal Code sec. 638.

Colorado–Limits use of automated sales devices. Colo. Rev. Stat. sec. 18-9-311.

"Trading in telephone records," is a misdemeanor. It is defined as the unauthorized buying or selling of a person's telephone information and the possession of a person's telephone records with the intent to do harm. The law applies to both land-line and wireless telephones and defines "lawful authorization." Sec. 18-13-125.

Connecticut–The Consumer Protection Agency operates a do-not-call list. Conn. Gen. Stat. Ann. sec. 42-288a.

It is unlawful to use a device that transmits an unsolicited telephone message and that does not hang up when the recipient of the solicitation hangs up. Sec. 16-256e. There is a right to sue for violations. It is unlawful to transmit unsolicited facsimile sales messages. Sec. 52-570c.

The law prohibits procuring "a telephone record" without consent, selling a record without consent, or receiving a record known to have been procured by pretext, without consent. Gen. Stat. Ann. sec. 18-13-125.

District of Columbia–Auto dialers are prohibited. D.C. Code Ann. sec. 43-1418.

Florida–The Department of Agriculture and Consumer Services maintains a do-not-call list. The charge to be listed is $10 initially and $5 a year to renew. It is published quarterly to telemarketers and they are prohibited from selling the information. Fla. Stat. Ann. sec. 501.059(3)(a).

State law prohibits the use of telephone solicitation systems that make use of automatic dialing devices and tape players, with limited exceptions. Sec. 365.165.

Telephone sellers must identify themselves and hang up upon a negative response. Telephone customers may have a listing of "No sales solicitation calls" in the directory. Sellers may not call them, nor persons who are unlisted. Sec. 501.059.

There is a $500 civil penalty for sending an unsolicited facsimile advertisement. Sec. 365.1657.

Florida's law on pretexting for calling records is similar to Connecticut's but exempts law enforcement and phone companies for specified purposes. Sec. 817.484.

Georgia–Automatic dialing and recorded message equipment may not be used if unattended by an operator, nor after 9 p.m. A permit is required. Ga. Code Ann. sec. 46-5-23.

The Public Service Commission maintains a quarterly do-not-call list that telemarketers must obey. Sec. 46-5-27. Phone numbers obtained through call number display or "Caller ID" may not be disclosed or used for sales. Sec. 46-5-173. Sec. 10-5B-4 prohibits blocking display of caller ID by telephone solicitors.

The state prohibits buying and selling a telephone customer's calling records. Code Ann. sec. 16-11-3.

Hawaii–The law prohibits all autodialers selling "goods and wares." Haw. Rev. Stat. sec 445-184.

The Office of Consumer Protection enforces the law that requires companies to have a procedure for deleting phone numbers of persons who are called and who ask to receive no more sales calls from that company. Rev. Stat. sec. 481P-5.

Idaho–The attorney general's office maintains the state's "do-not-call" list. Idaho Code sec. 48-1003A.

Illinois–Telemarketing is regulated. 815 ILCS 413/15.

No one may send an unsolicited facsimile message without believing he or she has permission. 720 ILCS 5/26-3.

The do-not-call list maintained by the Commerce Commission is merged into the federal list. 815 ILCS 402/10.

Indiana–A person who solicits whether live or through the use of an autodialer may not block display of number or identity. Ind. Code Ann. sec. 24-5-12-25.

A telephone solicitor may not make a sales call to a number listed on the attorney general's do-not-call list..Charities are covered by the law. Sec. 24-4.7-4-1. Telephone solicitors must be registered. Sec. 24-5-12.

Iowa–It is unlawful to disturb the right of privacy of any person by repeated anonymous telephone calls. Iowa Code Ann. sec. 708.7.

Kansas–The "pitchster" must ask within ten seconds, "Are you interested" and if the answer is no, hang up. Kans. Stat. sec. 50-670.

Kentucky–Certain companies that are *engaged primarily in the business of conducting telephone solicitations* must abide by a state-run do-not-call list. Citizens may register for the list through a written form. KRS 367.46951.

Use of automatic dialers is limited. Sec. 367.461.

Louisiana–Consumers may register for the state do-not-call list by toll-free telephone or on-line, and telemarketers must pay for the list and abide by it. La. Rev. Stat. Ann. sec 45: 844-14.

Maine–"Telephone subscribers have a right to privacy and the protection of this right to privacy is of paramount concern to the State." A telephone customer is entitled to free *per-call* blocking, to defeat the display of one's phone number to the person called by way of Caller ID. Customers asserting a specific need based on health or safety must be provided free *per-line* blocking. Me. Rev. Stat. Ann. title 35-A, sec. 7101-A through 5.

No sales calls may be made to persons who have said they do not wish them; only one call per eight hours; name and address of the telemarketer must be announced in the first minute of a call. Title 10, sec. 1498. See also title 35-A, sec. 7103.

Telemarketers doing business in Maine must consult a national do-not-call list before calling consumers in Maine. Title 69A, sec. 4690A.

Maryland–Automated devices for sales or surveys must disconnect when the called party hangs up. Prerecorded messages for sales are prohibited. Md. Pub. Util. Code 8-204. Using prerecorded devices to emulate an emergency is a crime. Md. Crim. Law sec. 9-603.

Unsolicited faxes are prohibited. Sec. 14-1313.

The law on accessing telephone-calling records is similar to Florida's. Crim. Code 7-304.

Massachusetts–A customer is given an opportunity to notify a telephone company and to prohibit automated sales calls. Mass. Gen. Laws Ann. ch. 159, sec. 19B-E.

Gen. Laws Ann. ch. 159C creates a do-not-call list in the Office of Consumer Affairs and Business Regulation and outlaws certain automated devices and solicitation practices.

Michigan–"A home solicitation sale shall not be made by telephonic solicitation using in whole or in part a recorded message." Harassment or stalking by telephone are offenses. Mich. Comp. Laws Ann. sec. 445.111a. Customer dialing information may be released to competitors. 484.2305. See also 484.125.

State law prohibits commercial ID blocking. Sec. 484.125.

The identity-theft act has been amended to prohibit using the personal information of another to obtain "a confidential telephone record" (narrowly defined) or procuring or receiving "the confidential telephone record of another" without consent. Comp. Laws sec. 445.65a, sec. 5.

Minnesota–Automatic dialing and announcing devices may not be used without consent; there must be a live operator; and the calling system must disconnect when the customer hangs up. Minn. Stat. Ann. sec. 325E.26-31.

All commercial telemarketers must subscribe to a do-not call list maintained by the Department of Commerce. Consulting the federal do-not-call list complies with the requirement. Exempted are calls from charitable and political organizations, businesses with a prior relationship, or a business that intended to complete the sale face-to-face. Telemarketers may not disable consumers' caller ID capability. Stat. Ann. sec.325E.311 to 316.

The law on calling records is similar to Connecticut's, disallowing "knowingly procuring, selling, or receiving customer phone records without the customer's authorization." Sec. 325F.675.

Missouri–A do-not-call list is maintained by the attorney general. Mo. Ann. Stat. sec. 407.1098. Telemarketers may not block caller ID. Sec. 407.1104.

Montana–A company may not use automated telephone equipment for dialing numbers and making recorded sales messages except to present customers under certain circumstances or if a live operator asks permission before a recorded message, according to a 1991 law. Mont. Code Ann. 45-8-216.

Nebraska–Solicitors must have a permit from the Public Service Commission to use automated devices and must agree to use a human operator beforehand and have the device disconnect when the person called hangs up. Neb. Rev. Stat. sec. 87-307.

Nevada–Unsolicited fax advertisements are prohibited. Nev. Rev. Stat. sec. 207.325.

New Hampshire–Users of automatic dialers must register with the state, automatically disconnect, and identify themselves to persons called. The law on commercial blocking of caller ID is similar to Indiana's law. N.H. Rev. Stat. Ann. sec. 359-E:1 through 6.

New Jersey–Automated dialing devices are prohibited, and there must be a live operator and the consent of a consumer before playing a recorded message for commercial solicitation. N.J. Stat. Ann. 17-48.

New Mexico–The telemarketer must identify itself. Calls between 9 a.m. and 9 p.m. only. N.M. Stat. Ann. sec. 57-12-22.

New York–A do-not call list is maintained by the Consumer Protection Board. N.Y. Gen. Bus. Law sec. 399-Z. The law on commercial blocking of caller ID is similar to Indiana's law. Sec. 399-P. It is illegal to send unsolicited facsimile messages. There is a $100 fine. Sec. 396-aa.

See also **Mailing Lists**.

The "consumer communication protection act" prohibits sales of a person's calling records and authorizes the state attorney general to bring enforcement actions, like injunctions. Gen. Bus. Law sec. 399-dd and Penal Law 250.30.

North Carolina–Automated devices are prohibited except with a live operator. Charitable groups and pollsters are exempt. N.C. Gen. Sta. sec. 75-30.

North Dakota–A telephone company offering call-number display (Caller ID) must also offer a free per-call blocking feature to any subscriber. The company must also advise all customers 30 days in advance before offering Caller ID. N.D. Cent. Code 49-21-01.6.

Unsolicited facsimile messages are prohibited. Sec. 51-07-23.

Oklahoma–Okla. Stat. title 21, secs. 1742.1 through 4 prohibits revealing telephone records, with exceptions. The attorney general maintains a do-not-call list. Title 20, sec. 775B.1.

Oregon–The attorney general maintains a do-not-call list that telemarketers must consult every month. Or. Rev. Stat. sec. 646.561. A telephone solicitor must identify him or herself within 30 seconds and hang up upon a negative response. Sec. 646.611. Auto dialers and recording devices are prohibited for sales. Sec. 759.290. No telephone sales agreement is valid unless written and signed. Sec. 83.715.

Once a person has sent a notice that he or she does not want to receive facsimile messages from someone, that person must discontinue the messages. Sec. 646.872.

Pennsylvania–Caller ID is permitted only when free per-line blocking is also offered. Pa. Stat. Ann. title 66, sec. 2906.

Telemarketers must abide by the attorney general's do-not-call list. Stat. Ann. title 73, sec 2241.

Rhode Island–Telephone sales devices must hang up when the consumer does. R.I. Gen. Laws sec. 11-35-26. Solicitors must be registered. Sec. 5-61-1.

Sending unsolicited fax advertisements is a misdemeanor. Sec. 11-35-27.

The nation's first law against disclosing or procuring telephone-calling records makes selling, obtaining, or disclosing calling records a crime and allows a victim to sue for damages. Disclosure of up to ten records is a misdemeanor; disclosing more is a felony. There are exceptions: with consent or a court order or to a law enforcement agency. Gen. Laws. 39-2-24.

Tennessee–Phone companies must tell customers twice a year how to get on a state-run do-not-call list. Telemarketers for businesses and non-profits must purchase the list each year. Tenn. Code Ann. sec. 65-4-405. The law on blocking caller ID is similar to Indiana's. Sec. 65-4-403.

There is a criminal penalty for unsolicited recorded messages. Callers must use a live voice to identify the company and the purpose of the call and to ask for permission to play a recorded message. Sec. 47-18-1501. Unsolicited fax messages are illegal. Sec. 47-18-1602.

Telephone sales devices must hang up when the consumer does. Sec. 39-6-1102.

Texas–The law on caller ID blocking is similar to Indiana's. 4 Bus. and Commerce Code Sec. 43.051. Telemarketers must abide by a do-not-call list. Sec. 43.101. The commission must approve uses of automated devices, which may not be "used for random dialing or to dial numbers by successively increasing or decreasing integers." The sales person must identify him or herself and disconnect within ten seconds of hanging up. No calls are permitted late at night or Sunday mornings. Tex. Rev. Civ. Stat. Ann. art. 1446c, sec. 111 through 119. See also Tex. Bus. & Comm. Code Ann. sec. 35.47.

Utah–The name, address and phone number of the telemarketer must be announced within 30 seconds, and there may be calls only between 9 a.m. and 8 p.m. Companies must register with the state. Utah Code Ann. sec. 13-25-1. Law on blocking caller ID similar to Indiana's. Sec. 13-25a-103(6).

Virginia–It is a misdemeanor to use "recorded solicitation calls which do not disengage or terminate when the party called replaces the receiver." Va. Code sec. 18.2-425.1. Law on blocking caller ID similar to Indiana's. Sec. 59.1-513.

Pretexting to get phone-calling records is a misdemeanor offense. Stat. Ann. title 18.2, sec.152.17.

Washington–No unsolicited faxes may be sent unless there is a previous relationship. No unsolicited faxes may be sent to government agencies. Wash. Rev. Code Ann. 80.36.540.

A customer may collect $500 in damages if unsolicited calls are made by automatic devices. Sec. 80.36.390 and 400.

The law prohibits sales of phone-calling records without consent. Victims may file lawsuits. Rev. Code sec. 9.26A, sec. 1.

Wisconsin–"No person may use an electronically prerecorded message in telephone solicitation without the consent of the person called." Wisc. Stat. Ann. sec. 134.72.

There may be no Caller ID offered without free per-call blocking and, in abuse cases, per-line blocking. Sec. 196-207(2).

The law on procuring telephone-call records is similar to Arizona's. Stat. Ann. sec. 100-525.

The Department of Agriculture, Trade, and Consumer Protection enforces the do-not-call list. Sec 100.52.

Wyoming–It is a misdemeanor to make sales calls with an automatic telephone system. Wyo. Stat. sec. 6-6-104.

Federal law–The Federal Trade Commission is empowered to create a national do-not-call list, whereby residential customers may call a toll-free number or go online and include their phone numbers on the list. Telemarketing companies must consult the list and not call numbers on the list. Wireless devices are protected. Some states enforce their do-not-call lists by incorporating their state list with the federal list. 15 U.S.C. 6101. One-time registration is permanent.

The Telephone Consumer Protection Act of 1991, 47 U.S.C. 227, requires prior express written consent for all autodialed or prerecorded telemarketing calls to wireless numbers and residential lines, according to 2012 rules of the Federal Communications Commission. Calls from health providers subject to the HIPAA law, political campaigns, and charities are exempt, as are emergency notifications.

The Telemarketing and Consumer Fraud and Abuse Prevention Act of 1994 and its regulations say that companies making sales calls to residences must promptly identify themselves and their product or service. They must announce the cost before asking for money. They must have express, verifiable authorization (in writing or tape-recorded) before debiting a consumer's checking account. They may call only between 8 a.m. and 9 p.m. and they may not call anybody who has previously told them that they do not want sales calls. Telemarketing may not be conducted in a pattern that is abusive of consumers' privacy. 15 U.S.C. 6101 to 6108.

A phone company must disclose to a customer (who requests in writing) the customer's calling information that the phone company must provide by law to its competitors (called "customer proprietary network information," CPNI). 47 U.S.C. 222(c)&(d).

It is a federal crime to buy or acquire or receive or sell "confidential telephone information," defined as information that appears on a customer's bill. Internet Protocol-enabled voice services are protected. State laws are not preempted. 18 U.S.C. 1039.

TESTING IN EMPLOYMENT
(Including Urinalysis, Genetic, and Blood Tests)

Arkansas–Employers may not request genetics tests. Ark. Code Ann. sec. 11-5-401.

Arizona–Employers may not use **genetic test results** in employment decision. Ariz. Rev. Stat. Ann. sec. 41-1463.

California–There may be no discrimination in employment based on "**genetic characteristics**." Cal. Gov. Code sec. 12940 and sec. 12926.

See also **Polygraphs**.

Connecticut–Employers may not ask about or discharge due to **genetic data**. Conn. Gen. Stat. sec. 46a-60.

Employers must inform persons in writing that a **urinalysis** test will be used. They must perform two tests to confirm a positive result. Employers may test only when there is a "reasonable suspicion that the employee is under the influence of drugs or alcohol which adversely affects or could affect such employee's job performance." Employees or applicants are entitled to copies of positive test results, and all results must remain confidential. Management may not observe employees when they provide specimens. Exceptions to the prohibition against random testing are government employees, those covered by federal law, those in employee-assistance programs, and those in "safety-sensitive occupations" labeled by the State Commissioner of Labor. Sec. 31-51t.

Testing for HIV must be confidential. Sec. 19a-581.

See also **Polygraphs**.

Delaware–Employers may not discriminate based on **genetic information**. Del. Code Ann. title 19 sec. 711.

Florida–**Drug testing** in the workplace, including random testing, is allowed, but restricted. Fla. Stat. sec. 440.102 . Drug testing of state employees is governed by sec. 112.0455.

A person must be informed if **genetic information** was used to deny employment, mortgage, credit, loan or educational opportunity. Sec. 760.40.

Hawaii–Before a **drug test**, employees must be told which illegal drugs will be tested and given an opportunity to declare which prescription drugs may show up in the test. Ha. Rev. Stat. sec. 329B.

Employers may not discriminate based on genetics results. Rev. Stat. 431:10A-118.

Illinois–An employer shall treat **genetic testing information** consistent with federal law, including the Americans with Disabilities Act. 410 ILCS 513/25.

Iowa–Iowa law limits testing for the HIV virus as a condition of employment. Iowa Code Ann. Sec. 216.6.

Employers may not solicit, require, or administer **genetic tests** as a condition of employment. Sec. 729.6.

See **Medical Records** for law on HIV testing.

Louisiana–All elected officials, welfare recipients, state contractors and vendors, college students receiving state aid, and most state employees operating vehicles must be tested for drugs, according to a 1997 law that will not take effect until the legislature allocates funds. La. Rev. Stat. Ann. sec. 49:1021.

The state workers' compensation law requires **drug testing** indirectly. Sec. 23:1601.

Employers may not require or request DNA testing. Rev. Stat. Ann. sec. 23:302.

Kansas–An employer may not seek or use **genetic information** to distinguish, discriminate or restrict an employee or prospective employee. Kans. Stat. Ann. sec. 44-1009.

Maine–Employers may require **urine testing** only after they have employee assistance programs, written policies, and proper procedures in place. Employees must be consulted in the development of drug-testing policies, and the state Department of Labor must approve. Me. Rev. Stat. Ann. title 26, sec. 681-690.

An employer may not fire or fail to hire a person based on genetic information or refusal to take a **genetic test**. Title 5 sec. 19302.

Maryland–**Testing of urine** specimens in places of employment must be conducted in a certified laboratory, which must be identified for employees. An employee may have an independent test, at his or her expense. Md. Gen. Health Law sec. 17-214.1.

Employers may not request DNA testing. Ann Code art. 49B, secs. 15 and 16.

Massachusetts–It is unlawful to use **genetic information** in hiring or setting terms and conditions of employment. Mass. Gen. Laws Ann. ch. 151B sec. 4.

Honesty testing in employment is prohibited. Ch. 149, sec. 19B.

See also **Polygraphs**.

Michigan–Employer may not require a **genetic test** as condition of employment. Mich. Comp Laws Ann. sec. 37.1202.

Requiring employees to submit to genetics tests is illegal. Comp. Laws Ann. sec. 37.1201.

See also **Polygraphs**.

Minnesota–Random **drug and alcohol testing** in the workplace may be conducted in "safety-sensitive positions." Otherwise, testing of employees must be part of a physical exam with two weeks' notice, pursuant to a reasonable suspicion of impairment or as part of a treatment program. If one applicant is tested, all applicants for the same position must be tested. Employers must have written policies. No adverse action may be based on an original positive result, and no discharge may be based even on a confirmed positive result if this was the first such result for the employee. Test results are confidential, and the individual has a right to inspect the information when it is in a personnel file. Minn. Stat. Ann. sec. 181.950.

See also **Polygraphs**.

No employer may request or collect genetic information. Stat. Ann. sec. 181.974.

Missouri–Employer may not require a test or use **genetic information** except "when such information is directly related to a person's ability to perform assigned job responsibilities." Mo. Rev. Stat. sec. 375.1306.

Montana–Urine and blood testing is permitted in safety-sensitive positions. State law is silent on testing of other employees. An employer's testing program must meet certain standards, and an employee must be given an opportunity to rebut an original test result. Mont. Code Ann. sec. 39-2-205.

Nebraska–Testing of breath or bodily fluids of employees is regulated; tests are permissible if the results are confirmed. Employees have a right to a retest. There are limits on disclosure. Tampering with specimens is a misdemeanor. Employees may be fired for refusing to take a **urine or breath test**. Neb. Rev. Stat. sec. 48-1901.

See also **Polygraphs**.

Employers may not require genetics tests nor discriminate based on them. Rev. Stat. sec. 48-236.

Nevada–An employer may not ask or encourage a person to get a **genetic test** nor deny employment based on genetic information. Nev. Rev. Stat. sec. 613.345.

New Hampshire–The law on **genetic tests** is similar to Rhode Island's N.H. Rev. Stat. Ann. sec. 141-H:3.

New Jersey–Employers may not screen employees or applicants based on **genetic information**. N.J. Rev. Stat. 10:5-12. [See 1997 book.]

New Mexico–Testing for HIV may not be a condition of employment. N.M. Stat. Ann. sec. 28-10A-1.

New York–Unlawful to discriminate based on "**genetic disposition** or carrier status." N.Y. Exec. sec. 296.

North Carolina–An employer may not deny employment or fire a person on the basis of any **genetic information** or if the person requires a genetic test or counseling. N.C. Gen. Stat. sec. 95-28.1A.

An employer may test for the AIDS virus (HIV) as part of an annual physical and may fire a person with the AIDS virus if there is a risk to others. Sec. 130A-148(i).

All laboratories for **urine testing** must be certified. Sec. 95-232.

North Dakota–All testing for HIV is to be confidential and conducted only with consent. N.D. Cent. Code sec. 23-07.5-01.

Oklahoma–An employer may not seek, obtain or use **genetic information** in hiring decisions nor require a genetic test Okla. Stat. title 36 sec. 3414.2.

Oregon–Discipline based on an unconfirmed positive **drug test** is not allowed. Or. Rev. Stat. 438.435.

The law on **genetic screening** is similar to Iowa's. Sec. 659A.303.

The use of breathalyzers in the workplace is severely limited. Sec. 659.225.

Pennsylvania–Testing for HIV is to be confidential and with consent. Pa. Stat. Ann. title 35, sec. 7601-12.

Rhode Island–Urinalysis and blood testing is permitted only when there are reasonable grounds (similar to Connecticut's law). Tests must be conducted in private and verified. The employee must have a chance to refute the results. R.I. Gen. Laws sec. 28-6.5-1.

An employer may not request or require **genetic testing** or use predictors based on genetic profiles. R.I. Gen. Laws 28-6-7.1.

See also **Polygraphs**.

South Dakota–Employers may not use the results of genetics tests for employment decisions. S.D. Codified Laws. Ann. 60-2-20.

Texas–It is unlawful to discriminate based on **genetic information** or refusal to take a test. Tex. Labor Code Ann. sec. 24.402.

It is unlawful to discriminate in hiring, discharging, or other employment decisions based on genetic information or an individual's refusal to submit to a genetic test. Lab. Code Ann. sec. 21.402.

Utah–Employers must have written policies on **alcohol and drug testing** and show due regard for employees' privacy. Testing is permitted, and the law limits the liability of employers because of incorrect test results or other causes, if the employer has complied with the law. Utah Code Ann. sec. 34-38-1.

See also **Polygraphs**.

Employers may not consider the results of genetics testing in employment decisions. Code Ann. sec. 26-45-101.

Vermont–No employer shall require **DNA tests**, use DNA information or results of DNA counseling of a person or a family member in employment decisions. Vt. Stat. Ann. title 18 sec. 9333.

The law on **drug testing** is similar to Connecticut's. As in Connecticut, an applicant must be given advance notice of a drug test. Title 21, sec. 511.

State law prohibits HIV testing as a condition of employment and prohibits discrimination based on a positive blood test result. Title 21, sec. 495(6) and (7).

Virginia–Testing for HIV is to be confidential and with consent. Va. Code sec. 32.1-36.1 and 32.1-37.2.

Employers may not request genetics tests. Stat. Ann. title.18, sec. 9333.

Washington–Similar to Vermont's law on HIV testing. Wash. Rev. Code Ann. sec. 49.60.172.

Wisconsin–The law on **genetic tests** is similar to Rhode Island's. Wis. Stat. Ann. sec. 111.372 and 111.39.

With exceptions, no AIDS testing is permitted in employment. Sec. 103.15.

See also **Polygraphs**.

Federal law–Access to and use of genetic information about individuals in employment (and in group health-insurance coverage) is restricted. 42 USC 2000 ff. The law does not preempt stricter state laws or limit the authority of a health-care professional to request an individual to undergo a genetic test.

TRACKING TECHNOLOGIES

Arkansas–The owner of a vehicle or long-term lessee owns the data in an "event-data recorder" in a motor vehicle and it may not be retrieved or used without consent. Ark. Code Ann. sec. 27-37-103.

California–Manufacturers that install "event-data recorders" in vehicles must disclose that fact in the owner's manual. Only certain persons may have access. Veh. Code sec. 9951. Vehicle-rental companies are prohibited from using, accessing, or obtaining information relating to a renter's use of a rental vehicle obtained using on-board electronic surveillance technology ("black boxes"), except in certain limited circumstances. A renter's consent is necessary before using or disclosing information about the renter's use of the vehicle. Civ. Code sec. 1936.

Bars, car dealers, and others may not collect information by swiping a driver's license for any purpose other than verifying age or authenticity of the license. Civ. Code sec. 1798.90.1.

It is a misdemeanor (with several exceptions) to steal data from radio-frequency identification (RFID) cards, called skimming, without the person's knowledge or consent. It also is a misdemeanor to reveal the operational system keys used in a contactless identification document. Civil Code sec. 1798.79.

"A person shall not require, coerce, or compel any other individual to undergo the subcutaneous implanting of an identification device." The law "shall not in any way modify existing statutory or case law regarding the rights of parents or guardians, the rights of children or minors, or the rights of dependent adults." Cal. Civ. Code 52.7. See also **Computer Crime**.

No person or entity shall use an electronic tracking device on a vehicle to determine the location or movement of a person, except with consent or by law enforcement. Violation could result in loss of an investigator's license and/or misdemeanor conviction. Penal Code sec. 637.7.

It is a tort to attempt to capture, in a manner that is offensive to a reasonable person, any type of visual image, sound recording, or other physical impression of a person even from afar. Civ. Code 1708.8 (a).

Colorado–"A manufacturer of a motor vehicle that is sold or leased with an event-data recorder shall in bold-faced type disclose, in the owner's manual, that the vehicle is so equipped and, if so, the type of data recorded." Colo. Rev. Stat. sec. 12-6-401.

Connecticut–"No person, except the registered owner of the motor vehicle that contains the event data recorder, or the registered owner's representative, may retrieve, obtain or use data stored on or transmitted from the event-data recorder unless [consent, by police with a warrant, by legal process in a civil action, by a dealer, or for motor safety]. Conn. Gen. Stat. Ann. sec. 14-164a.

Maine–The state restricts access to event-data recorders in autos. Me. Rev. Stat. Ann. title 29-A, sec. 1.

Missouri–"No employer shall require an employee to have [subcutaneous or surgically implanted] personal identification microchip technology implanted into an employee for any reason." This is a misdemeanor. Mo. Rev. Stat. sec. 285.035. 1.

Nevada–"Black box" recorders may not be installed in automobiles without consent of the owner or lessee. Nev. Rev. Stat. sec. 484.638.

New Hampshire–A manufacturer must disclose the presence of an event-data recorder in a new automobile. N. H. Rev. Stat. ann. sec. 357-G:1.

New York – In 2005 the state was the second to enact restrictions on information in auto event-data recorders. N.Y. Veh. & Traffic Law. tit. 4A16, sec. 416-B.

Missouri–"No employer shall require an employee to have [subcutaneous or surgically implanted] personal identification microchip technology implanted into an employee for any reason." This is a misdemeanor. Mo. Rev. Stat. sec. 285.035. 1.

North Dakota–Manufacturers must notify buyers of the presence of an event-recording device in an auto. The data may be used only for service or improving safety. N.D. Cent. Code sec. 51-07.28.

Sec. 12.1-15-06 says, "A person may not require that an individual have inserted into that individual's body a microchip containing a radio-frequency identification device. A violation is a class A misdemeanor."

Oregon–There is access to data in vehicle event-data recorders by search warrant, with owner consent and, with difficulty, in civil actions. Ore. Rev. Stat. sec. 644.

Rhode Island–There are restrictions on the use of radio-frequency identification devices (RFID) for the purpose of tracking the movement or identity of a student while on school grounds, at school functions or on school buses. RFID data in highway-toll transactions is not considered public information. R.I. Gen. Laws 27-5-3.7.

Texas–The law on event-data recorders in motor vehicles is similar to the law in Arkansas. Tex. Trans. Code sec. 547.615.

Virginia–The law provides a property interest to vehicle owners in event-data recorder information even after the vehicle is sold. Va. Code sec. 46.2-1088.6.

Washington–"A person that intentionally scans another person's identification device remotely, without that person's prior knowledge and prior consent, for the purpose of fraud, identity theft, or for any other illegal purpose, shall be guilty of a class C felony. The aim of the law is cover radio-frequency identification tags (RFID). Stated in the findings of the legislation: "The legislature finds that Washington State, from its inception, has recognized the importance of maintaining individual privacy." Wash. Rev. Code 19.300.020.

It is a misdemeanor to access data in a vehicle recorder device except as permitted in the statute. Sec. 46.35.

Wisconsin–"No person may require an individual to undergo the implanting of a microchip. Any person who violates [this law] may be required to forfeit not more than $10,000." Each day of continued violation constitutes a separate offense. Wisc. Stat. Ann. 146.25.

APPENDIX – CANADIAN LAWS

BANK RECORDS

Federal law–The Bank Act authorizes the government to make regulations "governing the use by a bank of any information supplied to the bank by its customers." S. C. 1991, c. 46.

COMPUTER CRIME

Alberta–See **Private Sector.**

Ontario–See **Medical Records.**

Federal law–Fraudulently obtaining a computer service or intercepting a system or using a computer in a crime or destroying data or obstructing data services is an offense. R.S.C. 1985, c. C-46. Sec. 430 (1.1) of the same chapter of the Criminal Code says that destroying or altering data or interfering with the use of data is criminal mischief.

CREDIT REPORTING

British Columbia–The credit reporting law is similar to Manitoba's. The consent of the consumer is necessary to conduct a credit check. There is a right to copy and to challenge one's own report. Credit bureaus must register with the province. R.S.B.C. 1979, c. 78.

Manitoba–Anyone who supplies personal investigatory reports for profit must register with the government and gather information only for specified purposes (generally credit, insurance, or employment) and only with the consent of the person involved.

There may be no reference to race, religion, ethnicity, or religious or political beliefs in a credit report. No bankruptcy older than 14 years may be reported. The individual has a right to see the report and to protest a report. Personal Investigations Act, S.M. 1971, c. 23.

Nova Scotia–The Consumer Reporting Act, S.N.S. 1973, C. 4, is similar to Manitoba's act, with a six-year limit on bankruptcies and a seven-year limit on criminal convictions. Credit bureaus must meet standards of accuracy.

Ontario–An Act to control the storage and supply of personal information for rating purposes, S.O. 1973, c. 97, resembles Manitoba's.

Prince Edward Island–The Consumer Reporting Act, R.S.P.E.I. 1974, c. C-18, is identical to Manitoba's.

Saskatchewan–The Credit Reporting Agencies Act, R.S.S. 1978, c. C-44, resembles Manitoba's.

ELECTRONIC SURVEILLANCE

Ontario–Disclosure of a telephone conversation by a person who is not intended to be a party to the conversation is prohibited. Telephone Act sec. 112 In addition the Criminal Code prohibits intercepting private conversations. R.S.O. 1985, c. C-46.

Federal law–The Canadian Radio-Television Communications Commission is authorized to act to protect the privacy of individuals. R.S.C. 1993, c. 38.

GOVERNMENT INFORMATION ON INDIVIDUALS

Alberta–The Protection of Privacy Act provides citizens access to their own data and limits disclosure of personal information by provincial agencies. S.A. 1994, c. F-18.5.

British Columbia–The Freedom of Information and Protection of Privacy Act is similar to Ontario's, with a Information and Privacy Commissioner authorized to resolve complaints and to issue orders. S.B.C. 1992, c. 61.

Manitoba–The freedom of information law permits access to government documents and a right to correct personal information. An ombudsman resolves complaints. S.M 1985-86, c. 6.

New Brunswick–The Right to Information Act prevents disclosure to third parties of personal information that was provided on a confidential basis to provincial government agencies. S.N.B., c. R-10.3. The act is not as comprehensive as the laws in Ontario or Quebec.

Newfoundland–The Freedom of Information Act is similar to New Brunswick's. S.N. 1981, c. 5.

Northwest Territories–The Access to Information and Protection of Privacy Act is similar to Ontario's. S.N.W.T. 1994, c. 20.

Nova Scotia–Citizens have a right of access and there are broad limits on disclosure of records in provincial agencies and educational organizations, according to the Freedom of Information and Protection of Privacy Act. S.N.S. 1993, c. 5. A review officer considers complaints.

S.N.S. 2008, c. 42 provides authority to a review officer to investigate breaches of privacy when persons and organizations are not satisfied with how information shared with government or public bodies such as hospitals, universities and school boards is handled.

Ontario–The Freedom of Information and Privacy Act, R.S.O. 1987, c. 25, provides a right of access to information about oneself in provincial agencies and provides for the protection of privacy of individuals whose information is stored in government files.

Some information may not be released except to the individual himself or herself: medical, psychiatric or psychological history, employment or educational history, tax information, financial information, racial or ethnic origin, sexual orientation or religious or political beliefs.

Information may be gathered only if expressly authorized by statute and mainly from the individual himself or herself. There is a right to correct or rebut information in the files. The act creates an Information and Privacy Commissioner to investigate complaints and identify problems.

The Municipal Freedom of Information and Protection of Privacy Act, R.S.O. 1987, c. M.56, extends the provisions of the provincial law to all municipalities in Ontario.

Prince Edward Island–The Freedom of Information

and Protection of Privacy Act has been passed by the Provincial Legislature but has not been proclaimed into law by the Lt. Governor-in-Council. Stats. P.E.I., 2001, c.37.

Quebec–The Act Respecting Access to Documents Held by Public Bodies and The Protection of Personal Information, R.S.Q. 1982, c. A-2.1, provides for access to provincial government documents and to provincial records about oneself, with a right to correction. The act is administered by a three-member Access to Information Commission created by the act.

Saskatchewan–There is a Freedom of Information and Privacy Act similar to Ontario's. S.S. 1990-91, c. F-22.01. The Local Authority Freedom of Information and Protection of Privacy Act, S.S. 1990-91, c. L-27.1, extends these provisions to local government agencies.

Yukon–The Access to Information Act, R.S.Y. 1986, c. 1, is similar to the laws in New Brunswick and Newfoundland.

Federal law–The Privacy Act, R.S.C. 1983, c. P-21, controls the collection, use, disclosure, retention, and disposal of personal information by federal departments, whether in computer or manual form. Federal departments must inform individuals how information will be used and must take steps to insure accuracy. Individuals may see and challenge information about themselves.

The act creates an independent Privacy Commissioner with tenure, to audit compliance with the law and hear complaints.

The Access to Information Act, R.S.C. 1985, c. A-1, provides citizens access to government documents, with exceptions, including "personal information that would violate another person's privacy" and creates a separate Information Commissioner.

IDENTITY THEFT

Federal law–Obtaining and possessing identity information with the intent to use it deceptively, dishonestly or fraudulently in the commission of a crime; trafficking in identity information for possible criminal use; and transferring or selling personal information with knowledge of, or recklessness as to, the possible criminal use of the information are offenses under the identity theft law. Bill S-4, 2009, c. 28.

MEDICAL RECORDS

Manitoba–The law provides an individual the right to examine and receive a copy of personal health information maintained by a trustee. Individual may request corrections. The law protects against unauthorized use of information. Act controls collection, use and disclosure of PHIN (Personal Health Information Number). Man. Rev. Stat. 1997 c. 33.5.

Ontario–The Personal Health Information Protection Act, S.O. 2004, c. 3, sched. A includes breach notice requirements "at the first reasonable opportunity," for custodians of personal health information (sec. 12(2)). It lays out guidelines for the collection, use, and disclosure of personal medical information and consent by patients. An individual may have access to his or her own medical file

and "request in writing that the custodian correct the record."

POLYGRAPH TESTS

Ontario–The Employment Standards Act permits an employee to decline to submit to a polygraph test. R.S.O. 1990, c. 14.

PRIVACY STATUTES AND CONSTITUTIONS

British Columbia–The Privacy Act, R.S.B.C. 1979, c. 336 as amended by S.B.C. 1982, c. 46, s. 32, states that it is a tort actionable without proof of damages for a person to willfully and without claim of right to violate the privacy of another. These violations include surveillance, wiretapping, use of likeness or voice for advertising and use of personal letters, diaries, and the like.

Manitoba–Privacy Act, R.S.M. 1987, c. P-125, is similar to the British Columbia statute on torts and surveillance.

Newfoundland–Privacy Act, S. Nfld. 1981, c. 6, is similar to the acts in British Columbia and Manitoba.

Quebec–Art. 5 of the Quebec constitution states, "Every person has a right to respect for his private life." R. S. Q. 1975, c. C-12.

The Respect of Reputation and Privacy Act, R.S.Q. 1985, c. 3, defines invasion of privacy to include unauthorized publicity, interception of private communications, and "observing a person in his private life by any means."

Saskatchewan–The Privacy Act recognizes a cause of action for the tort of invasion of privacy. S.S. 1979, c. P-24.

Federal law–Sec. 8 of the *Charter of Rights and Freedoms* states, "Everyone has the right to be secure against unreasonable search and seizure."

The Supreme Court in 1984 interpreted this provision broadly, saying its purpose is to "protect individuals from unjustified state intrusions upon their privacy."

In later years, the court ruled that Section 8 prohibits audio and video surveillance by the government and supports privacy claims against the government.

The 1985 Statute Law Amendment Act requires a warrant before the government may enter private dwellings.

PRIVATE SECTOR INFORMATION ON INDIVIDUALS

Alberta–The Personal Information Protection Act, 2004, S.A. 2003, c. P-6.5, provides fair information practices in credit bureaus and other private organizations. Its enactment means that entities in the province are not governed by the federal privacy law covering the private sector. Entities must send a notice of a breach of personal information to the provincial privacy commissioner, who will decide whether individuals will be notified.

British Columbia–The Personal Information Protection Act, SBC 2003, c.63, not federal law, regulates the private sector.

Ontario–The Consumer Reporting Act is patterned after the original U.S. Fair Credit Reporting Act, permitting consumers to know the nature and substance of their own credit reports, but not to have copies. R.S.O. 1990 ch. C.33. The Consumer Protection Branch of the Ministry of Government and Consumer Services monitors compliance. Consumers may place an alert on their credit records. Once informed of the alert, credit grantors must take action to verify the identity of the person before proceeding with transactions.

Quebec–The fair-information requirements in the Act Respecting Access have been extended to private businesses. An individual has a right to access (without charge) and to correct information about himself or herself in the hands of a private organization. Organizations must register their personal databases with the Access to Information Commission. R.S.Q., c. P-39.1.

Federal law–The Personal Information Protection and Electronic documents Act establishes a right to the protection of personal information collected, used, or disclosed in the course of commercial activities, federal contracts, or commerce between provinces or internationally. It imposes the following principles on data gatherers: accountability, identifying the purposes for the collection of personal data, obtaining consent, limiting collection, use and disclosure of data, ensuring accuracy, providing adequate security, announcing information management policies, providing individuals a right to access information about themselves and a right to challenge an organization's compliance with these principles. Provinces are obligated to enact comparable legislation. Part Two of the act covers use of electronic records and electronic signatures. S.C. 2000, c.5.

TELEPHONE SERVICES

Federal law–S.C. 2005, c. 50 (Bill C-37 in 2005), empowers the Canadian Radio-television and Telecommunications Commission to administer a do-not-call database. Charities, existing business relations, and political and polling solicitations are exempt from the requirement.

END

Copyright © 2013 Robert Ellis Smith

ISBN 978-0-930072-56-8

PRIVACY JOURNAL

PO Box 28577, Providence RI 02908
401/274-7861   fax 401/274-4747
orders@privacyjournal.net
www.privacyjournal.net

4-4

Our essential publications about privacy are available in electronic or hard copy from Privacy Journal, or from amazon.com, Kindle, and other electronic readers.

2285402

PRIVACY JOURNAL'S
Compilation of State and Federal Privacy Laws
2018 Supplement

This supplements the latest edition of the Compilation (issued in 2013) and includes entries from the 2014, 2015, 2016, and 2017 supplements. New material since 2017 are <u>underlined</u>. New section this year: INTERNET SERVICES

ARREST AND CONVICTION RECORDS
Including "Ban-the-Box"

California–In a state law patterned after an ordinance in Los Angeles, public and private employers with five or more employees are prohibited from "inquiring into or considering" the conviction history of the applicant until after a conditional offer of employment has been made. This means not asking questions about conviction history until an offer of employment is made and not utilizing background checks that reveal criminal conviction history until after an offer is made. Amendments in 2017 to the Fair Employment and Housing Act expand restrictions on an employer's ability to make pre-hire and personnel decisions based on an individual's criminal history, including a significant and far reaching "ban-the-box" component. Cal. Govt. Code sec. 12952.

Colorado–The law on pre-employment inquiries into crimes is similar to California, with additional language. It covers state employment. Colo. Rev. Stat. sec. 24-5-101.

Connecticut–The state prohibits employers from inquiring about a prospective employee's prior arrests, criminal charges or convictions on an initial employment application, unless the employer is required to do so by an applicable state or federal law, or a bond is required for the position. Conn. Gen. Stat. Ann. Sec. 31-51i. The law on employer inquiries applies to state entities and it applies to licensing.. Sec. 46a-80.

Delaware–The "ban-the-box law similar to California's applies to public employment. It postpones inquiries into credit histories as well as criminal histories. Del. Code title 19, sec. 710 and title 29, sec. 6909.

District of Columbia–An employer may not make an inquiry about or require an applicant to disclose or reveal an arrest; or a criminal accusation made against the applicant, which is not then pending against the applicant, or did not result in a conviction. An employer may not make an inquiry about a criminal conviction until after making a conditional offer of employment. D.C. Code sec. 24-1351.

Hawaii–The nation's first "ban-the-box" law (1998) permits an employer to inquire into conviction records for applicants only after the person has received a conditional offer of employment. It permits the conditional offer to be withdrawn if the applicant has a conviction record that bears a rational relationship to the duties and responsibilities of the position. Haw. Rev. Stat. sec. 378-2.5.

<u>**Illinois**–The "ban-the-box law is at 820 ILCS 75/10.</u>

<u>**Indiana**–A 2017 state law, first in the nation, effectively bans "ban-the-box" by prohibiting the enactment of restrictions on employers asking about criminal histories. Ind. Code Ann. sec 22-2-17-3.</u>

Maryland–The 2013 prohibition against premature inquiries into criminal histories applies to state employment. Md. Labor and Empl. Code sec. 2-203.

Massachusetts–The "ban-the-box" law exempts a position for which a law creates a disqualification based on a conviction or if the employer has a legal obligation not to employ persons convicted of an offense. Mass. Gen. Laws ch. 6, sec. 116c.

Minnesota–A 2009 state law prohibits premature inquiry into criminal records by public employers ("ban-the-box"). The law limits the admission of evidence of an employee's criminal history into a lawsuit against an employer. The law was extended in 2013 to include private employers. Minn. Rev. Stat. 364.01.

Mississippi–The state has a complex of laws concerning expungement of misdemeanor and felony records, notably Miss. Code Ann. 99-19-71.

Nebraska–"A public employer shall not ask an applicant to disclose information concerning the applicant's criminal record, including any inquiry on any application, until the public employer has determined the applicant meets the minimum employment qualifications." Neb. Rev. Stat. sec 48-202.

New Jersey–Public and private employers may not inquire into a candidate's criminal history until the employer has conducted the first interview with the candidate. Employers may not consider expunged or pardoned convictions when making an employment decision. N.J. Rev. Stat. sec. C.34:6B-11N.

New Mexico–The state, like others, bans premature inquiries by public employers into criminal records. Also, arrest records not leading to convictions may not be used in pre-employment inquiries. N.M. Stat. Ann. sec. 28-2-3.

North Carolina–A state licensing board may not automatically deny licensure based on the criminal history of the applicant. N.C. Gen. Stat. sec. 93B-8.1.

Ohio–State and local governments and school districts may not ask about an applicant's criminal history on employment applications. Ohio Rev. Code Ann. Sec. 9.73.

Oregon–An employer may not inquire into criminal convictions prior to making a conditional offer of employment. Ore. Rev. Stat. <u>659A.360</u>.

Rhode Island–The law on pre-employment inquiries is similar to the one in Massachusetts. R.I. Gen. Laws sec. 28-5-7.

Tennessee–Except for "covered" positions requiring a criminal check by law, a state employer shall not inquire about an applicant's criminal history on the initial application. Tenn. Code Ann. 8-50-112.

Vermont–Private and public employers are prohibited from requesting criminal history record information on an initial application form. If the employers violates this law, the applicant have an opportunity to rebut. 21 Vt. Stat. Ann. 495j.

Virginia–A governmental employer shall not, in any application, interview, or otherwise, require an applicant to disclose information concerning any arrest or criminal charge against him that has been expunged. Va. Code 19.2-392.4.

Note: Georgia, Illinois, Kentucky, Missouri, New York, Oklahoma, and Pennsylvania have enacted "ban-the-box" administratively and many cities have enacted it by ordinances.

BANK RECORDS

Federal law–<u>"Each financial institution has an affirmative and continuing obligation to respect the privacy of its customers." The law requires regulatory agencies (1) to ensure that financial institutions have safeguards "to insure the security and confidentiality of customer records and information; (2) to protect against any anticipated threats or hazards to the security or integrity of such records; and (3) to protect against unauthorized access. 15 U.S.C. 6801(a) and (b).</u>

COMPUTER CRIME
Including 'Security-Breach Notifications'

Alabama–<u>The state has become the final state among the 50 to enact a data breach notification law. Written notice must be made to affected individuals (and to the attorney general if more than 1000 Alabama residents are notified) within 45 days of a determination that the breach of security is reasonably likely to cause substantial harm to affected individuals. Notice to all consumer reporting agencies is also required "without unreasonable delay" if more than 1000 Alabama residents are notified. Also, third-party contractors are required to notify their clients within ten days of discovery. Covered entities that are subject to other federal or state notification requirements have reduced obligations under the 2018 law. "Personal or protected information" triggering the notice requirement is defined.</u>

<u>The law also requires entities to shred, erase or otherwise modify sensitive personally identifying information when the records are no longer to be retained pursuant to applicable law, regulations or business needs. SB 318 of 2018, Act 2018-396, Ala. Code 22-40.</u>

California–The data-breach notification law was amended expanding the definition of personal information to include online identifiers and license plate numbers. Because the breach-notification law is triggered by a breach of unencrypted personal information, the law was amended in 2015 to define encryption as "rendered unusable, unreadable, or indecipherable to an unauthorized person through a security technology or methodology generally accepted in the field of information technology." The law now specifies how the notice must be organized and standardizes the headings that must be used. Civ. Code sec. 1798.29 and 1798.82. Any firm collecting information on Californians is subject to the notification rules there.

Connecticut–The law on security breaches addresses biometric data such as a fingerprint, voice print, and an eye image and requires new security standards, as a result of amendments in 2015. Companies doing business in Connecticut need to provide identity-theft protection services for 12 months at no cost to a resident whose personal information is compromised. If the breach involves Social Security numbers and perhaps medical information, companies must provide two years of "appropriate identity theft prevention services and, if applicable, identity theft mitigation services" to Connecticut residents affected by a breach. Conn. Gen. Stat. sec. 36a-701b.

District of Columbia–<u>The breach notification law is at D.C. Code Ann. sec. 28-3851.</u>

Florida–Notifications are required of security breaches, Fla. Stat. Ann. Sec. 501.171. "Online account credentials" have been added to the list of personal information the breach of which triggers a notification requirement. The specifics of computer crime are found at sec. 817.568.

Illinois–"Online account credentials" have been added to the list of personal information the breach of which triggers a notification requirement. 815 ILCS 505/1.

Kentucky–When a data breach reveals unencrypted personally identifiable information, individuals must be notified in writing. Ky. Rev. Stat. Ann. sec. 365. 720-734.

Missouri–Entities must notify persons of a security breach only if there is a likelihood of identity theft occurring. Mo. Rev. Stat. § 407.1500.

Nebraska–"Online account credentials" have been added to the list of personal information the breach of which triggers a notification requirement. Neb. Rev. Stat. sec. 87-802

Nevada–The definition of personal information in the

breach-notification law has been expanded, with a 2015 amendment. "Online account credentials" have been added to the list of personal information the breach of which triggers a notification requirement. Many transfers of personal information must now be encrypted. Nev. Rev. Stat. sec. 603A.040.

New York–"Any state entity that owns or licenses computerized data that includes private information shall disclose any breach of the security of the system following discovery or notification of the breach in the security of the system to any resident of New York state whose private information was, or is reasonably believed to have been, acquired by a person without valid authorization." N.Y. Tech. Law sec. 208.

Oregon–The law on security-breach notification has been amended to require notification to the attorney general if 250 or more victims are involved. The following are included in personal data that triggers the protections in the law: biometric data, a consumer's health insurance policy number or medical history or mental or physical condition or diagnosis or treatment. Also, any combination of data without the consumer's first name or first initial and last name if encryption, redaction, or other methods have not rendered the data element or combination of data elements unusable and the data element or combination of data elements would enable an individual to commit identity theft. "Personal information" does not include publicly available data other than a Social Security number, that is lawfully made available to the general public from government records. Ore. Rev. Stat. 646A.

Rhode Island–The language in the 2005 breach-notification law, R.I. Gen Laws 11-49.2 (called an identity theft law), has been replaced by a 2015 law similar to California's. A government agency or private entity must have a security plan, may disclose personal data about a R.I. resident only pursuant to a written contract that the receiving party will implement and maintain reasonable security procedures and practices. Weak encryption may no longer meet state standards. An entity must disclose a breach [with very specific elements in the notice] if it poses a significant risk of identity theft. "Online account credentials" have been added to the list of personal information the breach of which triggers a notification requirement. R.I. Gen. Laws sec. 11-49.3-2. Harassment online is a crime. 11.52-4.2.

South Dakota–The 2018 law on breach notification defines "personal information" as a person's name in combination with a Social Security number, driver's license number or unique number issued by the government, account, credit card, or debit card with security, PIN or passcode, routing number or any other information that would allow someone to access a person's account, health information or an identification number assigned by an employer including a security code, access code, password or biometric data used in employment. Individuals must be notified within 60 days. The state attorney general is also to be notified if more than 250 residents are affected. All reportable breaches, no matter how many residents are affected, must be reported to the credit reporting agencies. S.D. Codified Laws Ann. sec. 22-40-19, effective Jul. 1, 2018.

Virginia–Breach notification must be made without reasonable delay. Va. Code sec. 18.2-186.6, amended in 2017 to include payroll information.

"It is unlawful for any person, other than a law-enforcement officer, to use a computer to obtain, access, or record, through the use of material artifice, trickery or deception, any identifying information. Sec. 18.2-152.5:1.

Washington–The law on breach notification is similar to California's. Wash. Rev. Code Ann. Sec. 19.255.010. Compliance with the federal HIPAA notification rule equals compliance with the state law. If a single breach impacts more than 500 state residents, the attorney general must also receive notice. Notification is to be within 45 days. Wash. Rev. Code Ann. Sec. 19.255010.

Wyoming–"Online account credentials" have been added to the list of personal information the breach of which triggers a notification requirement.

Federal law–Sec. 104 of the Cybersecurity Act of 2015, 6 U.S. C. 1503, authorizes but does not require private entities including Internet providers and communications carriers to monitor their information systems, operate defensive measures, and share and receive cyber threat information. Private entities must, prior to sharing cyber-threat information, review and remove any information not directly related to a cybersecurity threat known at the time of sharing to be personal information of a specific individual or that identifies a specific individual, or to implement and utilize a technical capability to do so. Sec. 103(b)(1)(E) requires development of procedures to identify and remove personal data and requires procedures to notify individuals whose personal information has been shared in violation of the law.

The act authorizes exchanges among government agencies.

The act directs the U.S. Department of Health and Human Services to develop cybersecurity best practices for organizations in the health-care industry, consistent with the current HIPAA Security Rule. Additionally, the act directs HHS to create a new public-private task force to review the challenges to securing networked medical devices and other software or systems that connect to electronic health records.

The U.S. Securities and Exchange Commission, using its statutory authority to require most publicly traded companies to annually disclose potential risk factors, 15 U.S. Code 77g, includes cybersecurity concerns in the requirement. The SEC says "Although no existing disclosure requirement explicitly refers to cybersecurity risks and cyber incidents, a number of disclosure requirements may impose an obligation on registrants to disclose such risks and incidents. In addition, material information regarding cybersecurity risks and cyber incidents is required to be disclosed when necessary in order to make other required disclosures, in light of the circumstances under which they are made, not misleading."

Federal regulations under 20 U.S.C. 1232g, encourage direct notification of a breach of personal information if the data includes student Social Security numbers or other identifying information that could lead to identity theft. The law does not require that an institution notify the Family Policy Compliance Office of a data breach but it believes it is good practice to do so.

The federal Gramm-Leach-Bliley Act law is interpreted as requiring regulatory agencies to ensure that financial institutions have safeguards "(1) to insure the security and confidentiality of customer records and information; (2) to protect against any anticipated threats or hazards to the security or integrity of such records; and (3) to protect against unauthorized access." Institutions must establish response plans that include notifications to affected individuals. 15 U.S.C. 6801(a) and (b).

CREDIT REPORTING
Including 'Credit Freezes,' 'Credit Repair,' 'Credit Clinics,' Check-Cashing, and Credit-Card Use

California–Use of credit scores requires certain disclosures to the consumer. Cal. Civ. Code sec.1785. 20.2.

Placing a security freeze on a consumer's credit report is covered by Civ. Code sec. 1785.11.2 et seq. Credit-report consolidators and check-authorization services not covered.

See also **Employment.**

Colorado–See **Employment.**

District of Columbia–Security freezes are authorized D.C. Code Ann. sec. 28-3861.

Georgia–"A consumer may place a security freeze on the consumer's credit report by making a request in writing." Ga. Code Ann. sec. 10-1-913.

Indiana–A consumer may prevent access to the consumer's consumer report by requesting that a credit bureau place a security freeze on the consumer report. Credit bureaus must allow for email requests. Ind. Code Ann. Sec. 24-5.

Nevada–An employer may not condition hiring on any credit information. Nev. Rev. Stat. sec. 613.

Massachusetts–Credit scores may not be used in the underwriting of auto coverage. Mass. Gen. Laws Ann. Ch. 175, sec. 4E.

Texas–"An insurer may not deny, cancel, or nonrenew a policy of personal insurance solely on the basis of credit information without considering any other applicable underwriting factor independent of credit information." The absence of credit data may not be a factor in underwriting. Tex. Ins. Code sec. 559.052.

ELECTRONIC SURVEILLANCE
Including Video Voyeurism and Camera Surveillance

California–The authority for limited wiretapping has been extended to 2020. Cal. Penal Code 629.98.

Connecticut–"Each employer who engages in any type of electronic monitoring shall give prior written notice to all employees who may be affected, informing them of the types of monitoring which may occur. Each employer shall post, in a conspicuous place which is readily available for viewing by its employees, a notice concerning the types of electronic monitoring which the employer may engage in. . . . When an employer has reasonable grounds to believe that employees are engaged in conduct which violates the law, violates the legal rights of the employer or the employer's employees, or creates a hostile workplace environment, and electronic monitoring may produce evidence of this misconduct, the employer may conduct monitoring without giving prior written notice." Conn. Gen. Stat. Ann. sec. 31-48d.

Delaware–"No employer shall monitor or otherwise intercept any telephone conversation or transmission, electronic mail or transmission, or Internet access or usage of or by a Delaware employee unless the employer either: provides an electronic notice of such monitoring policies to the employee at least once during each day the employee accesses the employer-provided e-mail or Internet access services; or has first given a one-time notice to the employee of such monitoring in writing." Del. Code title 19, sec. 705.

Massachusetts–The law on illicit "upskirting" prohibits photographing or "electronically surveilling" "the intimate area" of a person's body without consent. Mass. Gen. Laws. Ann. ch. 272, sec. 105.

Texas–State law allows for a warrant to authorize law enforcement to procure stored email content from other states and also requires a court warrant to procure email content. This is apparently the first state law requiring such a warrant. Tex. Code Crim. Pro. Art. 18.21, sec 4.

Utah–"A person is guilty of voyeurism who intentionally uses any type of technology to secretly or surreptitiously record video of a person: for the purpose of viewing any portion of the individual's body regarding which the individual has a reasonable expectation of privacy, whether or not that portion of the body is covered with clothing, without knowledge or consent, under circumstances in which the individual has a reasonable expectation of privacy. Enacted in 2017, replacing the statute in the 2013 book.. Utah Code Ann. sec. 76-9-702.7.

Federal law–The CLOUD Act of 2018 permits easier access by foreign governments to surveillance data held by U.S. companies and by the U.S. government to data held by U.S. companies overseas. Foreign governments may go directly to U.S. companies for such data, if they show an agreement with the U.S., a national privacy policy and a clean human rights record. Companies may move to quash the demand. 18 U.S.C. 2703.

EMPLOYMENT
Including Access to Social Media

Arkansas–Employers are prohibited from requiring applicants or employees from providing access to their personal social-media accounts. There are many exceptions, including a company's inadvertent discovery of social-media materials. Ark. Code Ann. sec. 11-2-124(b)(1)(A).

California–The limits on use of credit reports in employment decisions is at Cal. Labor Code 1024.5.

An employer may not take adverse action because an employee updates personal information based on a lawful change of name, Social Security number, or federal employment authorization document. Labor Code 1024.6.

Colorado–An employer may not suggest, request, or require an applicant or employee to disclose any user name, password, or other means for accessing the person's personal Internet account through the person's own device and may not compel adding anyone to his or her list of contacts with social media nor suggest or cause a person to change privacy settings. Colo. Rev. Stat. sec. 8-2-127.

The law prohibits an employer's use of consumer credit information for employment purposes if the information is unrelated to the job. The company must disclose to an employee or applicant when consumer credit information is used to take adverse action against a person and the particular credit information used. An aggrieved person may bring suit for an injunction, damages, or both. Sec. 8-2-12.

Connecticut–"Each employer who engages in any type of electronic monitoring shall give prior written notice to all employees who may be affected, informing them of the types of monitoring which may occur. Each employer shall post, in a conspicuous place which is readily available for viewing by its employees, a notice concerning the types of electronic monitoring which the employer may engage in. . . . When an employer has reasonable grounds to believe that employees are engaged in conduct which violates the law, violates the legal rights of the employer or the employer's employees, or creates a hostile workplace environment, and electronic monitoring may produce evidence of this misconduct, the employer may conduct monitoring without giving prior written notice." Conn. Gen. Stat. Ann. sec. 31-48d.

The law on employee social-media use is the same as Rhode Island's. Sec. 31-40x(b)(1).

Delaware–No employer shall monitor or otherwise intercept any telephone conversation or transmission, electronic mail or transmission, or Internet access or usage of or by a Delaware employee unless the employer either: provides an electronic notice of such monitoring policies to the employee at least once during each day the employee accesses the employer-provided e-mail or Internet access services; or has first given a one-time notice to the employee of such monitoring in writing." Del. Code title 19, sec. 705.

The entries in the 2013 book and 2015 supplement are replaced by: The state has a law making it unlawful for employers, subject to certain exceptions, to mandate that an employee or applicant disclose a password or account-information access. Title 19, sec. 709A.

Illinois–It is unlawful for an employer to request or require an employee or prospective employee to provide a password or other account information in order to gain access to the person's social-media accounts. Nor may an employer or prospective employer request or require an employee or applicant to authenticate or access a personal online account in the presence of the employer, to request or require that an employee or applicant invite the employer to join a group affiliated with any personal online account of the employee or applicant, or join an online account established by the employer. 820 ILCS 55, sec. 10.

Louisiana–The law prohibits employers or private and public educational institutions from requesting or demanding access to a person's Internet accounts. La. Rev. Stat. 51: 1951 through 1955.

Maine–Employers are limited in access to social media about individuals. Me. Rev. Stat. Ann. title 26, sec. 616.

Maryland–Private and government employers are prohibited from requesting or requiring an employee or applicant to disclose a user name, password, or other means to access a personal account or service through an electronic communications device. Md. Lab. and Employ. Code 3-712(a)(4)(i)(2) and (b)(1).

Massachusetts–"It shall be an unlawful practice for an employer to require that an employee refrain from inquiring about, discussing or disclosing information about either the employee's own wages, including benefits or other compensation, or about any other employee's wages; seek the salary history of any prospective employee from any current or former employer; provided, however, that a prospective employee may provide written authorization to a prospective employer to confirm prior wages." Mass. Gen. Laws Ann. ch. 149, sec. 105A (c)(1).

Michigan–The law prohibits employers from requiring certain individuals to disclose information that allows access to certain social-networking accounts and from taking certain retaliatory actions. Mich. Comp. Laws Ann. sec. 37.273.

Missouri–See **Tracking Technologies**.

Montana–State law prohibits requests for online passwords as a condition of employment. Mont. Code Ann. Sec. 39-2-3.

Nebraska–No employer shall require or request that an employee or applicant provide or disclose any user name or password or to log into a personal internet account in the presence of the employer in a manner that enables the employer to observe the contents of the employee's or applicant's personal internet account or . . . require an employee or applicant to add anyone, including the employer, to the list of contacts associated with the employee's or applicant's personal internet account or require or otherwise coerce an employee or applicant to change the settings on the employee's or applicant's personal internet account which affects the ability of others to view the content of such account; or take adverse action against, fail to hire, or otherwise penalize an employee or applicant for failure to provide or disclose any of the information or to take any of the actions specified." Neb. Rev. Stat. 48-3502.

Nevada–An employer may not condition hiring on access to an employee's social-media account. Nor may employment be conditioned on access to a person's credit report. The law covers entities that serve or represent employers. Nev. Rev. Stat. sec. 613.

New Hampshire–The law prohibits an employer from requiring an employee or prospective employee to disclose his or her social-media or electronic-mail passwords. N.H. Rev. Stat. Ann. Sec. 275:71.

New Jersey–There are limits on employers seeking access to individuals' personal social-media accounts. N.J. Rev. Stat. sec. 34:6B-6.

New Mexico–The law on employers' access to social-media passwords is similar to Utah's. N. M. Stat. Ann. sec. 50-4-34.

Oklahoma–No employer may require or request a person to disclose Internet information or access devices except in an investigation, as specified. A company may not take retaliatory action. A victim has a civil right of action. Okla. Stat. title 40, sec. 173.2.

Oregon–The law on employer's access to social-media sites is similar to Colorado's. No adverse action may be taken based on the prohibitions. If an employer inadvertently gets a password, it may not use the information it acquires. It is an unlawful employment practice for an employer to require that a person maintain a personal social-media account or authorize the employer to advertise on the social-media account of an employee or applicant. Or. Rev. Stat. sec. 659A. 330.

Rhode Island–An employer may not require, coerce or request a person to provide passwords or access to a social-media site; to change settings; or to add anyone like a boss to a social media site. R.I. Gen. Laws sec. 28-56-1.

Tennessee–An employer is limited in requesting access to an employee's Internet accounts except for investigations and other instances. Tenn. Code Ann. 50-1-1001 thru 1004.

Utah–The law prohibits an employer from asking an employee or applicant to disclose the user name and password that allows access to his or her "personal Internet account," as well as taking adverse action against the individual for failing to do so. Utah Code Ann. sec. 34-48-102 and 201 and 202 and 203 and 301. 53B-24-102 and 201 and 202 and 203 and 301 protects students.

Virginia–The law prohibits an employer from requiring, requesting, or causing a current or prospective employee to disclose the user name and password to a social-media account; and it prohibits an employer from requiring an employee to add an employee, a supervisor, or an administrator to the list of contacts, or changing the privacy settings. Va. Code sec. 40.1-28.7:5.

There are limits on employers' uses of genetics test results. 40.1-28.7:1.

Washington–The law on employer's access to social-media sites is similar to Colorado's. No adverse action may be taken based on the prohibitions. If an employer inadvertently gets a password, it may not use the information it acquires. Wash. Rev. Code Ann. sec. 49.44.

West Virginia–The law is similar to Nebraska's, adding that it does not prohibit an employee from using a personal account during work hours. W.Va. Code Ann. sec. 21-5G-1.

Wisconsin–With significant exceptions, employers are limited in access to passwords and other material concerning an employee or applicant's Internet accounts. Collective-bargaining provisions inconsistent with this are null upon expiration of the contract. The same law protects tenants. Wisc. Stat. Ann. sec. 995. 55. Also 106.54 (10)(a).

NOTE: See also **Arrest Records**. See also **Internet Services.**

GOVERNMENT RECORDS

Colorado–Government entities must have public policies on privacy. Col. Rev. Stat. sec. 24-72-501.

Iowa–The Fair Information Practices Act requires state agencies to permit persons to know about systems of records and to inspect and amend records about themselves. Iowa Code Ann. sec. 22.11.

Maryland–The law limits information collection by state agencies and says a person must be notified of "the person's right to inspect, amend, or correct personal records, if any." Md. State Govt. Code sec. 10-624.

New York–Agencies must develop privacy policies, safeguard personal data, and permit data subjects access to their own information. N.Y.S. Tech Law sec 201-208.

South Carolina–State agencies must develop privacy policies and display them on web sites. S.C. Code sec. 30-2-40.

Federal law–The Judicial Redress Act of 2016 (PL 114-126, amends the Privacy Act, 5 USC 552a (note), to give Europeans and Pacific Rim residents the right to sue the U. S. for unlawful disclosure of personal information and other rights in the Privacy Act 1974.

See also **Computer Crime, federal law**.

IDENTITY THEFT

Florida– Fraudulent use of another's ID elements is a crime. Fla. Stat. Ann. Sec. 817.568.

Rhode Island–Impersonating another is a crime. R.I. Gen. Laws 11-41-4.

breach-notification law has been expanded, with a 2015 amendment. "Online account credentials" have been added to the list of personal information the breach of which triggers a notification requirement. Many transfers of personal information must now be encrypted. Nev. Rev. Stat. sec. 603A.040.

New York–"Any state entity that owns or licenses computerized data that includes private information shall disclose any breach of the security of the system following discovery or notification of the breach in the security of the system to any resident of New York state whose private information was, or is reasonably believed to have been, acquired by a person without valid authorization." N.Y. Tech. Law sec. 208.

Oregon–The law on security-breach notification has been amended to require notification to the attorney general if 250 or more victims are involved. The following are included in personal data that triggers the protections in the law: biometric data, a consumer's health insurance policy number or medical history or mental or physical condition or diagnosis or treatment. Also, any combination of data without the consumer's first name or first initial and last name if encryption, redaction, or other methods have not rendered the data element or combination of data elements unusable and the data element or combination of data elements would enable an individual to commit identity theft. "Personal information" does not include publicly available data other than a Social Security number, that is lawfully made available to the general public from government records. Ore. Rev. Stat. 646A.

Rhode Island–The language in the 2005 breach-notification law, R.I. Gen Laws 11-49.2 (called an identity theft law), has been replaced by a 2015 law similar to California's. A government agency or private entity must have a security plan, may disclose personal data about a R.I. resident only pursuant to a written contract that the receiving party will implement and maintain reasonable security procedures and practices. Weak encryption may no longer meet state standards. An entity must disclose a breach [with very specific elements in the notice] if it poses a significant risk of identity theft. "Online account credentials" have been added to the list of personal information the breach of which triggers a notification requirement. R.I. Gen. Laws sec. 11-49.3-2. Harassment online is a crime. 11.52-4.2.

South Dakota–The 2018 law on breach notification defines "personal information" as a person's name in combination with a Social Security number, driver's license number or unique number issued by the government, account, credit card, or debit card with security, PIN or passcode, routing number or any other information that would allow someone to access a person's account, health information or an identification number assigned by an employer including a security code, access code, password or biometric data used in employment. Individuals must be notified within 60 days. The state attorney general is also to be notified if more than 250 residents are affected. All reportable breaches, no matter how many residents are affected, must be reported to the credit reporting agencies. S.D. Codified Laws Ann. sec. 22-40-19, effective Jul. 1, 2018.

Virginia–Breach notification must be made without reasonable delay. Va. Code sec. 18.2-186.6, amended in 2017 to include payroll information.

"It is unlawful for any person, other than a law-enforcement officer, to use a computer to obtain, access, or record, through the use of material artifice, trickery or deception, any identifying information. Sec. 18.2-152.5:1.

Washington–The law on breach notification is similar to California's. Wash. Rev. Code Ann. Sec. 19.255.010. Compliance with the federal HIPAA notification rule equals compliance with the state law. If a single breach impacts more than 500 state residents, the attorney general must also receive notice. Notification is to be within 45 days. Wash. Rev. Code Ann. Sec. 19.255010.

Wyoming–"Online account credentials" have been added to the list of personal information the breach of which triggers a notification requirement.

Federal law–Sec. 104 of the Cybersecurity Act of 2015, 6 U.S. C. 1503, authorizes but does not require private entities including Internet providers and communications carriers to monitor their information systems, operate defensive measures, and share and receive cyber threat information. Private entities must, prior to sharing cyber-threat information, review and remove any information not directly related to a cybersecurity threat known at the time of sharing to be personal information of a specific individual or that identifies a specific individual, or to implement and utilize a technical capability to do so. Sec. 103(b)(1)(E) requires development of procedures to identify and remove personal data and requires procedures to notify individuals whose personal information has been shared in violation of the law.

The act authorizes exchanges among government agencies.

The act directs the U.S. Department of Health and Human Services to develop cybersecurity best practices for organizations in the health-care industry, consistent with the current HIPAA Security Rule. Additionally, the act directs HHS to create a new public-private task force to review the challenges to securing networked medical devices and other software or systems that connect to electronic health records.

The U.S. Securities and Exchange Commission, using its statutory authority to require most publicly traded companies to annually disclose potential risk factors, 15 U.S. Code 77g, includes cybersecurity concerns in the requirement. The SEC says "Although no existing disclosure requirement explicitly refers to cybersecurity risks and cyber incidents, a number of disclosure requirements may impose an obligation on registrants to disclose such risks and incidents. In addition, material information regarding cybersecurity risks and cyber incidents is required to be disclosed when necessary in order to make other required disclosures, in light of the circumstances under which they are made, not misleading."

Federal regulations under 20 U.S.C. 1232g, encourage direct notification of a breach of personal information if the data includes student Social Security numbers or other identifying information that could lead to identity theft. The law does not require that an institution notify the Family Policy Compliance Office of a data breach but it believes it is good practice to do so.

The federal Gramm-Leach-Bliley Act law is interpreted as requiring regulatory agencies to ensure that financial institutions have safeguards "(1) to insure the security and confidentiality of customer records and information; (2) to protect against any anticipated threats or hazards to the security or integrity of such records; and (3) to protect against unauthorized access." Institutions must establish response plans that include notifications to affected individuals. 15 U.S.C. 6801(a) and (b).

CREDIT REPORTING
Including 'Credit Freezes,' 'Credit Repair,' 'Credit Clinics,'
Check-Cashing, and Credit-Card Use

California–Use of credit scores requires certain disclosures to the consumer. Cal. Civ. Code sec.1785. 20.2.

Placing a security freeze on a consumer's credit report is covered by Civ. Code sec. 1785.11.2 et seq. Credit-report consolidators and check-authorization services not covered.

See also **Employment**.

Colorado–See **Employment**.

District of Columbia–Security freezes are authorized D.C. Code Ann. sec. 28-3861.

Georgia–"A consumer may place a security freeze on the consumer's credit report by making a request in writing." Ga. Code Ann. sec. 10-1-913.

Indiana–A consumer may prevent access to the consumer's consumer report by requesting that a credit bureau place a security freeze on the consumer report. Credit bureaus must allow for email requests. Ind. Code Ann. Sec. 24-5.

Nevada–An employer may not condition hiring on any credit information. Nev. Rev. Stat. sec. 613.

Massachusetts–Credit scores may not be used in the underwriting of auto coverage. Mass. Gen. Laws Ann. Ch. 175, sec. 4E.

Texas–"An insurer may not deny, cancel, or nonrenew a policy of personal insurance solely on the basis of credit information without considering any other applicable underwriting factor independent of credit information." The absence of credit data may not be a factor in underwriting. Tex. Ins. Code sec. 559.052.

ELECTRONIC SURVEILLANCE
Including Video Voyeurism and Camera Surveillance

California–The authority for limited wiretapping has been extended to 2020. Cal. Penal Code 629.98.

Connecticut–"Each employer who engages in any type of electronic monitoring shall give prior written notice to all employees who may be affected, informing them of the types of monitoring which may occur. Each employer shall post, in a conspicuous place which is readily available for viewing by its employees, a notice concerning the types of electronic monitoring which the employer may engage in. . . . When an employer has reasonable grounds to believe that employees are engaged in conduct which violates the law, violates the legal rights of the employer or the employer's employees, or creates a hostile workplace environment, and electronic monitoring may produce evidence of this misconduct, the employer may conduct monitoring without giving prior written notice." Conn. Gen. Stat. Ann. sec. 31-48d.

Delaware–"No employer shall monitor or otherwise intercept any telephone conversation or transmission, electronic mail or transmission, or Internet access or usage of or by a Delaware employee unless the employer either: provides an electronic notice of such monitoring policies to the employee at least once during each day the employee accesses the employer-provided e-mail or Internet access services; or has first given a one-time notice to the employee of such monitoring in writing." Del. Code title 19, sec. 705.

Massachusetts–The law on illicit "upskirting" prohibits photographing or "electronically surveilling" "the intimate area" of a person's body without consent. Mass. Gen. Laws. Ann. ch. 272, sec. 105.

Texas–State law allows for a warrant to authorize law enforcement to procure stored email content from other states and also requires a court warrant to procure email content. This is apparently the first state law requiring such a warrant. Tex. Code Crim. Pro. Art. 18.21, sec 4.

Utah–"A person is guilty of voyeurism who intentionally uses any type of technology to secretly or surreptitiously record video of a person: for the purpose of viewing any portion of the individual's body regarding which the individual has a reasonable expectation of privacy, whether or not that portion of the body is covered with clothing, without knowledge or consent, under circumstances in which the individual has a reasonable expectation of privacy. Enacted in 2017, replacing the statute in the 2013 book.. Utah Code Ann. sec. 76-9-702.7.

Federal law–The CLOUD Act of 2018 permits easier access by foreign governments to surveillance data held by U.S. companies and by the U.S. government to data held by U.S. companies overseas. Foreign governments may go directly to U.S. companies for such data, if they show an agreement with the U.S., a national privacy policy and a clean human rights record. Companies may move to quash the demand. 18 U.S.C. 2703.

INSURANCE

Massachusetts–Collection and use of genetic information generally is governed by Mass. Gen. Laws Ann. Ch.111, sec. 70G.

Patients on someone else's insurance policy (like a former spouse or a parent) may have payment summaries customarily mailed by health-care providers to the holder of the policy to be sent to the patient directly instead. "Carriers shall not specify or describe sensitive health care services in a common summary of payments form." The so-called PATCH Act of 2018, for Protecting Access to Confidential Health Care, is the first such law in the nation. Ch. 1760, sec. 27.

See also **Credit**.

South Dakota–Genetic testing is governed by S.D. Codified Laws Ann. 34.14-22.

Utah–Health insurers are limited in collecting and using genetics information. Utah Code Ann. Sec. 26-45-104.

Virginia–Insurers are bound by a code of confidentiality. Va. Code sec. 38.2-613. Insurers may not generally use genetic information as the sole basis for decisions. Sec 38.2-508.4.

INTERNET SERVICES
Including "Phishing"

Alabama– "A person commits the crime of phishing if the person . . . using the internet, solicits, requests, or takes any action to induce another person to provide identifying information by representing that the person, either directly or by implication, is a business, without the authority or approval of the business." (The offenses are "phishing" and "whaling," a more sophisticated form of "phishing.") Sec 13A-8-114.

Arizona–State web sites must include "a privacy policy statement to disclose the information gathering and dissemination practices related to the internet" describing the service provided, the individual data obtained, user's options, the use of the information, what disclosures are made of the information, whether other entities collect personal data from the site, and the security measures in place. Ariz. Rev. Stat. 41-4152.

The law on phishing is similar to Alabama's. Sec. 18-541 to 544.

Arkansas–State web sites must post privacy policies. Ark. Code Ann. sec. 25-1-114.

"No person shall engage in phishing." Sec. 4-111-103(d).

California–An amendment to the Online Privacy Protection Act (OPPA) requires Web sites, mobile apps, and online services that collect personal information, broadly defined, from consumers in California to disclose how they respond to "do not track" signals and whether third parties collect such information on their sites or apps. Cal. Bus. & Prof. Code secs. 22575 et seq.

Web site operators and advertisers must post notices that they are forbidden from knowingly using, disclosing or compiling the personal data of minors to advertise products that minors are not legally allowed to purchase. Further, minors who are registered users of a Web site or mobile app may re- move content that they posted to that service. Bus. and Prof. Code sec. 22580.

State web sites must post privacy policies. Govt. Code sec 11019.9.

The law on phishing is similar to Alabama's. An individual or an internet provider may bring a civil action. Bus. & Prof. Code sec. 22948 to 22948.3.

Penal Code sec. 646.9 punishes "direct electronic harassment" or cyberstalking. Sec. 653.2 punishes "indirect electronic harassment," in which the defendant posts information on the internet that will encourage other people to harass or stalk the victim, with the intent to place that person in reasonable fear.

Colorado–The law requires a government agency to have a policy on email monitoring similar to what is required in Tennessee. Col. Rev. Stat. sec. 24-72-204.5. Government entities must have public policies on privacy. Sec. 24-72-501

Connecticut–Employers who engage in any type of electronic monitoring must give prior written notice to all employees, informing them of the types of monitoring which may occur. Conn. Gen. Stat. Ann. sec. 31-48d.

Phishing is a civil violation and a felony. Sec. 53-454.

Delaware–An operator of an internet website, online or cloud computing service, online application, or mobile application directed to children younger than 18 may not market or advertise tobacco, alcohol, firearms, fireworks, tattoos, or dietary products on the service. Del. Code title 29, sec. 1204c(a) Nor may the service market or advertise the products directed to a person it knows to be a child based upon information specific to that child, including the child's profile, activity, address, or location sufficient to establish contact with the child. The service shall not knowingly use, disclose, or compile, or allow another person to use, disclose, or compile the personal information of the child. Sec. 1204c(b).

The Online Privacy and Protection Act of 2015 requires operators of commercial web sites and apps that gather personal information on residents of Delaware to conspicuously post a privacy policy, which identifies the personal information collected and third parties that receive the data, identify and describe the process for correcting or amending information, if there is one; discloses how the operator responds to web browser "do not track" signals, and discloses whether other parties may collect personally identifiable information about online activity on that site across different web sites, services, or apps. Sec. 1205C.

A digital book service provider shall not knowingly disclose to any government entity or be compelled to disclose to any government or private entity any information about a user or his or her choices, except lawfully to law enforcement or to a government entity pursuant to a court order (after the service has an opportunity to resist the demand and the individual gets notification and an opportunity to resist). Non-government agencies may get access by court order after showing the information is not accessible elsewhere and the individual has an opportunity to resist or give written consent. Sec.1206(c).

The law prohibits employers from monitoring or intercepting electronic mail or internet access or usage by an employee unless the employer has first given a one-time written or electronic notice to the employee. Sec. 19-7-705.

State agencies must post internet privacy policies. Title 29, sec. 9017C.

Florida–Fraudulent use of person's identity to induce personal data is a civil violation. Fla. Stat. Ann. Sec. 668.701 through 705.

Georgia–Phishing is a crime. Ga. Code Ann. sec. 16-9-109.1.

Illinois–"State agency web sites may not use permanent cookies or any other invasive tracking programs that monitor and track Web site viewing habits; however, a state web site may use transactional cookies that facilitate business transactions." 5 ILCS 177/15.

Phishing is a civil violation. 740 ILCS 7/1 through 7/15.

Kentucky–Phishing, even from out of state, is punishable as a crime. Ky. Rev. Stat. Ann. sec. 434. 697.

Michigan–The anti-phishing law is similar to Louisiana's. Mich. Comp Law Ann. sec. 445.67a.

Louisiana–Phishing as well as creating a phony web page to further the scheme is an offense. La. Rev. Stat. 51:2021.

Maine–State web sites must have privacy policies. Me. Rev. Stat. Ann. title 1, sec. 541 and 542.

Minnesota–Internet service providers are limited in disclosing personal information and must get permission from subscribers before disclosing information about the subscribers' online surfing habits and internet sites visited. Minn. Stat. Ann. sec. 325M.01 to .09. Another law addresses cookies used by state agencies. Sec. 13.15.

Phishing is a crime. Sec. 609.527, subd. 5a.

Montana–Mont. Code Ann. 2-17-550 governs when state agency web operators may gather personal information.

The law against phishing is similar to Alabama's. Mont. Code Ann. sec. 30-14-1712 and 33-19-410.

Nebraska–State law regards as a deceptive trade practice, "Knowingly [making] a false or misleading statement in a privacy policy, published on the internet or otherwise distributed or published, regarding the use of personal information submitted by members of the public. Neb Rev Stat. sec. 87-302(15).

An internet service provider must keep subscribers' data confidential (except email addresses). Violation is a misdemeanor. Sec. 205.498.

Nevada–An internet service provider must keep subscribers' data confidential (except email addresses). Providers must post a conspicuous notice to this effect. Violation is a misdemeanor. Nev, Rev. Stat. ann 205.498.

Out-of-state operators of a web site or online service that collects certain information from residents of Nevada must provide a notice of privacy protections in the information. Nev. Rev. Stat. sec. 603A-010.

New Mexico– Entities experiencing "unauthorized acquisition of personal data" about a resident must notify the affected persons, the attorney general, and/or consumer-reporting agencies within 45 days N.M. Stat. Ann. sec. 57-12C-2.

New York–Phishing is a civil violation. N.Y. Gen. Bus. Laws sec.390-b. State web sites must abide by a model privacy policy. N.Y.S. Tech Law. Sec. 202.

Oklahoma–It is a violation of the state consumer protection law to transmit a commercial electronic mail message that falsifies information or other routing information or contains false or misleading information in the subject line, or to use a third party's internet address or domain name without the third party's consent. . . that makes it appear that the third party was the sender of such mail. Okla. Stat. title 15, sec. 776.6.

Oregon–Phishing is prohibited. Ore. Rev. Stat. 646A.808.

Pennsylvania–The law on false statements in privacy policies is similar to Nebraska's. It is a criminal deceptive or fraudulent business practice to "knowingly [make] a false or misleading statement in a privacy policy, published on the internet or otherwise distributed or published, regarding the use of personal information submitted by members of the public." Pa. Stat. Ann. title 18, sec. 4107(a)(10).

Rhode Island–Phishing is prohibited. R.I. Gen. Laws sec. 11-52.1-3.

Tennessee–Government agencies that maintain an email system must adopt a written policy on any monitoring of email and the circumstances for it. The statement must alert an employee that email may become public under the public records law. Tenn. Code Ann. sec. 10-7-512.

The anti-phishing law is at sec. 47-18-5201 to 47-18-5205.

Texas–The anti-phishing law is at Tex. Bus. and Comm. Code sec. 325.001 to 006.

Utah–State agencies must post policy policies. Utah Code Ann. sec 63D-2-102.

The law prohibits phishing and pharming, defined as operating a web page that represents itself as belonging to a legitimate business, without approval of the legitimate business, to induce any user of the internet to provide identifying information or property; or the alteration of a setting causing a user to reach a phony web site. Sec. 13-40-201.

Virginia–State agencies must post internet privacy policies limiting collection of personal information.

Va. Code sec. 2.2-3803.

"It is unlawful for any person, other than a law-enforcement officer, to use a computer to obtain, access, or record, through the use of material artifice, trickery or deception, any identifying information. Sec. 18.2-152.5:1.

Washington–Phishing is prohibited. Wash. Rev. Code Ann. sec. 19.190.080 et seq.

Federal law–Sec. 230 of the Communications Decency Act was amended in 2018 to no longer provide immunity from federal or state criminal charges or civil claims for web sites distributing content defined as sex trafficking and prostitution. "Knowingly assisting, supporting, or facilitating a sex trafficking is a criminal violation." HR 1865 of 2018, 47 U.S.C. 230 (e)(5).

LIBRARY RECORDS

Arizona–The library confidentiality law is at Ariz. Rev. Stat. 41-151.22.

California–Records that identify a borrower's activities in a public library are confidential. Govt. Code sec. 6267.

Hawaii–The state's Uniform Information Practices Act (Modified), Haw. Rev. Stat. 92F, has been interpreted as protecting borrowing records in public libraries but not records of fines assessed.

Ohio–"A [public or private] library shall not release any library record or disclose any patron information except in the following situations: to a minor child's parent; in accordance with a subpoena, search warrant, or other court order; or to a law enforcement officer. Ohio Rev. Code Ann. Sec. 149.432.

Texas–The 1973 Public Information Act, Tex. Gov. Code Ann. Chap. 552, has been interpreted as protecting borrowers' records in public libraries.

Utah–Records of public libraries are private, Utah Code Ann. sec. 63-2-302, with exceptions , 63-2-202.

MEDICAL RECORDS

California–The medical confidentiality law has been extended to mobile apps. Cal. Civ. Code sec. 56.06.

Massachusetts–See Insurance.

Nevada–Genetic information must be protected generally. Nev. Rev. Stat. Ann. Sec. 629.171.

New Mexico–Genetic information is protected by N.M. Stat. Ann. Sec. 24-21-1 through 24-21-7.

New York–Results of genetic tests are to be kept confidential, with exceptions. N.Y. Civ. Rt. Law sec. 79-l.

Oregon–The genetic privacy statutes are at Ore. Rev. Stat. sec. 192.531 through 549.

Rhode Island–Health insurers are prohibited from sharing genetic information. R.I. Gen. Laws sec 27-18-52. And health plans. Sec. 27-19-44, 27-20-39, and 27-41-53.

South Carolina–Insurers use of genetic information is governed by S.C. Code sec. sec. 38-93-10.

Texas–Collection and use of genetic information is governed by Tex. Vernon's Code Chap 20, tit. 132.

Washington–Compliance with the federal HIPAA notification rule equals compliance with the state law. If a single breach impacts more than 500 state residents, the attorney general must also receive notice. Notification is to be within 45 days. Wash. Rev. Code Ann. Sec. 19.255010.

See also **Computer Crime, Federal law.**

MISCELLANEOUS
Including Breast-Feeding Protections

California–Information about utility consumers using "smart grid" technologies is protected by law. Utilities need consent to share or market personal information. They and their contractors must meet data security standards. Cal. Civ. Code sec. 1798.98.

Wisconsin–With significant exceptions, landlords are limited in access to passwords and other material concerning a tenant. Wisc. Stat. Ann. sec. 995.55.

See also **Employment.**

PRIVACY STATUTES

California–The state has increased the penalties for violation of the "celebrity paparazzi law," which makes it a crime to harass a child because of a parent's employment. Cal. Penal Code sec. 11414. Knowingly entering into the airspace above the land of another person without permission is equivalent to a physical invasion of privacy. Civ. Code sec. 1708.8.

Florida-The open-records law shall not include disclosure of certain images from a police body camera in a private place, with a provision opening this up to further consideration in the future. There are many exceptions. Fla. Stat. Ann. sec. 119.071.

SOCIAL SECURITY NUMBERS

Connecticut–See **Computer Crime.**

New Hampshire–The Department of Education may not obtain or use a Social Security number as an identifier for any pupil. N.H. Rev. Stat. Ann. Sec. 193-E-5.

Oregon–"A public university may not disclose the Social Security number of a student," except to law enforcement or a family-support enforcement agency. Ore. Rev. Stat. 326-585 through 589.

<u>**South Carolina**–State agencies are limited in collecting Social Security numbers. S.C. Code sec. 30-2-310.</u>

Federal law–The U.S. Department of Education and Department of Justice interpret the provision on Social Security numbers in the Privacy Act, 5 U.S.C. 552a (note), as prohibiting a public school district from *re-quiring* a pupil or parent to provide an SSN or denying admittance because a pupil does not provide a Social Security number. Presumably this applies to public higher education as well.

The Social Security Administration "shall establish cost-effective procedures to ensure that a Social Security number (or derivative thereof) is not displayed, coded, or embedded on the Medicare card issued to an individual." 42 U.S. Code 405(c) (2) (2) (xiii)

STUDENTS AND STUDENT RECORDS
Including Access to Social Media

Arkansas–Colleges and universities may not request access to personal social-media accounts or students and applicants. There are significant exceptions, including a company's inadvertent discovery of social-media materials. Ark. Code Ann. sec. 6-60-104.

California–"Public and private postsecondary educational institutions shall not require or request a student, prospective student, or student group to disclose a user name or password for accessing personal social media, access personal social media in the presence of the institution's representative, or divulge any personal social media information." Cal. Ed. Code, Sec. 99121 (a).

The operator of a Web site, online service, online application, or mobile application may not knowingly target advertising to K-12 students or their parents, sell or disclose information provided by students using a school-based commercial service (including identifiers, health information and locator information). An operator must maintain reasonable security procedures to protect student information and to delete it when a school or school district requests it. Bus. & Prof. Code 22584

Colorado–The law on student online data resembles Georgia's. Colo. Rev. Stat. sec. 22-2-309.

Delaware–An institution of higher education may not require or request a password or other social-media account information. Del. Code title 14, sec. 8103.

The state law on access to pupil data in an online system, Title 14, sec. 8102a, is modeled after California's law.

<u>**District of Columbia**–An educational institution shall not take or threaten to take action against a student or prospective student, including discipline, expulsion, unenrollment, refusal to admit, or prohibiting participation in a curricular or extracurricular activity, because the student or prospective student refused to disclose a username, password, or other means of account authentication used to access the student's personal media account or personal technological device; access the student's personal media account or personal technological device in the presence of school-based personnel in a manner that enables the school-based personnel to observe data on the account or device; add a person to the list of users who may view the student's personal media account or access a student's personal technological device; or change the privacy settings associated with the student's personal media account or personal technological device.</u>

<u>If an educational institution inadvertently receives the prohibited information on a student, it shall not use the information to access the personal media account or personal technological device of the student or prospective student; not share the information with anyone; and delete the information immediately or as soon as is reasonably practicable. Suspicion-based searches of social media are permissible. Schools may monitor usage for unauthorized use if a student is notified. D.C. Code Ann. sec. 38-831.04 and 05.</u>

<u>Schools may conduct investigations based on reasonable suspicion, monitor use on an institution's network or prohibit social media use during the school day.</u>

Georgia–Online services are barred from selling or sharing elementary and secondary pupils personal data, test scores, grades, or socioeconomic or disability information. The data may not be used to target ads to students. The State School Superintendent shall designate a chief privacy officer. Ga. Code Ann. sec 20-2-661.

Idaho–The state must notify students or their parents when there is unauthorized access to the state database of student information. Idaho Code sec. 33-133.

Illinois–A post-secondary educational institution is limited in requesting or requiring social media passwords and materials, with significant exceptions. Also "an elementary or secondary school must provide notification to the student and his or her parent or guardian that the school may request or require a password or other related account information in order to gain access to the student's account or profile on a social networking website if the school has reasonable cause to believe that the student's account contains evidence that the student has violated a school disciplinary rule or policy. The notification must be published." 105 ILCS 75/15.

Kentucky–A cloud computing service gathering student information may not use it for advertising. Ky. Rev. Stat. Ann. 365.734.

Louisiana–The law prohibits employers or private and public educational institutions from requesting or demanding access to a person's Internet accounts. La. Rev. Stat. 51: 1951 through 1955. Parents have access to student records. 17:3136.

Maryland–An educational institution may not cause a student to grant access to a personal electronic account or to add individuals to a list of contacts or to change privacy settings. Md. Educ. Code sec. 26-401.

Michigan–"An educational institution shall not request a student or prospective student to grant access to, allow observation of, or disclose information that allows access to or observation of the student's or prospective student's personal internet account nor discipline, fail to admit, or otherwise penalize a student or prospective student for failure to grant access." Mich. Comp. Laws Ann. sec. 37.274.

New Hampshire–The law limits access to social-media materials of present or future students. N.H. Rev. Stat. Ann. Sec 189:70.

Individual pupil names or codes in the statewide assessment results, scores, or other evaluative materials shall be deleted for the purposes of records maintenance and storage unless a parent or legal guardian provides written authorization otherwise. Sec. 193-C:11.

The state may maintain no information to link a pupil ID number with a student's identity, nor may the Department of Education obtain or use a Social Security number as an identifier for any pupil. Sec. 193-E-5.

There are limits on disclosure of and collection of pupil information in the statewide database. Sec. 189:67.

New Jersey–There are limits on institutions of higher education seeking access to individuals' personal social-media accounts. N.J. Rev. Stat. sec. 18A:3-30.

New Mexico–The law on institutions' access to social-media passwords of students is similar to Utah's. N. M. Stat. Ann. sec. 21-1-46

New York–Parents are provided a Bill of Rights on Privacy and Security. A chief privacy officer is appointed in the Department of Education. There are limits on sharing pupil data with a "shared learning infrastructure service provider." N.Y. State Educ Law sec 2-c.

Oklahoma–The student DATA Act requires public reporting on data collected on pupils by the state, mandates the creation of a statewide student data security plan, and limits the data that can be collected on individual students and how that data can be shared. It establishes new limits on the transfer of data, including de-identified data, to federal, state, or local agencies and organizations outside Oklahoma. It further restricts the state from requesting delinquency, criminal, and medical records, Social Security numbers, and biometric information as part of student data collected from local schools and districts. Okla. Stat. title 70, sec. 3-168.

Oregon–A public or private educational institution may not require, request or otherwise compel a student or prospective student to disclose or to provide access to a personal social media account. Ore. Rev. Stat., sec. 326.551.

See also **Social Security Numbers.**

Rhode Island–An educational institution may not require, coerce or request a person to provide passwords or access to a social-media site; to change settings; or to add anyone like a teacher or coach to a social-media site. R.I. Gen. Laws sec. 16-103-3. Organizations providing cloud computing services may not use student data for commercial purposes. 16-104-1(b).

Utah–The law prohibits a private or public institution of higher education from asking a student or applicant to disclose the user name and password that allows access to his or her "personal Internet account," as well as taking adverse action against the individual for failing to disclose. Utah Code Ann. sec. 53B-24-102 and 201 and 202 and 203 and 301.

Virginia–Public institutions of higher education may not require a student to disclose the user name or password to any personal social media accounts, except possibly campus police. Va. Code sec. 23-1-405 D.

West Virginia–The Student Data Accessibility, Transparency and Accountability Act appears at W. Va. Code sec. 18-2-5h.

Wisconsin–With significant exceptions, educational institutions are limited in access to "access information" concerning a student's Internet accounts. No adverse action may be taken if a student declines to provide passwords and other access information. Wisc. Stat. Ann. sec. 995.55. Also 106.54 (10((a).

Federal law-See **Social Security Numbers**. See **Computer Crime** (Data Breaches).

TELEPHONE SERVICES

Minnesota–See **Tracking Technologies**.

Montana–"A government entity may not obtain the location information of an electronic device without a search warrant" except in an emergency, with consent, or when the device is reported stolen. This limits seeking to establish a person's location through "metadata" maintained by a provider of cell-phone services. Mont. Code Ann. sec. 46-5-110.

Rhode Island–State law requires a warrant prior to obtaining location or other information from a service provider for cellular devices. It also establishes exceptions, including emergencies and consent of the owner, and would impose various notice requirements. R.I. Gen. Laws 12-32-1.

Texas–A warrant is required to access email and other stored electronic communications content. Tex. Code of Crim. Pro. art. 18.02(a)(13).

Federal law–"Every telecommunications carrier has a duty to protect the confidentiality of proprietary information of, and relating to, other telecommunication carriers, equipment manufacturers, and customers, including telecommunication carriers reselling telecommunications services provided by a telecommunications carrier. A telecommunications carrier that receives or obtains proprietary information from another carrier for purposes of providing any telecommunications service shall use such information only for such purpose, and shall not use such information for its own marketing efforts. Except as required by law or with the approval of the customer, a telecommunications carrier that receives or obtains customer proprietary network information by virtue of its provision of a telecommunications service shall only use, disclose, or permit access to individually identifiable customer proprietary network information in its provision of (A) the telecommunications service from which such information is derived, or (B) services necessary to, or used in, the provision of such telecommunications service, including the publishing of directories." Exempted: caller location services and emergencies. 47 U.S. Code sec. 222.

TESTING IN EMPLOYMENT

Idaho–"Private genetic information may not be used in employment decisions. Idaho Code sec. 39-8301 to 8304.

South Dakota–Genetic testing is governed by S.D. Codified Laws Ann. 34.14-22.

Virginia–There are limits on employers using genetics test results. 40.1-28.7:1. Correcting citation in 2013 book.

TRACKING TECHNOLOGIES
Including Unmanned Aircraft (Drones) and 'Stingrays'

California–It is an infraction to operate an unmanned aircraft system on or above the grounds of a public school. Penal Code sec.4577-79. It is an invasion of privacy to take images or recordings over private property by drones, Civ. Code 1708.8

No state law enforcement agency or other investigative entity may compel a business or individual to turn over any "metadata" or digital communications, including emails, texts, and documents stored in the cloud – without a warrant approved by a judge. The law also requires a warrant to track the location of electronic devices like mobile phones, or to search them. It seems to address concerns about law enforcement's unfettered access to "Stingray" technology, which mimics a cell tower to force all nearby mobile devices to connect to it so that they may be monitored. Cal. Penal Code sec. 1546.

Florida–Law enforcement may not use "a powered, aerial vehicle (a drone) to gather evidence or information" without court authorization. A citizen may sue for redress. Fla. Stat. Ann. sec. 934-50. Nor may a person, a state agency, or a political subdivision use a drone to capture an image of privately owned real property or of the owner or occupant of the property, with the intent to conduct surveillance without written consent if a reasonable expectation of privacy exists. The law authorizes use of a drone by a person or entity engaged in a licensed business in certain circumstances. Fla. Stat. Ann. sec. 934.50.

Localities may enact ordinances relating to nuisances, voyeurism, harassment, reckless endangerment, property damage or other illegal acts involving drones. Sec. 330.41.

Idaho–"Absent reasonable, articulable suspicion of criminal conduct, no person, entity or state agency shall use an unmanned aircraft system to conduct unwarranted surveillance or observation of [nor to photograph] an individual or a dwelling owned by an individual." Idaho Code sec. 21-213.

Illinois–The Freedom from Drone Surveillance Act prohibits law enforcement from using a drone to gather information, except with a warrant issued to counter a terrorist attack, prevent harm to life, or prevent the imminent escape of a suspect, among other situations. If a law enforcement agency uses a drone, the agency must destroy all information gathered by the drone within 30 days with certain exceptions. It must report annually on the drones that it uses. A "drone" is defined as any aerial vehicle that does not carry a human operator. 725 ILCS 167. It is illegal to use a drone to interfere with a person's lawful taking of wildlife or aquatic life. 5 ILCS 48-3(b)(10).

An entity must not transfer or sell personal biometric identifiers and must take special precautions to protect them in storage. Consent is required. 740 ILCS 14.

Indiana–A court warrant is required for law enforcement to gather "geolocation information" by access to electronic devices like cell phones, Wi-Fi computers, or GPS navigation. 35-31.5-2-143.3. And to gather information by drones. 35-33-5-9.

As of 2017, a sex offender may not use an unmanned aircraft to follow, contact, or capture images or recordings of someone if the offender is subject to conditions that prohibit them from doing so. The law creates the misdemeanors of "remote aerial harassment" and "remote aerial voyeurism." This becomes a felony if the person publishes the images, makes them available on the internet or shares them with another person. Sec. 14-22-6-16.

Iowa–Drones may not be used for traffic enforcement. Iowa Code Ann. sec. 321.492B.

Maine–State law requires a warrant before law enforcement may seek the location of a person's electronic device and it specifies the procedure for granting a warrant. Similar to Montana's law, the nation's first regulation of drones. Me. Rev. Stat. Ann, title 25, sec. 4501.

Minnesota–Law enforcement, with five exceptions, requires a "tracking warrant" based on probable cause to harvest calling data from certain high-tech cell towers. Minn. Rev. Stat. 626A.42.

The existence of all technology maintained by a law enforcement agency that may be used to electronically capture an audio, video, photographic, or other record of the activities of the general public, or of an individual or group of individuals, for purposes of conducting an investigation, responding to an incident or request for service, monitoring or maintaining public order and safety, or engaging in any other law enforcement function authorized by law is public data. Sec. 13-82, subd. 31.

Data from automatic license plate readers is limited and non-public and must be destroyed within 60 days. "Automated license plate readers must not be used to monitor or track an individual who is the subject of an active criminal investigation unless authorized by a warrant." Law enforcement must maintain a public log detailing the use of readers. Sec. 13.824.

Montana–"A government entity may not obtain the location information of an electronic device without a search warrant" except in an emergency, with consent, or when the device is reported stolen. This limits seeking to establish a person's location through "metadata" maintained by a provider of cell-phone services. Mont. Code Ann. sec. 46-5-110.

Information from a drone is not admissible in court nor may be used as the basis for a warrant. 46-5-109.

New Hampshire–State law prohibits determining the ownership of a motor vehicle or the identity of a motor vehicle's occupants on the public ways of the state through the use of a camera or other imaging device or any other device, including but not limited to a transponder, cellular telephone, global positioning satellite, or radio frequency identification device" but there are many exceptions. N.H. Rev. Stat. sec. 236:130.

North Carolina–The state prohibits use of unmanned aircraft to conduct surveillance of private property or a dwelling without consent or a warrant. N.C. Gen. Stat. sec. 15A-300.1.

Oregon–All uses of a drone must be registered with the Oregon Department of Aviation. It is an offense to fire from a weaponized drone. Ore. Rev. Stat. 837.360 and 837.365.

South Dakota–Intentional use of a drone to observe, photograph or record someone in a private place with a reasonable expectation of privacy and landing a drone on the property of an individual without that person's consent is unlawful surveillance. Local government may enact ordinances relating to nuisances, voyeurism, harassment, reckless endangerment, property damage, or other illegal acts. S.D. Codified Laws Ann. sec. 22-21-1.

Tennessee–The law bans law enforcement use of a drone to gather information unless there is a court warrant, an imminent danger to human life, the need to search for a missing person, or a declaration by the U.S. Secretary of Homeland Security that a risk of terrorist attack exists. A drone is defined as a powered, aerial vehicle without a human operator on board, uses aerodynamic forces to provide lift, can fly autonomously or by remote control, and can be expendable or recoverable. Tenn. Code Ann. sec. 39-13-609. It is a misdemeanor to use a drone to conduct video surveillance of private citizens lawfully hunting or fishing without written consent 70-4-302(a)(6).

Texas–It is unlawful to capture an image using an unmanned aircraft except for research or mapping or planning by utilities, or military purposes, FAA-approved testing, pursuant to a warrant or consent, Law enforcement is generally exempt but must make public reports every two years about use of drones or photo satellites. Tex. Gov. Code sec. 423.001.

State law, defining a biometric identifier as "a retina or iris scan, fingerprint, voiceprint, or record of hand or face geometry," has similar protections as the law in Illinois. Bus. & Prof. Code sec. 503.001.

Utah–The law on drones was reorganized in 2017, replacing the statute in the 2017 Supplement. Weaponized unmanned vehicles are prohibited. A person is not guilty of what would otherwise be a privacy violation if the person is operating an unmanned aerial vehicle for legitimate commercial or education purposes consistent with FAA regulations. Utah Code Ann. sec. 72-14-101.

Virginia–No law enforcement agency may use a drone, unless with a search warrant or under other circumstances. Private use of drones is not affected. Va. Code sec. 19.2-60.1. It is a misdemeanor to use a drone to trespass upon the property of another for the purpose of secretly or furtively peeping, spying, or attempting to peep or spy into a dwelling or occupied building. 18.2-130.

"The [state] shall not comply with any federal law or regulation that would require the [state] to use any type of computer chip or radio-frequency identification tag or other similar device on or in a driver's license or special identification card." 46.2-323.01.

A search warrant is required before accessing telecommunications content or location data by way of a "Stingray" device (also known as "cell site simulators" or "IMSI catchers," Va. Code Sec. 19.2-70.3.

Washington–Law enforcement officials are required to get a warrant before deploying a "Stingray" and must describe the cell-tower technology to the judge, despite any non-disclosure agreement with the FBI or manufacturer.

Wisconsin– "No Wisconsin law enforcement agency may use a drone to gather evidence or other information in a criminal investigation from or at a place or location where an individual has a reasonable expectation of privacy without first obtaining a search warrant." Wisc. Stat. Ann. sec. 175. 55. "Whoever operates any weaponized drone is guilty of a felony." 941.292. "Whoever uses a drone [except for law enforcement] with the intent to photograph, record, or otherwise observe another individual in a place or location where the individual has a reasonable expectation of privacy is guilty of a misdemeanor." 942.10.

APPENDIX – CANADIAN LAWS

COMPUTER CRIME

Alberta–The Personal Information Protection Act is the only provincial statute in Canada to impose mandatory notification to the Privacy Commissioner in case of a data breach. The Privacy Commissioner may require that the organization notify affected individuals. The law, 34.1(1), requires the notice of "any incident" where there is "a real risk of significant harm to an individual."

New Brunswick–Custodians of health information have a breach notification requirement. See **Medical Records**.

Newfoundland–Custodians of health information have a notification requirement. See **Medical Records**.

Federal law–Organizations are required to notify the Privacy Commissioner and affected individuals of "any breach of security safeguards involving personal information under [the organization's] control if it is reasonable in the circumstances to believe that the breach creates a real risk of significant harm to an individual." Bill S-4 2015 amending S.C. 2000, c. 5. Effective Nov. 1, 2018.

MEDICAL RECORDS

New Brunswick–The Personal Health Information Privacy and Access Act (S.N.B. 2009, c. P-7.05) provides individuals with a right to examine and request correction and receive a copy of personal health information, and a right to be notified of security breaches adversely affecting them.

Covered entities must establish information practices promoting openness, transparency of policies and procedures to the public.

Newfoundland–The Personal Health Information Act SNL2008 chapter P-7.01 establishes rules that custodians of personal health information must follow when collecting, using and disclosing individuals' confidential personal health information. PHIA also sets out the rights of residents of the province regarding obtaining access to and exercising control of their personal health information. It came into force in 2011. Custodians must report breaches to an individual if an adverse impact is reasonably expected. In addition, custodians are required to report material breaches to the provincial Office of the Information and Privacy Commissioner.